Additional Praise for *Leading with IT: Lessons from Singapore's First CIO*

"Alex has the battle scars from his digital journey, starting from an era of mainframe computing to the current situation where everyone is connected and (almost) everything can be achieved digitally. It is great to have him share his experience and insights in a candid and humble manner."

– Saw Ken Wye, CEO, CrimsonLogic

"The only constant is change. Without change, an organisation will be made obsolete in a rapidly-evolving ecosystem. Alex Siow's book addresses the challenges and strategies in change management. The lessons in the book are based on experience and are therefore practical and transcend theories. Although the narratives are IT-related, anyone involved in change management can benefit from the examples cited. This book is now part of my reference sources, as all of my roles involve managing change."

– Gerard Ee, Chairman, Agency for Integrated Care

"Digitalisation has become a crucial driver of competitiveness and survival for organisations. This book is, therefore, an essential read for the C-Suite so that they understand how ICT can transform their organisations – and how leaders can leverage digitalisation to serve their stakeholders better."

– Peter Lam, Principal and CEO, Temasek Polytechnic

"Alex Siow has made such a significant impact on the IT industry and the organisations he has served through his visionary, practical, unassuming, and humorous style of leadership. This book reflects Alex's practical nature of combining stories of his experience and the learnings gleaned from them. A worthwhile read indeed."

– Dr. Chong Yoke Sin, President, Singapore Computer Society

"It is always pleasant and enlightening when having discussions with Alex Siow. He has vast experience in IT across various roles as a seasoned practitioner and the first CIO in Singapore. Drawing on his lifetime of experience and practices, he offers today's IT leaders a practical roadmap to building an effective digital organisation to face the new challenges arising from the unprecedented rate of change in the world."

– Leong Chin Yew, Group Director (Retired), Information Systems, HDB

"This is a must-read book for all budding CIOs in Singapore. It portrays the journey of a young civil engineer into the world of IT who becomes Singapore's first CIO. Alex is Singapore's pioneering IT leader who has shaped the CIO profession and has been instrumental for the growth and development of the IT community in Singapore with his leadership in ITMA and the SCS. This is a practical field book for the practitioner CIO."

— **Yap Chee Yuen**, Group CIO, Surbana-Jurong

"I have known Alex since his days as a CIO at HDB during the 1990s. He was instrumental in shaping the role of a 'CIO' when the term was at a very nascent stage. Fast-forward to today, and Alex is still very active in shaping the new expectations of a modern-day CIO. Changing mindsets, business models, agility, and resilience are hallmarks of the new IT. The pandemic has accelerated digital transformation efforts and CIOs are at the forefront of this digital revolution. CIOs must recognise that with this new-found power comes great responsibilities. This book is an essential guide for both existing and budding CIOs who wish to make an impact not only in the backroom operations, but also in the business."

— **P. Ramakrishna**, CEO, CIO Academy Asia

"Alex Siow is a well-respected pioneer and veteran of Singapore's IT Industry. His journey is rich with experiential stories – from having tackled mainframe computing to the current ubiquitous digital world. The book contains great insights and offers very practical tips."

— **Siew Yim Cheng**, Chief Digital Officer, ComfortDelGro

Leading with IT

Leading with IT

Lessons from Singapore's First CIO

ALEX SIOW

WILEY

For general information on our other products and services or for technical support,
please contact our Customer Care Department within the United States at (800) 762-
2974, outside the United States at (317) 572-3993, or fax (317) 572-4002.

Wiley publishes in a variety of print and electronic formats and by print-on-demand.
Some material included with standard print versions of this book may not be included
in e-books or in print-on-demand. If this book refers to media such as a CD or DVD
that is not included in the version you purchased, you may download this material
at http://booksupport.wiley.com. For more information about Wiley products, visit
www.wiley.com.

Library of Congress Cataloging-in-Publication Data is Available:

ISBN 9781119797401 (cloth)
ISBN 9781119797418 (ePDF)
ISBN 9781119797425 (ePub)

Cover image: © M Four Studio/Shutterstock
Cover design: Wiley

SKY10023488_011121

Dedicated to cancer researchers worldwide.
(Cancer claimed my parents, wife, and cousin.)

Contents

Foreword   xi
Tan Chin Nam

Preface: How to Handle Herculean Tasks   xv

Acknowledgments   xxvii

About the Author   xxix

Introduction: The Mission and the Vision   1
Raju Chellam

Part I: Legacy   13

Chapter 1: How to Deal with Legacy Systems   15

Chapter 2: How to Deal with Data Centres   25

Chapter 3: How to Deal with Data   35

Part II: Information   45

Chapter 4: How to Handle Info Overload   47

Chapter 5: How to Optimise Outsourcing   63

Chapter 6: How to Plan for Effective BC-DR   77

Part III: Motivation   87

Chapter 7: How to Motivate and Mentor Your Staff   89

Chapter 8: How to Train and Certify Your Staff   103

Chapter 9: How to Resolve Conflicts Amicably   115

Part IV: Change   127

Chapter 10: How to Ensure Good Governance   129

Chapter 11: How to Help Your End Users   141

Chapter 12: How to Handle Change   153

Part V: Innovation   163

Chapter 13: How to Foster Innovation   165

Chapter 14: How to Manage Big Data   179

Chapter 15: How to Ensure Enterprise Security   191

Part VI: Future   207

Chapter 16: The Future of Money   209
  Keith Carter

Chapter 17: The Future of Work   221
  Teo Chin Seng

Chapter 18: Why Ethical AI Matters   233
  James Lau Oon Beng

Epilogue: Innovating in the Trenches   247
  Jim Lim Shien Min

Index   259

Foreword

Tan Chin Nam

WAS GLAD WHEN ONE of my close friends, Alex Siow, asked me if I would write the Foreword to his book, *Leading with IT: Lessons from Singapore's First CIO*. I first met Alex in 1980 when he came for an interview for an open position in the Systems and Computer Organisation (S&C) at the Ministry of Defence.

Alex had just returned from Germany after completing his engineering degree. He still had to complete his national service stint in the army. I interviewed Alex and a few others. He turned down the offer to join S&C and said he wanted to be a structural engineer in the Housing and Development Board (HDB).

But fate played its hand, and Alex switched his career from engineering to IT in a few years. We kept in touch with each other, and Alex was invited to join as a member of the board at the National Computer Board (NCB) Society in 1998.

When I read through the chapters in Alex's book, I found a strange déjà vu; to some extent, the learnings from his book reflected mine, even though our career trajectories have been very different.

Leadership is about creating purpose and meaning in work and life, and aligning people to achieve greater things together for the organisation or the benefit of society. I was fortunate and honoured to have been given many opportunities to create, reposition or transform organisations in the Singapore Civil Service, where I spent 33 years serving the nation. Alex, likewise, evolved into a worthy leader, working in HDB and StarHub, and leading organisations like the Singapore Computer Society (SCS), the IT Management Association (ITMA), and others.

I started my career in the public sector as a systems engineer in the Ministry of Defence, applying modern management approaches in solving complex problems, including computerising the ministry. This paved the way for my active involvement in the national computerisation effort, which led to the formation of the NCB. Throughout this journey, I observed that everyone is in a position to make a difference, irrespective of the level of responsibilities. Alex, likewise, honed his leadership skills as he climbed the corporate ladder.

The NCB was set up in 1981 with the vision to drive Singapore into the Information Age with a series of national IT plans to follow. That was motivational for the staff. They found this national-level movement meaningful and engaging and were equally inspired by the 3P philosophy of professionalism, partnership, and people. The "NCBians" were emotionally connected with their work and users; Alex, in performing his chief information officer (CIO) role, reflected this philosophy fully.

When I was appointed permanent secretary of the Ministry of Labour, some colleagues offered their sympathy, suggesting that managing work permits for domestic helpers and construction workers could not be very exciting. But with the Manpower 21 Plan, the ministry was repurposed as the Ministry of Manpower (MOM) with the vision to make Singapore a talent capital in the knowledge economy.

This involved re-looking at human resources as capital for the country's knowledge, innovation, emotional well-being, and social relations. Efforts were underway to cultivate an engaged workforce, including transforming the workplace into one in which staff can have an emotional connection. Naturally, this mission riding on the strong foundation of the Labour Ministry, was a big boost for the motivation and morale of MOM staff.

That was akin to Alex being asked to head the Computer Services Department (CSD) at the HDB and the subsequent issues he had to deal with, totally unprepared. But he rose to the challenge, transforming the CSD – and thereby the way IT was perceived in the HDB – which eventually made him Singapore's first CIO. It's a journey of grit and confidence, and the ability to motivate a team to work as one.

I was directly involved overseeing the various versions of the National IT Plan from the beginning with the exception of the very last version. The evolution of the National Computerisation Programme (1980) into National IT Plan (1986), IT 2000-Intelligent Island (1991), Infocomm 21 (2000), Connected Singapore (2003), Intelligent Nation 2015 (2006), and finally Infocomm Media 2025 (2019) paralleled the development of info-communications technology (ICT) and digital media technologies in the world.

It was an exciting journey and I could sense the zealous efforts of all those who were involved in this partnership between the public, private, and people sectors in our concerted national transformation for economic competitiveness, better quality of life, and a better tomorrow. Successive leaderships have been able to achieve good alignment in this purpose-driven national undertaking, which had been the highlight of my journey in the public sector.

We had a very humble beginning with meagre IT manpower of 850. Today, at 220,000 strong, our IT talent pool is providing an accelerated thrust to launch Singapore into the digital economy with a bright future for all. Our vision and aspirations of successive IT plans, and now with an overlay of Singapore as a Smart Nation in the transforming global economy, are being realised. Chief information officers, chief digital officers, and IT professionals can expect even more challenging and fulfilling times ahead.

This book is essential reading for anyone who aspires to lead, whether in the ICT industry or elsewhere. After all, all industries are ICT industries today; no business can survive without ICT. This book contains important lessons – and examples – in vital areas such as innovation and change management, motivation, and mentoring, and the future of work and money.

Leadership is a journey with its ups and downs. What sustained me in difficult times was my personal motto – to be a useful person and to make tomorrow better than today. It is a journey about making a more significant difference in what we do. For Alex, it was about respecting others, never looking down on others, and treating others, whether employee or vendor, fairly.

The final point: When the going gets tough, think of the meaning of your job, and work creatively and collaboratively to make it more meaningful. Every one of you is a leader in your own way. There is no need to wait for a CEO or a leadership position before you make a meaningful difference. After all, we are the stewards of functions entrusted to us by our destiny – a privilege – and ultimately, it is about making tomorrow better for our children and our grandchildren.

Dr Tan Chin Nam retired from the Singapore Administrative Service in 2007 after 33 years. Since 2008, he has been a senior corporate adviser, serving on various boards and advising companies. He has held top management positions, including Chairman of the National Computer Board; Managing Director of the Economic Development Board; CEO of the Singapore Tourism Board; Chairman of the Media Development Authority; Chairman of the National Library Board; Permanent Secretary of Singapore's Ministry of Manpower; and Permanent Secretary of the Ministry of Information, Communications, and the Arts. He is a Fellow of the Institution of Engineers, Singapore; Fellow Member of the Singapore Institute of Directors; Honorary Fellow of the Singapore Computer Society, and Distinguished Fellow of the EDB Society.

Preface: How to Handle Herculean Tasks

VER SINCE THE ROLE of CIO (chief information officer) began to become commonplace in the IT industry as well as in IT user organisations, it was subject to snide remarks, the key one being "Career Is Over." That's because the typical CIO needs to be multihatted: technocrat, businessperson, cheerleader, and as the custodian of the ITD (IT Department) finances. Some have even likened the duties and tasks of a CIO to the Twelve Labours of Hercules.

Who was Hercules? Most people would have some idea of Hercules from the many Hollywood films since 1957 that dramatized the heroic exploits of Hercules. The movies portray Hercules as a Roman hero. However, not many would know that the Roman hero's real name was Heracles and that his country of birth was Ancient Greece, not Ancient Rome.

According to Greek mythology, Heracles was the son of Zeus (King of the Gods) and Alcmene (granddaughter of Perseus). King Zeus had sworn that the next son born in the Perseid House should become Ruler of Greece. However, due to a trick played by Zeus' jealous wife, Hera, it was not Heracles but another child, the sickly Eurystheus, who was born first and became heir. When Heracles turned 18, he had to serve King Eurystheus and also suffer the vengeful persecution of Hera.

How did the Twelve Labours of Hercules come about? According to an epic Greek poem written in 600 BC by Peisander, in a fit of rage and madness induced by Hera, Heracles killed his wife and children. He then prayed to the God Apollo for guidance and went to the Oracle at Delphi. The Oracle told Heracles to serve his half-brother (and the King of Mycenae), Eurystheus, for 10 years. During that time, he had to perform 12 difficult feats, called "Labours". After completing his tasks, Heracles became a hero in the Greco-Roman world for his combination of physical strength, ingenuity, and bravery.

What's the connection with ICT? After joining the IT profession, I was often warned by friends and colleagues that developing large and complex ICT systems was a Herculean task. Considering what Hercules had gone through, I thought that they might have been exaggerating. But when I started to gain more experience and knowledge, I realised that there were indeed reasons to compare the rigours of systems development with the Labours of Hercules, albeit on a different scale.

To solve every problem, Heracles had to rely on hard skills, such as physical strength and stamina – and soft skills, such as bravery, ingenuity, and teamwork. Similarly, in the large, complex, and rapidly changing world of ICT systems, CIOs have to turn into Heracles almost daily and employ technical knowledge (hard skills) as well as problem-solving and teamwork (soft skills) to be successful.

Let us take a look at the analogy between the Twelve Labours of Heracles and the 12 skillsets of a CIO.

NEMEAN LION

- **Heracles' Labour:** Get the skin of the feared Nemean Lion. When Heracles found the Nemean Lion and shot arrows at it, they bounced harmlessly off the creature's impenetrable golden fur. When the lion returned to its cave, Heracles blocked one of its two entrances and entered through the other. He stunned the beast with his club. Using his immense strength, Heracles then strangled it to death. He attempted to skin the lion with a knife from his belt, but the blade was not sharp enough. He sharpened it on a stone and even tried to skin the lion with the rock, in vain. Athena, noticing his plight, told him to use one of Lion's claws to skin the pelt; that worked.
- **ICT Analogy:** Keep the lights on. The ICT environment is as complex as the Nemean Lion. The ITD supports many mission-critical apps that help run the business. The CIO needs to "keep the lights on" first, which is to ensure that all routine functions are working well, and then resolve complex issues such as carrying out a major systems upgrade or shut down critical systems for a major software patch. Like the Nemean Lion's ferociousness, IT has to be ferociously alert.

The Nemean Lion's skin is akin to the high availability and quality cloak of the IT environment. The sharp claws of the lion are equal to the defences that the ITD has to maintain to protect the company from attacks, including malware, DDOS (distributed denial of service), or ransomware. Even when such complex tasks are in process, the CIO's first key performance indicator (KPI) is to "keep the lights on" so that the company can continue to function.

LERNAEAN HYDRA

- **Heracles' Labour:** Slay the Lernaean Hydra. The Lernaean Hydra was raised by Hera just to kill Heracles. When Heracles cut off one of the hydra's heads, two others grew back in its place. To add to this complication, one of the hydra's heads – the middle one – was immortal. Heracles turned to his nephew Iolaus for help. Iolaus came up with the idea (possibly inspired by Athena) of using a firebrand to scorch the hydra's neck stumps after each decapitation. Heracles cut off each head; Iolaus cauterised the open stumps, thereby killing the Lernaean Hydra.
- **ICT Analogy:** Find the root cause of problems. The ICT environment is composed of many technologies, often from different vendors. The ITD's technical resources similarly come from multiple sources. When these diverse systems and technologies are not synchronised, it can result in a hydra-headed monster of solutions trying to work together, and some-times crashing. The CIO and the ITD team may try to fix one problem (cut off one head), and two issues may crop up, much like the Lernaean Hydra.

To address these myriad heads of the hydra, the CIO cannot just slice off one head; that would be like fixing a temporary patch or asking IT vendors to solve a specific problem without realising how it may impact other systems. As CIO, you need to identify the root causes, the base issues, and maybe even engage independent external expertise to troubleshoot and resolve tough technical problems. If you don't find the root cause of the problems and get them fixed, the heads of the hydra will reappear.

CERYNEIAN HIND

- **Heracles' Labour:** Capture the Ceryneian Hind. The Ceryneian Hind was a giant female deer, which lived in the region of Keryneia. It was sacred to the Hunting Goddess, Artemis. Although female, it had male-like antlers, which were made of gold, while its hooves were bronze. It could outrun a flying arrow. Heracles awoke from sleep and saw the hind by the glint of sunlight on its antlers. Heracles chased the hind on foot for a full year through Greece, Thrace, Istria, and the Hyperboreans. In some versions, he captured the hind while it slept, rendering it lame with a trap net.

■ **ICT Analogy.** Persistence pays. It took Heracles a year to capture the Ceryneian Hind. Heracles had to chase the creature across multiple geographies; he had to persist in getting to this goal. Likewise, in the ICT space, some projects will take longer to mature, will require teams to jump through technical hoops, often coming close to "throwing in the towel" and going back to status quo ante. For example, many projects involving big data analytics, AI and DX (digital transformation) are tough to do, require long periods of testing and fine-tuning, and need the persistence of the entire ITD as well as the organisation.

As CIO, you have to be the cheerleader of your team. You have to get them to carry on the tasks, no matter how challenging, until you reach the goal. You can, of course, take help from external parties, vendors, consultants, SMEs (subject matter experts). Your team will otherwise give up. You as CIO have to persist with the plan, and get your team not to lose hope.

ERYMANTHIAN BOAR

■ **Heracles' Labour:** Bring the Erymanthian Boar. This task was to bring the Erymanthian Boar back alive to King Eurystheus. A boar is a huge, wild, fierce pig with tusks growing out of its mouth. The Erymanthian Boar lived on the Erymanthus mountain. Every day it would come crashing down from its lair, attacking people and animals all over the land, gouging them with its tusks, and destroying everything in its path. Heracles had visited Chiron for advice on how to catch the creature. Chiron told him to drive it into thick snow during winter. Heracles caught the boar, bound it, and carried it to King Eurystheus, who was scared of the beast and fled into his half-buried storage, called Pithos, and begged Heracles to get rid of the creature.

■ **ICT Analogy.** Negotiate and seek expert advice. Heracles was not shy to seek advice or external expertise. The CIO would likewise be required to introduce new technology or solutions and might have no knowledge or talent in-house to get it done. Don't be shy to ask for advice, either from your vendors, industry bodies, or consulting companies.

Capturing the wild Erymanthian Boar is akin to introducing major IT solutions. IT projects come in waves: mainframes to client/server systems to Y2K migration, to e-commerce and mobile computing. Adopting and implementing these widely differing technologies requires different types of resources and IT talent. The only way to obtain both of these is to negotiate and seek expert advice.

AUGEAN STABLES

- **Heracles' Labour.** Clean the Stables of King Augeas. Getting Heracles to clean the stables of King Augeas was designed to be very humiliating (rather than impressive, as the previous tasks had been) and impossible, since the livestock was gifted with divine health (and immortality) and therefore produced an enormous quantity of dung. For more than 30 years, nobody had cleaned the Augean Stables, and more than a thousand cattle lived there. Heracles successfully rerouted two massive rivers, Alpheus and Peneus, to wash out the filth and clean the stables of King Augeas.
- **ICT Analogy.** Think outside the box. There was no feasible way to clean the dung that had accumulated for 30 years. If Heracles had not "thought out of the box" and managed to divert the paths of two major rivers, the dung would keep accumulating. Cleaning it piecemeal would complicate the issue, not solve it.

In an implementation of ERP (enterprise resource planning), the first in Asia, I faced a major dilemma: how to handle a new, central, enterprise-wide technology solution within budget and with the Y2K issue staring us in the face. I had to think out of the box. We proposed a plan, we asked for vendor time, expertise, and investment, we tweaked the contracts and worked together with multiple and diverse teams to get the ERP done on time and budget – and were Y2K compliant.

STYMPHALIAN BIRDS

- **Heracles' Labour.** Defeat the Stymphalian Birds. These were man-eating birds with beaks made of bronze and sharp metallic feathers that could tear apart their victims. The birds were sacred to the god of war, Ares. Their dung was also highly toxic. Heracles could not wade too far into the swamp, for it would not support his massive weight. Athena noticed his plight and gave Heracles a rattle, which Hephaestus had made for an occasion like this. Heracles shook the loud rattle and frightened the birds. When they tried to fly away, Heracles shot a bunch of them with his arrows. The rest of the flock flew far away, never to return.

■ **ICT Analogy.** Break down the problem. Heracles had a complex problem to solve, with multiple moving parts. He had to break down the problem into smaller components and solve each first, before going for the "big kill". That's also true in the ICT environment. Sometimes a problem looks huge, and it could be huge, such as a significant DDOS or ransomware attack. You can't solve it in one go. You must break it down into smaller components and fix each small issue first before you can go after that big mountain.

Take one example: a significant system slowdown. That could be due to legacy applications, or massive loading on the servers, or inadequate storage, or some servers not functioning, or malware in an application, or a dozen other reasons. Sometimes it's a mixture of multiple reasons. When the IT landscape is vast, the natural tendency is to leave it alone, as any change may create a disruption. As the CIO, you must have a bird's-eye view of your ITD systems and narrow down the possible causes of the problem. It could be something simple, like adding additional storage during month-end to handle the load.

CRETAN BULL

■ **Heracles' Labour.** Capture the Cretan Bull. The Cretan Bull had been wreaking havoc on Crete by uprooting crops and breaking down orchard walls. Heracles sneaked up behind the bull and used his hands to throttle it; he did not kill it. The hero then shipped it back to King Eurystheus, who got so scared of the creature that the King stayed hidden in the Pithos dungeon. He wanted to sacrifice the Cretan Bull to Hera, who hated Heracles. She refused the sacrifice because it would reflect glory on Heracles. The Cretan Bull was tamed and released; it wandered into the city of Marathon and was then known as the Marathonian Bull.

■ **ICT Analogy.** Nip the problem in the bud. Heracles knew that he had to nip the problem (the destructive bull) before it continued to do more damage. If he waited too long, the problem would be compounded and get out of control. But once the problem got resolved and the issues straightened out, there was no need to keep the bull captive, for it could not do any more damage. So it was released and allowed to wander wherever it wished.

For the CIO, problems may occur from many quarters. Key talent is resigning, or some specific software is slowing down other systems, or a piece of malware that has infected one application and might infect the whole ITD if not nipped in the bud right away. The CIO has to take charge immediately and instruct his team to resolve the issue (not patch it) as soon as possible. Letting a problem carry on – hoping it will resolve by itself – could be a fatal error of judgement.

MARES OF DIOMEDES

- **Heracles' Labour.** Steal the Mares from Diomedes. The Mad Mares of Diomedes were four horses that ate humans. They belonged to a giant named Diomedes, King of Thrace, son of Ares and Cyrene. The names of the mares were Podargos (swift), Lampon (shining), Xanthos (yellow), and Deinos (terrible). Some versions of the myth mention that the mares also exhaled fire. Heracles brought several volunteers to help him capture the giant horses. After decimating Diomedes' men, Heracles broke the chains that tethered the horses and drove the mares out into the sea.
- **ICT Analogy.** Get teams to collaborate. Heracles enlisted volunteers to help out with a pesky problem; the volunteers decided to chip in for three reasons: One, the Mad Mares were causing issues across the city that affected everyone. Two, it was apparent that the volunteers by themselves could not tackle the Mad Mares. Three, they believed in the leadership skills of Heracles to lead them to victory.

Those three points are precisely similar to issues that most organisations face in dealing with complex ICT problems, which are akin to the mares that impact all stakeholders. The ITD by itself cannot handle all of the issues because it may have roots in other business units (BUs), such as finance, sales, marketing, and logistics. You, the CIO, have to become Heracles, the leader, and get teams from all specific BUs to collaborate to solve ICT problems. Most often teams work in silos; the CIO has to get them to collaborate and work in diverse groups to "fight the Mad Mares of ICT".

HIPPOLYTA'S BELT

- **Heracles' Labour.** Procure the Belt of Hippolyta. King Eurystheus' daughter, Admete, wanted the Belt of Hippolyta. Hippolyta was the Amazonian queen who possessed a magical waist belt that she received from her father Ares, the God of War. The myth mentions that Hippolyta was impressed with Heracles and his exploits, and agreed to gift him the belt. However, Hera disguised herself and walked among the Amazonians, sowing seeds of distrust. She claimed that strangers were plotting to kidnap the Queen of the Amazons. Alarmed, the women rode off on their horses to confront Heracles. When Heracles saw the herd, he mistakenly thought Hippolyta had been plotting such treachery all along. He killed her, grabbed the belt and returned to Eurystheus.
- **ICT Analogy.** Beware of saboteurs. This episode offers insights into saboteurs as well as the earliest example of fake news. Saboteurs can be external or internal to the organisation, or even within teams. The CIO has to navigate these waters using soft skills (negotiations, persuasion, teamwork) and hard skills (get tough on saboteurs, negative thinkers, fake news spreaders, gossipers, and others).

Other than being measured on the management of the IT team, the CIO's credentials depend on their success in delivering major projects. Projects can be new implementations or upgrading of existing systems. Often, the project teams comprise a diverse mix of IT staff, vendors, and critical users. The success of the project depends on team members being able to work together within and outside their teams. Identify saboteurs early and find solutions to overcome problems.

 ## CATTLE OF GERYON

- **Heracles' Labour.** Grab the cattle from Geryon. The task was to get the cattle from Geryon. Geryon was a three-bodied, four-winged giant who lived on the island of Erytheia. He possessed a fabulous herd of cattle whose coats were stained red by the light of the sunset. Heracles drove the cattle over the Aventine Hill to the future site of the City of Rome. A giant called Cacus lived there; he stole some of the cattle as Heracles slept. Cacus did this by making the cattle walk backwards, so they left no trail. When Heracles drove his remaining cattle past the cave, where Cacus had hidden the stolen animals, they began calling out to each other. In another version, Cacus' sister Caca told Heracles where he was. Heracles killed Cacus and set up an altar on the spot; this spot would later be the site of Rome's "Forum Boarium" (the cattle market).

■ **ICT Analogy.** Watch out for hidden agendas. This episode illustrates the need for the CIO to keep an eye out for the hidden agendas of others, who may either be part of the ITD or even from other BUs. Usually, those with hidden agendas cloak their real intent behind credible curtains and may appear to have the well-being of the organisation at heart. Much like Cacus making the cattle walk back, they didn't leave any trail on their path.

It is challenging for the CIO to figure out everybody's real intent, especially since there are multiple parties and stakeholders involved, each with his or her perceptions and needs. Running large projects is like managing a herd of cattle; everyone needs to move in the same direction and work as a unified team. It is at such times that hidden agendas crop up. If aligned to the goal of the ITD or the organisation, it's ideal. If not, it's time to spot these outliers and deal with them directly.

GOLDEN APPLES OF HESPERIDES

■ **Heracles' Labour.** Steal three Golden Apples. The task was to steal three Golden Apples from the Garden of the Hesperides. When Heracles got to the garden, he encountered Atlas who was holding up the heavens on his massive shoulders. Heracles cajoled Atlas to get the three Golden Apples and offered to hold the sky for him. When Atlas returned, he did not want to take the heavens back and offered to deliver the Golden Apples himself. Heracles had to trick him by asking Atlas to hold the sky for a moment while Heracles adjusted his cloak. Atlas agreed. Heracles heaved the heavens back on Atlas' shoulders and fled with the Golden Apples.

■ **ICT Analogy.** Transfer ownership. There are two lessons here: One, the need to delegate effectively. The other is to ensure that the right person or team takes responsibility for the task and its outcome. Digitalisation has changed business processes and allowed the BUs to buy software and cloud instances directly, bypassing the ITD and creating what's called the "Shadow IT Syndrome". But the support function is dumped on the ITD without allowing the ITD to carry out adequate checks during the purchasing process.

Much like Heracles, who took over the chore for a while and transferred the heavens back to its rightful owner, the ITD must transfer the ownership back to the original BU after implementation. The CIO should involve key stakeholders and BUs early on with a clear understanding that the "Golden Apples" do not belong to the CIO or the ITD, and will revert to the rightful BU.

CERBERUS

▪ **Heracles' Labour.** Capture Cerberus. The most dangerous task of all was this one: King Eurystheus ordered Heracles to go to the Underworld, called the Kingdom of Hades, and kidnap its guardian, Cerberus. Ancient Greeks believed that when one dies, his or her spirit goes to the Underworld and lives there forever. All souls, whether they were good or evil humans, are destined for the Kingdom of Hades.

Cerberus guarded the entrance to Hades and kept the living from entering the world of the dead. Cerberus was a fearsome creature with three heads of wild dogs, a dragon for a tail, and snakeheads all over his back. After much rigour, Heracles reached Hades. He grasped all three heads of Cerberus at once and wrestled the beast into submission. After a long fight, Hercules captured Cerberus and carried it to Eurystheus, who fled once again to his lair, Pithos. Eurystheus then begged Heracles to return Cerberus to the Underworld, offering in return to release him from any further labours. The story has a happy ending: Cerberus was released back to rule the Kingdom of Hades, and Heracles got released from all future "Labours".

▪ **ICT Analogy.** Aim for a win-win outcome. The best deals in business, and ITD, are ones where all the parties feel they have contributed to the win individually and collectively. That is ideal, and not as rare as it seems. Key stakeholders should come together in the initial phases and chalk out what success should look like, and how each party can contribute to a successful outcome. It's then likely that the high level of trust and transparency may lead to everybody getting credit if the project succeeds, or everybody pitching in if the project goes through challenging phases.

On the flip side, Cerberus presents the dark forces of conflict management. In every organisation, there are always boundaries of political turf and the hidden walls of pride. These creep in as false objections, sabotage, fake news, and canvassing others to rebel. The CIO should face each of these stakeholders to address their complaints. The CIO needs charisma, integrity, and humility. The more effectively that you or your team can directly address these objections, the more buy-in you can achieve – and the better will the win-win outcome be for all stakeholders.

Acknowledgments

I WAS AN "ACCIDENTAL CIO" and inadvertently became Singapore's first CIO. This book, likewise, is an accidental product and was conceived from a series of articles I was invited to write for *The Straits Times* (*ST*) in the 1990s. The credit for those articles goes to Grace Chng, who was then the special projects editor in *ST*; the credit for this book goes to Joelle Choo, executive education fellow at the NUS School of Computing, who suggested I compile and update the articles into a book to document my journey from a structural engineer to a CIO at HDB.

This book aims to inform and educate the C-suite on the crucial role that IT plays in organisations and why the C-suite should take the CIO seriously enough to accord him or her a seat on the top decision-making body or board. Given the digital transformation that's occurring across the world, the book also deals with AI, the future of work, the future of money, and lessons learnt from managing the pandemic. For this, I thank my friends and fellow ICT professionals, Professor Keith Carter, Mr Teo Chin Seng, Mr James Lau and Mr Jim Lim for contributing guest chapters in the book. Special thanks to Mr Teo for helping with the extensive background research for this book.

I would not have been able to succeed in my job as a CIO without the continued support of my late wife, Ms Chew Sok Chuang. I'm grateful to my son Ivan and my daughter Iris, both of whom were my inspiration. My present wife, Marilyn Lew, continually encouraged me to work on this book when the task seemed daunting and challenging.

I also wish to thank all my former colleagues at the HDB, StarHub, Accenture, and the NUS School of Computing, as well as my many friends and former students. They have always been patient with me and encouraged me to continue to develop my skills in IT strategy and governance. I'm very grateful for the help given by May Ho for the transcriptions, and Stephanie Viki Thegarajan, my trusted secretary.

Last but not least, this book would not have been possible without the editing and rewriting skills of Raju Chellam. He was the BizIT Editor of *The Business Times* and the first to interview me as Singapore's first CIO. It's serendipitous that he also offered to edit the book and make it readable for the business executive.

About the Author

ALEX SIOW IS A professor (Practice) in the School of Computing at the National University of Singapore (NUS) as well as director of the Advanced Computing for Executives (ACE), the Strategic Technology Management Institute (STMI), and the Centre for Health Informatics (CHI). He is also chairman of Toffs Technologies Pte Ltd, an independent director of Tee International Ltd, a member of the Board of Governors at Temasek Polytechnic, a member of the Board of Trustees at Singapore University of Social Sciences (SUSS), and a member of the Board of Directors of the Ang Mo Kio Thye Hua Kwan Hospital. He is also chairman, Cloud Security Alliance, Singapore Chapter. He is a strategic advisor to Nityo Infotech, and consultant to U3Infotech. Professor Siow's expertise is in IT governance, enterprise risk management, management of emerging technologies, and technology roadmap planning. He is also active in the project management, fintech, blockchain, and cybersecurity communities.

Introduction: The Mission and the Vision

*Raju Chellam**

O N A CHILLY FRIDAY afternoon on June 12, 1987, at 2 p.m., US President Ronald Reagan delivered a speech at the historic Brandenburg Gate in West Berlin that had this iconic line: "Mr Gorbachev, tear down this wall!"

It was a bold and open call to the General Secretary of the Communist Party of the Soviet Union, Mikhail Gorbachev, to open the Berlin Wall, which had separated West and East Berlin since 1961.

It took 28 months and 28 days for the wall to come down after Mr Reagan's speech. The Berlin Wall fell on November 9, 1989. An end to the Cold War was declared at the Malta Summit three weeks later, and the reunification of Germany took place in October 1990.

On a cool Monday night on October 12, 1987, at 2 a.m., another wall, albeit not as iconic, was broken in the heart of Singapore, overseen by a young structural engineer who had studied civil engineering in Germany. The wall was in the new HDB headquarters at Bukit Merah Central. The reason was to move a mammoth mainframe into the facility. And the young structural engineer was 33-year-old Alex Siow.

They had to remove a portion of the wall facing Bukit Merah Central. An industrial crane had to be put into service to move the mainframe computer into the new building through the wall because the lifts were too small

*Raju Chellam is a Fellow of the NUS ACE (Advanced Computing for Executives) and Fellow of the Singapore Computer Society (SCS). He is Chief Editor of the AI Ethics and Governance Body of Knowledge, an initiative by the SCS and IMDA to infuse ethics in the development and deployment of AI solutions. Raju has been in the ICT industry for 40 years. He is Chair of the Cloud and Data Standards on Singapore's IT Standards Committee, Vice President of the Cloud Chapter at SCS, Vice President of New Technologies at Fusionex International, and former Vice-Chair of the Cloud and Data Chapter at SGTech. He was previously regional head of Cloud and Big Data at Dell and BizIT editor of *The Business Times*, Singapore. His book, *Organ Gold*, published by the Straits Times Press, is about the illegal sale of human organs on the Dark Web.

to accommodate the mainframe. The hoisting work started around midnight, and the police had to close two lanes of the road. The new DC (data centre) was located on the sixth floor of the building, and they had to deploy a supersized crane to get the job done.

That operation – and that day – left a deep impression on Alex Siow; he had joined the HDB in September 1980. "Breaking the wall to move in the mainframe was the right solution, but a costly solution," Mr Siow says. "It could not have been avoided because the building was not purpose-built to house the HDB HQ. It was supposed to be an office complex, with units that were offered for rent."

But HDB's HQ in Maxwell Road was running out of space to house all the employees. So a new spacious HQ was required. The Bukit Merah Central building was not in the initial list, so no provision was made to house a DC. "Hence, a decision was made to crack an opening in the wall to move in the equipment," Mr Siow says. "This operation taught me a lesson about getting things done by breaking walls. And that nothing is impossible if there is a will to find a solution, no matter how complicated the problem."

 ## ACCIDENTAL CIO

By 1990 Mr Siow had taken over as CIO of HDB. That was also accidental. "I thought I was a good structural engineer and was focusing on building design and going deep into construction technology," Mr Siow reminisces about the late 1980s. "However, from the early days of my career, I was fascinated with how computer software could help increase the productivity of engineers. I wrote a few software programs for my structural engineering colleagues to use."

That proved he had an aptitude for computing. The result: Mr Siow was roped into the computer unit of the structural engineering department to work on engineering software. Two years later, HDB decided to introduce a CADD (computer-aided design and drafting) system to improve the productivity of the drafting teams in its building and development division.

"They asked me to join the CADD team and, eventually, to take charge of it," he says. "In 1986, the management told me to introduce a computer-aided project management system. That project ran on the mainframe, which introduced me to a whole new world of mainframe computing."

In September 1989, Mr Siow was called to the CEO's office and told to relocate to the CSD to understudy the job of the head of the CSD. Mr Siow was stunned; he was neither prepared nor interested in changing his career from engineering to IT. Moreover, he knew that the CSD was facing many issues, both technical and administrative. The former head had quit abruptly, and a global search for his replacement bore no fruit. So the CEO Mr Chuang Kwong Yong, told Mr Siow to spend a "couple of months in the CSD and figure out how to fix it."

Fate sometimes works in strange ways. As it turned out, Mr Siow and Mr Chuang had met each other 16 years ago in 1973. Under Singapore's compulsory military service for males, Mr Chuang was for a period a trainee under Mr Siow.

"I was the platoon sergeant in the School of Section Leaders in the army, and Mr Chuang was a trainee in my platoon," Mr Siow says. "I maintained a high standard of training and discipline in the platoon and had a reputation as a tough guy. So I thought he had a tough time under my leadership. Maybe he wanted to put me to the test to see if the guy he trained under 16 years ago was that tough after all."

Once Mr Siow got to the CSD, he realised the extent of the problem that needed fixing. The CSD had 220 staff, mostly systems analysts. Mr Siow didn't exactly get a warm welcome. Here was a structural engineer who knew nothing about the intricacies of mainframe computing – and how dare he would be the boss of the CSD.

"I was used to managing large teams; the army had taught me how to manage a large number of people," Mr Siow says; in 1989, he was a battalion commander with about 800 soldiers in the reserve force. "That didn't matter at this point. The question was whether I could fix the sad state of affairs in the CSD, which had always operated in a silo. Staff morale was low; the attrition rate was 25 percent. The CSD staff were located in three different HDB sites with the HQ being at Maxwell Road."

A more significant concern was the potential clash of egos. Some team members were more senior and had a "superscale" status in the CSD; they resented having to report to a senior structural engineer. "I had been a follower of the concept of 'servant leadership' that was first embodied by the Prussian King Frederick II," Mr Siow says. "I now needed to muster all that learning to get my team to work with me – and not kill me."

SERVANT LEADERSHIP

Germany – of which Prussia was a historical province – was figuring once again in Mr Siow's life. Historically, King Frederick the Great ruled the Kingdom of Prussia from 1740 until 1786, the longest reign of any of the Hohenzollern kings, for 46 years. He called himself "the first servant of the state" and oversaw a stunning transformation akin to today's digital transformation.

Frederick the Great modernised the Prussian bureaucracy and civil service, tolerated religious freedom, reformed the judicial system, encouraged immigrants of various nationalities and faiths to come to Prussia, supported artists and philosophers, allowed complete freedom of the press and literature, and believed in a true meritocracy. For the first time in Europe, he made it possible for men not of noble status to become judges and senior bureaucrats.

The phrase "servant leadership" was first popularised by author Robert K Greenleaf in his 1970 essay, *The Servant as Leader*. Mr Greenleaf credited the book, *Journey to the East*, published in 1932 by Hermann Karl Hesse (another connection to Germany) as his inspiration.

Journey to the East is about Leo, a servant just like all the others. All the servants work well together. One day, Leo disappears. The servants then figure out that things aren't the same without Leo; they then realise that Leo was far more than a servant; he was in effect their leader. Taking a leaf from that book, Mr Greenleaf advocated that a leader should be someone that servants or workers can relate to. Mr Greenleaf first put his idea of servant leadership to use while he was working as an executive at AT&T Corp.

When Mr Siow took over the CSD, he met all of his staff: "I am here to work with you, to help you. So you need to help me to help yourself." The talk – and his style of management – made a deep impression on the staff.

"He did not micromanage, he walked around and talked to the staff, he knew everyone – that's more than 200 – by name," says Christina Lim, Mr Siow's secretary at HDB. She had been the previous CSD head's secretary and found Mr Siow's management style refreshing. "He delegated and trusted the staff to do their work. He talked to everyone in the CSD, even the cleaners. Alex was my fifth boss and probably the best."

HDB was her first job after Ms Lim did her O-Levels and a private secretary course; she later attended night classes to complete her A-Levels and earned a diploma in Human Resource Management at the PSB Academy. "Alex was kind to all his staff and me," Ms Lim says. "He was stricter with senior staff. He was a forgiving person and willing to listen. The door to his office was always open. He treated women equally as men. If you were good at your job, he would show his appreciation whether you were male or female. That was quite refreshing."

Ms Lim recollected an episode that left an impression on her. "Once, our cleaner aunty told me that Alex saw she was carrying some heavy stuff and helped her to carry it," Ms Lim says. "She said that my boss was so humble and she was very *paiseh* (shy) to be helped. Alex always said it is better to be friends with people, no matter who they are. That was one of the lessons he had learnt in Germany."

 ## GERMAN OMEN

Germany was where Mr Siow spent five years, from 1974 to 1979, studying civil engineering at the Stuttgart University of Applied Sciences. which had the German name, Hochschule für Technik (HFT) Stuttgart. Located in downtown Stuttgart, it is one of 10 institutes for higher education in Stuttgart, which is the capital of southwest Germany's Baden-Württemberg state. Stuttgart is a manufacturing hub; Mercedes-Benz and Porsche's headquarters and museums are located in the city.

How did Mr Siow strut from Singapore to Stuttgart? Serendipity. Singapore's Public Service Commission (PSC) had advertised overseas undergraduate engineering scholarships to Japan and Germany. He was friends with a woman he had met in high school, and she applied for the German scholarship – without informing him. So when the PSC called him for a scholarship interview, he was surprised. He went for the interview, and the PSC subsequently approved the scholarship.

"I was surprised, not shocked," Mr Siow laughs. "Many major events in my life, like going to study in Germany, was something quite unexpected. But I learnt to take such events as a good omen. Germany certainly was."

The HFT University was founded as a winter school for building craftspeople in 1832. By 1918, it was the largest of the then 67 construction schools in Germany with 923 students. The original winter school has long since become a modern University of Applied Sciences and is characterised by inter-faculty projects and contacts to numerous companies in Stuttgart and Germany.

Other than civil engineering, Mr Siow learnt about servant leadership, meritocracy, and, most importantly, treating women as being equal to men. HFT applies the principles of "gender mainstreaming". That means that all plans, concepts, and activities of the university are examined for their impact on gender equality.

The "Gleichstellungsbeirat", in which professors from all faculties are involved, works on university-wide concepts for the actual implementation of equality between women and men. HFT reports on its website. "The comparatively high proportion of women among the students, even in the very technical disciplines of the university, shows that the HFT Stuttgart is particularly attractive for female students."

Mr Siow was awarded a Bachelor in Civil Engineering degree – *DiplomIngenieur Bauingenieurwesen* – equivalent to a Bachelor of Engineering degree. "I spent the first six months learning German at the Goethe Institute in Germany," he says. "I also spent six months as a construction intern at a worksite."

 ## THE MISSION

In 1972 when he turned 18, Alex Siow was called to enrol in Singapore's mandatory National Service military training. When he went for his enlistment, the army conducted his medical check-up, and the doctor said he weighed 90 pounds (40.82 kg); the minimum weight was 100 pounds (45.36 kg). How could he make up the difference? The recruiting officer gave him two weeks to "fatten up" and return for another check-up.

"That became my first mission, to get myself in shape," Mr Siow sighs. "In those two weeks, I began a strict regimen. I ate five bananas and two bowls of rice at every meal and got my weight up to 95 pounds. The recruitment officer said, 'Wow! You really are determined to enlist; we will take you in.' All my friends and peers were in the army; if I didn't qualify, I would lose face, as the Chinese say. I dived in and suffered like hell because I was physically unfit and couldn't handle the hard training regimen."

But he did survive his basic military training. He went on to complete the Section Leaders' course and was then posted to the School of Section Leaders as an instructor. That's where he met Chuang Kwong Yong, who was posted as a trainee under Mr Siow and would one day become his boss.

"He was a Colombo Plan scholar and quite brilliant," Mr Siow reminisces. "After graduating, he went for further studies and later joined national service. So he was four years older than me. Both of us went on to join the Officers' Cadet course and were in the same platoon. Our friendship developed from there."

While the theory of management may have come from the German model, the practicality came entirely from the army. "I honed a lot of my management theory in the army; it was my foundation for picking up project management skills," Mr Siow says. "I made it my mission to be punctual, be meticulous about things, and to keep motivating my team. The army taught me that. My mission was to be a good project manager. Project management is about process control. Project management skills, in turn, helped me become a good CIO."

But there was an unexpected bump around the bend. When Mr Siow was suddenly whisked out of his comfort zone and asked to manage the CSD, he wondered whether he would be the fall guy. "Don't worry, I'm behind you," Mr Chuang assured Mr Siow. "I will give you three years to turn the CSD around. You can do it."

The very next year, Mr Chuang was posted out of HDB. Mr Siow was left wondering whether he could survive without the CEO's backing. But fate was kinder. Mr Chuang's replacement was Mr Siow's schoolmate from the Raffles Institution, Mr Lim Hng Kiang.

Mr Lim was born in April 1954 (Mr Siow was born in June 1954). Mr Lim won a President's Scholarship and a Singapore Armed Forces Scholarship to study at the University of Cambridge, where he completed a degree in engineering in 1976. In 1985, he won a scholarship for a Master of Public Administration degree at the John F Kennedy School of Government at Harvard University.

In due course, Mr Lim would serve as Singapore's Minister for National Development (1995–1999), Minister for Health (1999–2003), Minister in the Prime Minister's Office (2003–2004), and as Minister of Trade and Industry (2004–2018). He was a member of Parliament from 1991 to 2020.

With Mr Lim's backing and support, Mr Siow had a free hand to begin transforming the CSD as Singapore's first CIO (chief information officer). "In 1990, after becoming CIO of HDB, I reorganised the CSD and renamed it as the ISD (Information Services Department)," Mr Siow says. "I created several IS units responsible for creating and maintaining various applications that served the town councils and the administration teams. These units got support from the infrastructure, operations, security, and administration BUs."

In HDB, the CSD provided IT support services; it was divided into mainframe systems support and office systems support. In the early days, when the number of office systems users were few, the CSD had no problem supporting the users directly. With the coming of client-server systems and increasing uptake of office automation, it became untenable for a small CSD team to support 17 end-user departments and more than 5,000 office system users.

"The CEO approved our setting up PC support units in all the BUs," Mr Siow says. "These units consisted of two to three technical staff who reported to a senior officer, called the PC officer. The PC support unit was the first line of support when end-users in their BUs encountered problems. All complicated issues were escalated to the CSD. We held regular meetings and training sessions to ensure that the PC support units were upskilled."

Mr Siow was empowered to make the changes necessary to reengineer the department within three years.

"This was not an easy task, and the only way to do it was to attack on all fronts," Tung Lai and Efraim Turban wrote in the *Singapore Business Development Series* in 1996. "Mr Siow had a special relationship with staff members, resulting from his emphasis on people-orientation. He had the support of top management, and because he sat on several important committees in HDB, he knew various changes in policies and projects. According to Tan Poh Suan, a team leader in the ISD, Mr Siow not only reorganised the people and the systems, he also imparted a sense of freshness and motivation."

Mr Siow held quarterly departmental gatherings to improve staff communication and morale. "Staff members interviewed said that they felt a greater sense of departmental spirit than before and that there was a sense of belonging," the authors noted. "Mr Siow made it a point to send a personalised card to each staff on their birthday, and also called them in to help them to prepare for their promotion interviews. He also attended unit informal gatherings. Unit meetings were also instituted to promote interaction and information sharing at the unit and team levels."

One significant achievement was HDB's painless transition during the much-feared Y2K (Year 2000) rollover. "HDB enjoyed a smooth and trouble-free transition into the new millennium, thanks to the careful planning and preparation led by Alex," says Randy Lim, HDB's assistant CEO and chief data officer. "Alex steered HDB to win the National IT Awards in 1996 under the 'Public Sector' and 'Excellence in IT Training' categories. Alex was also instrumental in helping HDB win the Singapore Quality Award in 1997."

During his tenure, HDB also launched its online presence, called InfoWeb. Mr Lim says despite his taxing portfolio, Mr Siow also found time to serve in leadership positions in the Singapore Computer Society as president; and at the Information Technology Management Association, as the founder-president. He also held directorships in the National Computer Board and Institute of Systems Science. For his outstanding contribution to the HDB, the government awarded him the Public Administration Medal (Silver) in 2000.

THE VISION

But it was not always smooth sailing. An HR system that was outsourced to an external vendor ran into problems; it was overdue, over budget, and came under the Ministry of Finance (MOF) oversight. Mr Siow studied the case and found that the users were changing the requirements multiple times. "I wrote to the MOF and explained the reasons for the delay and said we would not impose liquidated damages," Mr Siow says.

The outsourced company was Asian Computer Service (ACS), an IBM business partner; the ACS CEO was Edward Lim. "I met Alex in 1998 as a result of ACS' failure to deliver a payroll project to HDB," Mr Lim says. "We explained the reasons for our failure and to request HDB for their understanding. Alex listened to both sides – the HDB team and us – and realised that the fault lay with both parties. He waived our penalties."

That incident left a lasting impression on Edward Lim. Years later, he could return the favour in an equally dramatic fashion. In 2001, Mr Lim was general manager at Veritas Software, a US software firm that was acquired by Symantec in 2004. Mr Siow was then head of enterprise sales at StarHub; his team had been trying in vain to get an appointment at Veritas, but their procurement manager was always busy.

Mr Siow called Mr Lim to request a meeting. "I rolled out the red carpet for Alex and his team, I had our procurement manager be present at the meeting and even organised a luncheon as a show of respect for Alex," Mr Lim says. "Soon, Veritas Software Singapore became a StarHub customer."

The StarHub enterprise sales team was impressed. "It was highly unusual for a prospect to host lunch for a vendor," Mr Siow says. "My team had never experienced anything like this before. I explained to my staff that treating people fairly and equitably will always pay dividends. Instead of bullying your vendors, make them your partners. Get them to help you. Make it a win-win situation. That's the best business model."

The "win-win" formula became Mr Siow's unstated vision that even his staff recognised and appreciated. "He liked mentoring and was very active in the IT community," says Serene Tan, Mr Siow's secretary at StarHub. "He was president or chairman of many IT-related entities. I remember updating the awards that he had earned and the list of boards that he sat on; it filled an A4-size page. He was also licensed to solemnise marriages and would do so quite often when requested by couples."

Serene Tan held a series of jobs and took part-time classes to pass a secretarial course. She worked as a secretary with Singapore Technologies before joining StarHub. "I supported Alex from 2005 until he retired in 2015," she says. "I remember he had a fantastic memory. When he was heading the CSD, we had many Indian and Myanmar staff. He would greet them by name whenever they walked past him and at team social events."

In 2013, her father was diagnosed with bone cancer and had to undergo surgery. "During my dad's stay at the hospital, I often had to bring lunch to him as he refused to eat the hospital food," Ms Tan says. "Alex knew the pressure I was under. He would often grant me the afternoon off so I could spend more time with my dad. I can never forget that act of compassion and empathy."

FAIL FAST

Another person who preferred working directly with Mr Siow was Dr Chong Yoke Sin. She was a systems engineer at IBM and part of Big Blue's team to service the HDB account. "Alex transformed the CSD in HDB and made it a vibrant organisation with many firsts," she says. "These included using a bank-style booklet that families could use to record payments made to the HDB, setting up the first client-server environment in Singapore, and one of the first to do regular BC-DR (business continuity, disaster recovery) trial runs. Alex was not afraid of failure; his motto was to fail fast, fix quickly and get things going."

Dr Chong Yoke Sin holds a PhD in chemistry and attended the Advanced Management Programme at the Harvard Business School. She has excellent credentials, among them: the founding CEO of Integrated Health Information Systems; CEO of NCS; Head of Enterprise Business at StarHub; Board Member of the Singapore Land Authority; Board of Governors of Republic Polytechnic, SG Enable and the National Kidney Foundation; Managing Partner at iGlobe Partners; and President of the Singapore Computer Society, which has 41,000 members, the largest ICT association in South-East Asia.

"Even as I moved on in my career from IBM to NCS and then to IHIS and StarHub, Alex and I have always been in touch," she says. "We also worked together in industry associations such as the IT Management Association and the Singapore Computer Society. Alex was willing to try new tech, which was a very refreshing attitude."

That attitude made Dr Chong invite Mr Siow to advise her on a deal at the Hong Kong Housing Authority in 2000. By then Dr Chong had taken over as the chief operating officer at NCS, a subsidiary of Singtel. Dr Chong and Mr Siow made a few trips to Hong Kong to present their solution, but the deal didn't materialise. "We were trying this for the first time, and we failed to win the deal," Mr Siow says. "However, I learnt a lot about doing business in Hong Kong."

On one of his trips to Hong Kong, he brought along his daughter, Iris. "We went to Hong Kong Disneyland together," Iris says. "During my university years, my dad gave me a lot of freedom to do the things I wanted to do. When I needed help, I would ask, and he would always try to help me out. We could talk about anything. He always encouraged me to pursue my dreams."

Iris says her earliest memories of her dad were about playing educational computer games like *Freddy the Fish* and *Putt-Putt*. One hidden talent: Cooking. "On Saturday nights, Dad would cook the most delicious meals for the whole family," Iris says. "On Sundays, we would travel all around Singapore, looking for the best food and different cuisines. These are some of the happiest moments that we had as a family. My parents always ensured that both my brother and I were treated equally. My brother and I were very close growing up; we still are. If my brother and I did not do well in a test or exam, we would not get scolded; we always received encouragement to do better. This positive reinforcement meant a lot to me."

Iris was four years younger than her brother, Ivan. His first memories of his dad was visiting HDB on special occasions like a family day or taking a bus to Malaysia. "All his colleagues were very friendly with us and spoke well of my dad," Ivan reminisces. "This memory stuck with me because I was very impressed at how his subordinates regarded him as a good friend, but at the same time, looked up to him with respect. It showed me that my dad was a good boss and treated his subordinates well."

Iris says she was closer to her mother because her father was busy at work or travelling. Her mother, Chew Sok Chuang, passed away from breast cancer when Iris was 16 and just about to enter junior college. "It was a hard time because it was a transition into a new school, my brother was just about to enter the army; it suddenly felt like I was all alone," Iris says. "But my dad was always making sure that I was fine. We got closer to each other. He helped me through school, and he encouraged me to obtain my driving license. Sometime in 2011, Dad suffered from a slipped disc and had to undergo surgery. I was not able to drive him to the hospital, but it made me determined to do well on my driving test, which I eventually did."

It was the serendipitous German connection that had bought the two together: Alex Siow and Chew Sok Chuang first met in 1980 at a Germany alumni event in Singapore. Ms Chew worked at the Department of Statistics, which had sponsored her trip to Germany to do a course in statistics. It turned out that Ms Chew had also studied at the Raffles Institution, and was just a year behind Mr Siow. They got married in 1982.

In November 1996, the entire family – Alex Siow, Chew Sok Chuang, son Ivan and daughter Iris – went to Europe on vacation. Their first stop was in Frankfurt where they rented a car and drove to Stuttgart to visit the Stuttgart University of Applied Sciences – or Hochschule für Technik (HFT) – where Alex Siow had studied civil engineering 20 years earlier. The German connection had come full circle.

PART ONE

Legacy

CHAPTER ONE

How to Deal with Legacy Systems

 INTRODUCTION

On June 14, 1822, a 31-year-old British maverick, Charles Babbage, announced the world's first computer – called the Difference Engine – in a paper at the Royal Astronomical Society, titled *Note on the Application of Machinery to the Computation of Astronomical and Mathematical Tables*. This revolutionary machine used the decimal number system and worked by cranking a handle. The British government was immediately interested, since producing tables was time-consuming and expensive; the Difference Engine was just what was required.

And the world's first digital programmable computer was born. And a legacy was created.

Charles Babbage lived to the ripe old age of 80 years; he died on October 18, 1871. He was a polymath, a mathematician, philosopher, inventor and mechanical engineer. Parts of Mr Babbage's incomplete mechanisms are on display in the Science Museum in London. In 1991, a functioning Difference Engine was constructed from Mr Babbage's original plans. The finished engine, built to tolerances achievable in the nineteenth century, indicated that his machine would have worked.

The legacy that Mr Babbage left behind continues its run in the current period as well. Computers have "graduated" from the mechanical to the mainframe, and the minicomputer. Then the PC came along and started another big revolution, leading to notebooks, notepads, iPads, tablets, smartphones, smart devices, and finally to IoT (Internet of Things).

The next primary visionary after Charles Babbage was Gordon Earle Moore. He was born on January 3, 1929, is the co-founder and chairman emeritus of Intel Corp, and is most well-known for Moore's Law, with which every computer professional is familiar. Here's the story:

In 1965, Mr Moore was working as the director of research and development at Fairchild Semiconductor Corp. He was asked by *Electronics* magazine to predict what was going to happen in the semiconductor components industry over the next decade. Mr Moore wrote in an article – published on April 19, 1965 – that the number of components (transistors, resistors, diodes, or capacitors) in a dense IC (integrated circuit) had doubled every year. He speculated that it would continue to do so for at least the next 10 years. In 1975, he revised the forecast to every two years; that would result in effectively halving the cost of ICs.

How does this impact you, the CIO? Moore's Law is a benchmark for the CIO (chief information officer) and the ITD (Information Technology Department) to keep upgrading not just the processes continually, but also the skillsets of the staff. Your objective is to determine how you can exploit these technological developments to benefit your ITD as well as your organisation.

That's because you're often challenged with delivering services based on high computing speeds and high availability. The technology landscape is laced with Moore's Law for hardware, and, therefore, software. You need to regularly keep updating and upgrading software such as ERP (enterprise resource planning) with new functionality that requires faster computing resources. The underlying assumption is that companies will continue to upgrade to the latest systems to get better performance.

To meet customer demands for performance, speed and functionality, you need to replace or upgrade your systems every two years ideally. However, replacing hardware is both expensive and disruptive. The ITD needs time to shut down processes, build up new systems and restore the apps and data. If you choose the cheaper component upgrade, you will have issues with compatibility. Moreover, vendors may no longer offer support for the older hardware or software used in legacy systems or applications.

For example, an upgrade of a hard disk may involve changing the entire disk farm controllers. However, keeping legacy systems functioning presents a problem. If you do not upgrade, your service levels and cost will suffer; if you do, then it will be expensive and disruptive to the organisation. That's a dilemma every CIO faces in almost every organisation.

There are two factors in legacy. The first is machine-related. You need to address the current inventory of what you already have, which is your existing technology legacy. It's not limited to the hardware and software that your ITD has. It could be multiple projects and implementations that your ITD may have deployed over the years. All of this is, therefore, a legacy for you.

The second is the human factor. That is an important step: having a competent workforce that is ready to adapt, learn and change.

The Third Dimension

As a CIO, you need to consider the third dimension of legacy, which is about change management. It involves both technology and HRM (human resource management). For example, during my tenure at HDB (Housing and Development Board), my ITD was very comfortable in the batch processes of our IBM mainframe. We had adapted to spending many days that were required to complete month-end closing statements. We were comfortable using punch-cards, we knew how to load multiple reels of tapes to back-up data, and how to change numerous drums of disk-packs to get our work done.

The minis ran faster, but it became an organisational nightmare to inform the IT operators that their jobs had now become obsolete. The minicomputers needed just a room, not the entire floor. The HDB's nontechnical staff could handle the closing of the month-end accounts; there was no need for data centre operators. Legacy is about people's work parameters and about changing established processes. It involves changes in technical knowledge, HRM and change management.

- **Organisational knowledge.** You have an army of people in your organisation who use computer systems to do their work. They form habits, have adapted to the organisation's culture and are knowledgeable using these systems. These older systems could be inefficient in the current environment, but to your senior employees, they are "efficiently inefficient".
- **Technical integration.** You have multiple generations of systems deployed in your organisation, integrated at the hardware, software and data levels. That becomes your legacy as it involves the knowledge of numerous teams in your ITD, BUs (business users) and your services providers. Some of your staff would meanwhile have left your company; some

others would have forgotten the work they have done or lost the manuals and documents. However, nobody dares to touch these interfaces as it may disrupt the systems, create errors, and generate faulty output.

▪ **Trusted business processes.** Your ITD has automated the business processes in your firm. Therefore, your IT systems represent the trusted business processes of your company; your existing employees – whom you trust – have vouched for these systems. So when you introduce a new technology or software, you will be challenging the comfort levels and knowledge of your staff. If your team does not change and adapt to the new ways, your new implementations will fail.

THE Y2K SCARE

The most significant legacy issue – and the biggest scare – was the Year 2000 problem, also called the Y2K problem, the Millennium bug, and the Y2K glitch. They all referred to events related to the formatting and storage of calendar data for dates beginning in the year 2000.

The issue: many software programs represented four-digit years with only the final two digits – making the year 2000 indistinguishable from 1900. Moreover, some legacy programmers had misunderstood the Gregorian calendar rule that determines whether years that are exactly divisible by 100 are not leap years, and assumed that the year 2000 would not be a leap year. In reality, there is a rule in the Gregorian calendar system that states years divisible by 400 are leap years – thus making 2000 a leap year.[1]

Fixing all this was not the core part of the problem. The real Y2K scare was that all of this would need changes at the source code. In 1997, AT&T had estimated that up to 60 per cent of the time and money required for its total compliance efforts would be devoted to testing the source code changes made to address the issue.

Organisations in many countries checked and upgraded their computer systems to address the anticipated problem. The reality: there were very few computer failures when the clocks rolled over at midnight on December 31, 1999.

---

[1] https://bit.ly/3jjBkAx.

In Singapore, in preparation for the Y2K crossover, many organisations took the opportunity to revamp their legacy systems and give them a new lease of life. One of the most impactful learnings from the Y2K transition was the coming together of C-level executives, finance, IT and stakeholders to address any IT issue that could potentially stop services and bring the company to a halt. It was probably the first time that CEOs saw IT as being strategic to the business.

In due course, the definition of legacy included mainframes and minicom puters. They were mainstream a couple of decades ago, but would they continue to be deployed in the new millennium? It was feared that many of the legacy systems would not survive the Y2K Bug or be around during the "dot-com generation". However, most of them did, once they were carefully analysed, modified and upgraded.

It was during this time that the companies followed three main types of migration strategies:

1. **Patch.** Some companies patched the mainframes or proprietary systems to remove the Y2K Bug. At HDB, we ploughed through millions of lines of code and still faced a danger of oversight. The rubbish in our existing systems consisted of patched routines, workarounds, temporary subroutines, and others. With staff turnovers, incomplete handovers, and insufficient or missing documentation, many companies had accumulated a tonne of IT rubbish. Making modifications to a legacy system was often impossible because of inadequate documentation, and was prone to bugs due to oversight. So a few organisations overcame the Y2K Bug by temporary patching until they could upgrade the systems.

2. **Migrate.** Some companies migrated to modern commercial systems like ERP, SCM (supply chain management), CRM (customer relationship management), sales, and distribution. These projects were expensive and disruptive as they were to be implemented company-wide. Most of these next-gen systems could support the mainframe environments as well as the lower-cost client-server architecture of minicomputers. Therefore, the risk was more to do with change management and change of attitude issues. It was also an excellent opportunity to discard the mainframe legacy and migrate to new sets of computer hardware.

3. **Segregate.** Some companies segregated the systems and created interfaces to new financial and accounting applications. That was a hybrid approach intended to maintain as much of the status-quo as possible in operations, manufacturing, sales and distribution. The focus was to ensure robust and accurate financial reporting and accounting.

Case Study

In HDB, we went with the second option, which was to migrate to commercial Y2K systems. We had support from all levels across the organisation. We considered this an opportunity to not only upgrade technology but also to revamp or reengineer our internal and customer processes. We got the top management to agree to our plan. We formed teams to chart out the methods and systems for migration.

The result was that the HDB got a new, modern technology platform from which many of our customer-friendly services got successfully launched, giving HDB the label of being ground-breakers and trail-blazers. In another example, during the Y2K transition, Parkway Healthcare Group was able to reduce its IT operational cost by 66 per cent by migrating from its old proprietary platform to a modern one.

LEGACY OF ITD

Right from the mainframe era, there was a need for skilled IT talent. The lack of talent became critical as most countries ramped up their computerisation efforts. Some nations even changed their immigration laws to attract ICT (info-communications technology) talent.

Once organisations upgraded from the mainframes to minicomputers, IT solutions expanded in reach and scope. At the start of the minicomputer migration, companies began to adopt ERP systems. That started the commoditisation of IT tools in programming, databases and the eventual emergence of PCs to replace the old green dumb terminals.

These changes in the technology landscape led to a massive shift in business processes and units; in many companies, the finance and accounting departments shrank. Most companies also saw considerable changes in their ITD to adapt to these new generations of technology. But at the core, one factor remained constant: the need for IT talent.

The situation in Singapore was not much different as compared to other rapidly developing nations. In 1990, there were about 37,000 ICT professionals in Singapore, but the demand was more than double that. To alleviate the shortage, many companies in Singapore resorted to pushing non-IT professionals to learn IT skills. If that didn't work, they began hiring IT professionals from other countries.

With the advent of the Internet, there was a massive demand for ICT professionals with skillsets in webpage design, e-commerce enablement, virtual presence and online security. The paradox: most ICT professionals in large organisations had no training in these new skills.

Most staff in the ITD possessed traditional skillsets in business, systems and data analysis, or structured programming. While these skills were still in demand, some people considered them to be "outmoded" and "archaic". It was no wonder then that new entrants to the ICT industry were reluctant to take up the "old-time" skills. At the same time, existing ICT staff were also leaving companies to pursue jobs in the new e-commerce areas that were opening up. As a result, many companies, especially large ones with legacy systems and applications, found it hard to fill vacancies in their ITD.

My colleagues, friends and peers in the ICT industry held long debates on how we could tackle the staff shortages. One easy way was to outsource or pass the problem to somebody else, to the outsourced contractor. That was not the right solution because it assumed that the outsourced firm had staff who were skilled to work on legacy systems. Therefore, outsourcing would, at best, be a temporary fix. We had to find a more permanent solution.

Retooling ITD

Before a massive rejuvenation exercise can happen, the IT staff must be trained and equipped with new skills. The organisation must invest in reskilling and training of its IT staff. Top management's commitment to change is most necessary; they should communicate this to the team. The ITD should realise that the ability to marry legacy skills with new economy skills would eventually be more valuable than just possessing new skills.

Legacy systems do not need to disappear; they can be given a new lease on life and remain relevant to businesses even in the new economy. It is worthwhile trying to rejuvenate legacy systems and marry them where possible to the latest technologies in the new economy. That is called "retooling". Eventually, the health of an organisation's digitalisation journey will depend on the effectiveness and relevance of its ITD.

The ITD would need constant retooling in the following areas:

▪ **Structures and capabilities.** When I first started my career in IT, the structure of the ITD was simple; it rested on the mainframe as the underlying system. Each department denoted a function, like systems administration, for example. That structure has since been transformed.

Companies are now grouping departments by business value, not by functions. Teams that do projects may consist of multiple disciplines, such as security, systems analysis, and testing. Accordingly, the skills specialisation has also evolved because ICT employees now have an array of tools to do more. There are also SMEs (subject matter experts) available either in-house or from outsourced vendors, or contractual or temporary staff for handling specific projects.

■ **Technology and delivery.** Unlike the mainframe environment where technology was unique and often proprietary, the solutions available today can be modified for the needs of the ITD. There are also specialised tools for specific functions. The ITD, therefore, doesn't need to be a jack of all trades.

Instead, the ITD needs to continually keep itself updated on each evolving technology so that it can select or create tools to adapt and deploy. That will have a cascading effect on training employees, purchasing hardware, software and tools, and defining the development or deployment strategy. If the ITD requires a new solution with different technology, the ITD should consider migrating the platform/tools/solutions to usher in these new technologies.

■ **Business and operating models.** Companies need to look at their operating models always. External service providers are useful if there is a lack of talent in-house. Even if the outsourced suppliers are efficient, the ITD must set up internal audit and governance structures to manage the outsourced supplier, to ensure compliance with the SLA (service level agreement). The ITD can outsource many services, but it should not outsource IT governance.

Outsourcing, as a business model, has evolved over the years. It now includes offshoring, contracted services, and managed services, including cloud-based services. That means applications that used to be available within the physical perimeters of the ITD are now available from external services providers, including CSPs (cloud service providers). Which business or operating model is suitable for your ITD depends on an array of options that you need to shortlist and consider.

■ **Mainframe maintenance.** Having many legacy systems in the organisation creates several problems. The maintenance costs for legacy systems generally increase with time because the expertise in out-of-date technologies becomes less available and costly.

The price of mainframe systems in the early days of computing was a few million dollars, compared to the more common client-server systems. Thus, the annual maintenance cost (about 20 per cent of the purchase price) was much higher for mainframes. Moreover, as mainframes were proprietary, services such as changing the hard disk was an additional cost. Client-server systems were more "open", and some even used Linux as the operating system. That helped lower prices across the ITD.

■ **Rejuvenate or replace.** The organisation has to take the bull by its horns and revamp its legacy systems. As was evident during the Y2K scare, there were two ways the ITD could achieve this: replace or rejuvenate. In the modern context, a replacement strategy is appropriate for legacy systems that can't keep pace with the company's business needs. Replacement involves building systems from scratch and could be very resource-intensive. You also need to carry out extensive and exhaustive testing of new systems.

Rejuvenation is expensive and needs a depth of technical knowledge. Legacy systems were generally well-tested and tuned and had encapsulated considerable business expertise. So for some companies, rejuvenation might be a better alternative. Legacy systems are costly to maintain and need resources for upkeep; the strategy could be to retain the legacy for a while to manage unforeseen disruptions in the new system. It can also validate the new system or do parallel financial closing with both old and new to ensure data integrity. It is essential to plan for the proper switching-off of the legacy system.

Rejuvenation involves more extensive changes than maintenance, but it retains a significant portion of the existing system. Renewal is ideal when a legacy system requires more pervasive changes than possible during the maintenance phase but has business value. Rejuvenation includes providing users with a modern GUI (graphical user interface), which improves usability. Some people call this process "creating a new façade" to the legacy system. You could also add an Internet-ready frontend so that data residing in the legacy databases can be used to power the new e-commerce applications.

From my experience, this approach is adequate to meet short-term demand, but it is a maintenance nightmare in the long term; it just accumulates more legacy. Using a patch for a GUI, or using patches to connect legacy databases to new e-commerce apps may work in the short term. However, it will be tough to extend these to mobile apps or the latest e-commerce platforms for seamless integration.

The bottom-line: IT management approaches need to change with time. That's because the evolution of tech is transforming business, government and consumer behaviour and services. It becomes a legacy if you don't change and adapt your organisation to support new advances in technology. The tech industry changes rapidly, as Moore's Law has shown; so should your ITD.

CHAPTER TWO

2

How to Deal
with Data Centres

 ## INTRODUCTION

The first-ever mainframe computer, called ENIAC (Electronic Numerical Integrator and Computer) was built in 1946 for the US Army to store artillery firing codes. It was the first general-purpose electronic digital computer. The ENIAC was big enough to require a hall-sized room, which in due course morphed to become the DC (data centre).

DCs began cropping up during the late 1950s when American Airlines and IBM Corp partnered to create a passenger reservations system offered by Sabre, automating one of its key business areas. The idea of a data processing system that could generate and manage airline seat reservations and instantly make that data available electronically to any agent at any location became a reality in 1960, opening the door to enterprise-scale DCs.

Since then, physical and technological changes in computing and data storage have led us down a winding road to where we are today. The traditional DCs, as is evident, has its roots in mainframes. A DC is a specially constructed building with reliable electricity, air-conditioning, cooling and security.

The DC buildings were huge, as was the case with the CPF (Central Provident Fund) or HDB (Housing and Development Board) in Singapore, which

25

required high computing power. The mainframes housed in those DCs were power-hungry, generated lots of heat and were massive in size. They also housed peripherals like disk drives, backup tape drives, and large batch printers. DCs needed operators who used a DC control centre to manage the computer systems and networks.

A lot has changed in the last couple of decades. Miniaturisation using semiconductors has reduced the size of computers following Moore's Law. Smaller size equals generating less heat. It also decreases the size of magnetic media like disk drives, backup tapes and networking equipment. Therefore, logically, the big DCs should have been reduced in area to data closets. But that has not happened.

The use of computing resources and apps has grown exponentially with the surge in PCs, tablets, mobile devices, and automation. Likewise, the network, which was once limited to a company's premises, has now extended to include LANs (local area networks), WANs (wide area networks), and the Internet. To collate, store, and analyse the mounds of data generated, DCs have not shrunk, but grown in size and scope.

At the same time, the need for human involvement in DC operations has shrunk. In the old days, DC operators were required to maintain the systems, carry out batch process jobs, mount storage media, and get printing jobs done. Today, automation has taken over much of these functions.

Own or Lease?

The key question for organisations: Should you own your own DC or lease it from another supplier? The cost to build a DC gets usually calculated on a price-per-square-foot basis. Depending on the city, this cost could range from US$200 per square foot to US$1,000 per square foot. DCs should have adequate access to network connections, electricity and failover resources.

"Electricity is a primary cost consideration. DCs require a great deal of power, and some parts of the world may charge as much as US$10,000 per megawatt," according to a TEP (The Engineering Project) blogpost. "You'll need a battery backup or generator, too, so that your data is protected in the event of a power outage."[1]

---

[1] https://bit.ly/2W1m2qb.

DCs have complexity and need expensive infrastructures like chilled-water systems, redundant power supplies and network connections, among others. That makes DCs a major Capex project. So it makes sense for large players such as banks, insurance companies and government organisations to build DCs.

For others, leasing DC space is a better option. Leasing began to take off in the mid-1990s. Companies could use leased DC facilities and equip them with systems, networking equipment and peripherals. Huge independent DC players such as Equinix, Digital Realty, Rackspace and Megaport began offering leased and managed DC services to large and medium enterprises.

After 2010, with the emergence of cloud computing, other companies such as AWS (Amazon Web Services), Microsoft, CenturyLink and Google began offering cloud-based services, including IaaS (Infrastructure as a Service), PaaS (Platform as a Service), SaaS (Software as a Service), and StaaS (Storage as a Service). They also spawned services such as on-premise to cloud migration. One example: Microsoft Office and email from the customer-owned software licenses and emails to a cloud-based platform, including Office 365, which is the entire Microsoft Office Suite on Azure on the cloud.

The CSP (cloud service provider) marketplace now includes players such as AWS, Microsoft, Google, Alibaba, Huawei and other niche players. The economies of scale offered by the CSPs made it increasingly attractive for the CIO to operate their IT infrastructure and systems on their platforms.

In-House or Outsource?

You have an option of outsourcing the management of your DC as well. That means you transfer the entire operations of your computing resources to external parties. Outsourcing will relieve you, the CIO, from the headache of managing a DC, but it also exposes the ITD to external risks of poor service delivery if not managed well. You may, therefore, want to keep the governance functions within your ITD team.

You can outsource IT systems, but you can't outsource the responsibilities of IT governance or ownership. There can be cost savings in an outsourcing contract. Still, there are substantial nonmonetary factors such as QoS (quality of service) that could reflect on your company's reputation if these services fail.

When your DC is running in a leased space, the service provider should be responsible for redundancy of facilities services such as HVAC (heating, ventilation and air-conditioning) data cables, and electricity. In a worst-case scenario with zero services availability, you will need to have effective BC-DR (business continuity and disaster recovery) built-in with selective redundancies, especially for critical systems.

You will need to have SLAs (service level agreements) that will state the schedule of events that need to happen when a systems disaster occurs. The outsourced or leased DC should provide a "Project Room" or a "War Room" that could double up as a command centre for an effective implementation like ERP (enterprise resource planning) or during a major upgrade. But you should not limit these facilities to just projects.

The proximity to your primary computer resources makes leased DCs a critical nerve centre for your BC-DR. You could connect your switches and routers to the alternate site to run your ERP. The secret to implementing such strategies depends on whether your team has complied with current standards and is practising the strict discipline of enabling secured application sockets, web services and APIs.

These are "peacetime housekeeping" procedures that your ITD should continuously revisit, change and upgrade. In reality, such issues are addressed during implementation or crisis – and forgotten after that. In due course, a new team comes in and eventually, the organisational knowledge is diluted or lost.

EVOLUTION OF DATA CENTRES

DCs have been evolving from the day they became part of the large enterprise, from a single room containing a single computer to enormous facilities filled with rows of racks. DCs are now evolving even more, as businesses move more of their data and apps to cloud-based systems. DC technologies have grown in different forms and architecture – in computing hardware and software, networking, systems, applications and development tools – since the mainframe days.

In the early days of computing, mainframes ran on proprietary environments (such as IBM MVS) and required a team of systems and business analysis to document user requirements. Other groups worked on COBOL and FORTRAN, two popular languages of that era.

The IT world has since moved on to open systems, commodity servers, standard apps, new development tools and more intelligent programming languages. These are the building blocks for the new generation of DCs. The design and continuous upgrade of DCs should include these developments.

For example, you may deploy VMs (virtual machines) that can run in an IDE (integrated development environment) like JAVA and PERL, or use cloud-based storage for ERP systems that serve your company's global operations. CSPs have cropped up to provide services and solutions to all kinds of enterprise apps and ops. There is a strong case to locate your virtual DC on the cloud.

Managing DCs

In the old days, you had a homogenous environment of mainframes that served the needs of the company via dedicated and secure terminals located at end-user stations. Even PCs had a window to emulate these "green" terminals and enabled users outside the company to access computer resources.

In due course, international access to systems and apps was enabled through dial-in modems, VPNs (virtual private networks), leased lines from telcos, and others. The Internet changed all that. Not only did it boost network connectivity, but it also enabled armies of users, suppliers, customers, partners and other stakeholders to connect to your computing resources.

The mass connectivity has made DC management more complex and insecure. So how do you manage these challenges as the CIO? How do you ensure regulatory compliance and offer legitimate users seamless access while keeping malware and malicious users out? Here are 10 tips on managing your DC:

1. **Location.** For a start, choose the location of the DC carefully. You should locate your DCs at separate sites, away from the business district, and save hugely on real estate cost. Since DCs don't need customers to access it physically, you can locate DCs where the rental or leasing prices are low. Ensure the location or building can handle the loading of heavy equipment. The site should have access to adequate and reliable electricity and networking/telecom facilities. Some computer equipment may not be able to fit into the elevators and would need to be hoisted by crane if the DC is on a higher floor.
2. **Flooring.** Ensure that you equip the DC with raised flooring. The cables need to be placed under the raised floor to provide interconnections between servers, storage and the telecom hub. A structured cabling system that runs under the floor-boards provides a neat and professional image and is easier to maintain. Place the cables on trays, carefully label and colour-code them.

3. **Power.** Protect the DC from unplanned power outages. It is therefore essential that there should be alternative sources of power supply. Ideally, all sensitive equipment in the DC should be protected by a UPS (uninterruptible power supply), which provides up to 30 minutes of electrical power to computer equipment in case the primary electricity fails.

   The UPS should provide enough time for the generator to start running. If a standby generator is not available, then the UPS should offer sufficient time for the servers to shut down properly so that data is not lost or corrupted. Some UPS also acts as a power conditioner, which filters spikes and troughs in the power supply. Power surges or dips may damage sensitive equipment or cause them to shut down abnormally; valuable customer or transaction data could be lost if this occurs.

4. **BCP.** The continuous availability of data and apps is critical to the business. So it's necessary to have a DRP (disaster recovery plan) or a BCP (business continuity plan) for the DC. The BCP spells out the steps to be taken when a disaster strikes. That could be environmental disasters such as a fire, earthquake, flooding or power outage. Or it could be human such as an irresponsible employee, hackers or malware. When normalcy is unlikely to be restored in the next few hours, it would be prudent to switch computer operations to an alternative site. Some companies maintain a "Secondary DC" to be used as a failover DC when required. Others subscribe to BC-DR services provided by third-party vendors, who may offer a standby DC for use in times of emergency.

5. **Security (Physical).** The physical security of the DC is an area of concern. Secure the DC against any form of unauthorised intrusion or sabotage. It is therefore crucial that you have stringent controls or checks over who is authorised to enter the DC or have access to specific areas or sectors in the DC. Security cameras should be set up at all critical areas within and outside the DC to monitor all movements, record entries and exits, and check against authorisation databases. Visitors should be asked to sign a logbook and must be accompanied by DC staff during their visit.

6. **Security (Virtual).** You may have the best physical security in place, but the bulk of attacks on DCs come virtually, from viruses, malware, ransomware, spyware, spy-bots and hackers. You need to have more stringent protocols to ensure virtual security. Security in the virtualised DC is between VMs. In the virtual network, the physical firewall cannot see traffic between VMs. In such cases, install a virtual hypervisor security appliance to enable security between VMs.

7. **EMS.** An EMS (environmental monitoring system) is crucial for the health of the DC. Most equipment in the DC generates heat and needs to be kept cool by the air-conditioning or the HVAC. Any buildup of heat in any part of the DC should trigger an alarm in the EMS. It should also detect the presence of water under the raised flooring. Water can cause the cables to short-circuit; the floor must be kept dry.

On the other hand, should a fire break out, there should be fire-fighting equipment handy – that should not use water – to put out the fire. Install a sprinkler system to help put out fires. However, ensure all the equipment is dry thoroughly before the DC can function again.

8. **Staffing.** Installing good infrastructure is half the battle; humans are the other half. Staff the DC with reliable, professional, efficient and well-trained staff. Modern DCs are far more complicated compared to the early days of computing when the computer inside the DC was just the mainframe.

It is not uncommon today to find dense and mid-range servers, SAN (storage area networks) and NAS (network-attached storage), print and file servers, voice-response systems, Internet servers, firewalls, desktop and laptop PCs. DC personnel need to be continuously updated on the latest technology so that they can manage the equipment in the DC efficiently and quickly.

9. **Ops.** Many organisations do not place sufficient emphasis on their DC operations, especially on BC-DR procedures. Some teams still think that a DC is only for organisations that have mainframes. In the client-server world, servers need to be running all the time, primarily if they cater to Internet services. The best bet is to house them in a DC and continually monitor the equipment. As all companies now use the Internet to serve customers 24/7, you should ensure systems run smoothly.

10. **PaaS and SaaS.** For a long time, ITDs needed to build DCs to run services like ERP, email, office automation and CRM. Now there are alternatives, and they have changed the way DCs are run and managed. Take email as an example: Companies like Microsoft and Google offer email with office automation as a service. That takes away the headache of doing regular updates, upgrading disk drives and implementing security, confidentiality and privacy management. You can use PaaS and SaaS instead of your own DC.

The moot question: Should you treat these as part of your DC, or should they be part of ICT governance managed by SLAs and contracts? Your BCP and BC-DR will be impacted depending on your approach.

The ideal would be to treat them as part of your DC because these systems would include the integration of workflows, ID (identity management), and security profiles. During a significant disruption (like the pandemic), you could extend the workflows to another interim system or even share secure folders with your partners, suppliers and vendors. PaaS and SaaS would help simplify the IT landscape during peacetime. However, if you don't plan it well beforehand, it can become a liability during a disruption or disaster.

 ## DC AND BC-DR

When you're dealing with a DC that houses your organisation's computing needs, be prepared when something fails. You need to plan for BC-DR and ensure that your business can resume as quickly as possible. Technology is the backbone of modern business, society and government. But it can fail or be compromised. BC-DR is no longer about tech disruption; it includes the use of tech to mitigate the risk of a disruption to business, society and government.

Having a good DR is a strategy to create redundancy. One approach is to set up a mirrored DC that is a copy of the primary DC. That can be expensive to build, equip and maintain. To save cost, and for practical reasons, you could take a "critical systems" approach. You identify the critical software apps and the system components that your ITD uses. You create redundancies for these systems in the secondary DC. This approach will be less expensive and can provide faster recovery times.

All good DR includes BCP. A good BCP should incorporate DR and layout the critical business processes that need to continue operating under a disaster. An effective DR creates redundancy on critical systems; a functional BCP maps out how the business processes will work under a reduced IT systems environment. For example, your customer service team can have manual forms that they can use during a DR phase, and these forms can be input into the system when the system recovers.

Case Studies

Here are three relevant case studies to learn from:

1. Maersk. Danish shipping giant Møller-Maersk fell prey to NotPetya on June 27, 2017, in an attack where Kremlin-backed hackers remain the prime suspects, according to media reports. At a WEF (World Economic Forum) in late 2017, Maersk Chairman Jim Hagemann Snabe lauded the "heroic effort" that went into the company's IT rescue operation.

From June 27, 2017, when he was first awakened by a 4 a.m. phone call in California, ahead of a planned appearance at a Stanford conference, it took just 10 days for the company to rebuild its entire network of 4,000 servers and 45,000 PCs. Full recovery took far longer; some staffers continued to work 24/7 for two months to rebuild Maersk's software. "We overcame the problem with human resilience," Snabe said.

NotPetya was delivered through a mock ransomware virus and wiped out data from the servers of banks, utility companies, government departments and an international airport. The Russian military spy agency GRU created NotPetya, the CIA concluded with "high confidence", according to classified reports cited by US intelligence officials.[2]

The learning? Since then, Maersk has consistently worked to improve its cybersecurity and turn it into a competitive advantage. "Indeed, in the wake of NotPetya, IT staffers say that practically every security feature they've asked for has been almost immediately approved," *Wired* magazine reported on August 22, 2018. "Multifactor authentication has been rolled out across the company, along with a long-delayed upgrade to Windows 10."[3]

2. Sony Pictures. On November 24, 2014, a bunch of hackers called "Guardians of Peace" leaked confidential data from Sony Pictures. The data included PII (personally identifiable information) about Sony Pictures staff and their families, emails between employees, executive salaries, copies of unreleased Sony films, plans for future Sony films, and scripts for certain films. The hackers then employed a variant of the "Shamoon" wiper malware to erase Sony's computer infrastructure.

The hackers demanded that Sony withdraw its then-upcoming film, *The Interview*, a comedy about a plot to assassinate Kim Jong-un, and threatened terrorist attacks at cinemas screening the film. After many major US cinema chains opted not to screen the movie, Sony decided to cancel the film's premiere and mainstream theatrical release; it opted to allow downloadable digital copies followed by a limited theatrical release the next day.

The lesson? When news of the Sony Pictures hack began to leak, the company's response showed a lack of planning. "Actions taken were sometimes contradictory or inflammatory. In short, the company lacked an appropriate incident response plan. Why this should be, is hard to fathom," wrote Stephen Cobb in a blog on December 22, 2014. "One of the most consistent themes

---

[2] https://wapo.st/2YYGiKK.
[3] https://bit.ly/2ArnxGl.

in IT security publications over the past few years has been: it's not if you get hacked but when. In other words, any responsible organisation will put in place a plan for responding to a breach. And stick to it when a breach occurs."[4]

3. Covid-19. When the Covid-19 pandemic struck, all the computer systems were working with no disruptions; the disruption was in the work processes. Software and procedures designed around a place of work were not equipped for remote work. Once Covid-19 began its run, and the Singapore government applied an extended CB (circuit breaker), almost all work environments were remote or virtual.

That resulted in an application mismatch in many companies, as business workflows moved to support working from home. DCs that were not architected with "open" connectivity with web services or secure APIs faced considerable challenges. That was because most employees were connecting from insecure home Wi-Fi routers and modems.

There was also a massive adoption of mobile technologies in the "Gig Economy." Modern BC-DR plans therefore needed to include protocols to handle external disruptions to business processes as well. Covid-19 not only disrupted employees' workflow but the entire supply chain. That is where the Gig Economy came into play: ad hoc essential services that needed to get integrated into corporate workflows. That could only happen if the IT architecture supported it.

The learnings? Quick responses are needed to adopt, adapt and integrate during a significant disruption like a pandemic. It also presents other challenges like securing PII, offering strong malware protection to home users, effective identity management, protocols to deal with new external systems, temporary ID management and procedures to ensure regulatory compliance.

---

[4] https://bit.ly/31VtA1t.

CHAPTER THREE

How to Deal with Data

INTRODUCTION

Ever since the massive mainframes began to bulldoze into large public and private sector companies, businesses have always sought insights and intelligence from the data captured by the machines. Initially, finance and accounting demanded these insights. That is why the initial phases of computing saw a large focus on financial, accounting and audit tools to manage cashflows better, to prevent fraud, and to create traffic-light notification systems to provide a degree of insight into specific areas that needed attention.

FLOW OF INFO

There is a subtle difference between data and information. Data consists of facts or details from which information gets derived. Individual pieces of data are rarely useful. For data to become information, software systems need to put data into context. The management of data – and therefore, information – has gone through waves of innovation. It's worthwhile going through a brief history of data management:

▦ **First Wave.** The mainframes were the first wave of data management. The management of data became an issue in the 1950s, when computers were slow, clumsy, and required massive amounts of manual labour to operate. Entire floors were required to warehouse and manage the punch cards that stored their data. On other levels, there were sorters, tabulators and banks of card punches.

Programs were then written in a binary or decimal form. They were read from toggled on/off switches at the front of the computer. Sometimes, magnetic tape or punch cards were used. This form of programming was called absolute machine language, later changed to 1GL (first-generation programming language).

Second-generation programming languages (formerly called assembly languages) got used as a first method for organising and managing data. Some of these languages became popular in the late 1950s. They used letters from the alphabet for programming instead of a complex string of ones and zeros.

Because of this, programmers could use assembly mnemonics, making it easier to remember the codes. These languages are now antiquated, but helped to make programs much more readable for humans, and freed programmers from tedious, error-prone calculations.[1]

▦ **Second Wave.** When client-server computing began to take off, specialised applications such as CRM (customer relationship management), ERP (enterprise resource planning), MRP (manufacturing resource planning) and SCM (supply chain management) began to get developed. That formed the second wave of the insights and intelligence journey as companies used data to understand their operations, customers, products, cost structures, supply chains and customer trends better.

The concept of data management began to take shape in the 1980s. RAM (random access memory) made it possible to store a discrete fact and quickly access it. But then, RAM-based processing was relatively slow. Therefore, there was more emphasis on "process management" rather than "data management". Batch processing was the norm. If the data was not well defined, the data could be incorrectly used in software applications. If you did not specify the process correctly, it was impossible to meet your users' needs.

---

[1] https://bit.ly/2C6uJIk.

- **Third Wave.** In the 1990s, the Internet was born, and data management took on a new life. That saw the rise of e-commerce and the integration of SCM with e-commerce. Companies began to use tools to understand user trends, behaviours, the security of transactions and emergence and detection of digital fraud. The customer base broadened. That was also the time when supply chains, manufacturing and electronic payment systems began to get integrated. Customers were getting closer to suppliers.

  The 1990s saw more work getting done in BI (business intelligence). As the Internet boom began, the emergence of big data concepts also took shape, with computing systems getting stretched to full capacity. By the late 1990s, business management software had become so advanced that predictive analytics was being discussed in the ITD, more in areas such as CRM and ERP.

- **Fourth Wave.** We are now in the fourth wave of data management, where data has become a science. Information sources now include data from social media, locations, search engines, website navigation and others. End-user behaviour and insights can be culled from the Internet, or with data from service providers like Amazon, Twitter, Google and Facebook. Real-time data is managed and coordinated on Google Maps or other platforms.

  The science of data is all-encompassing. It includes data from mobile devices, browsers, websites, social media platforms, Google and other search engines, IoT devices and embedded sensors such as pacemakers and wearable devices. New ways of collecting, collating, analysing and managing data to influence customer behaviour are possible. The science of data now works across many disciplines, including economics, sociology, psychology, analytics and statistics.

MDM

Corporate data now includes texts, scanned images, multimedia files and searches from engines like Google, Bing and Yahoo. But all data is not equal, nor is it equally structured. As CIO, your team will have access to multiple databases with different types of data (Chapter 4 deals with structured, unstructured and semi-structured data). To handle the massive amounts of disparate datasets, you need an excellent MDM (Master Data Management) solution just to keep track of what data is where.

An MDM tool can be used to remove duplicates, standardise dataset structures, and include rules to eliminate incorrect data from entering the system. Master data consists of the products, accounts and parties for which the business transactions are completed. The objective of MDM is to provide processes for collecting, aggregating, matching, consolidating, quality-assuring, persisting and distributing accurate data throughout an organisation to ensure a common understanding, consistency, accuracy and control.

MDM is required as more applications get introduced into an organisation. MDM can help merge the world of business and IT. MDM is a structured process to organise, store and analyse data. It can also include a data dictionary. MDM holds the information about your data. Besides the standard data attributes, MDM should consist of data transformation rules, business rules, assumptions and constraints of data. It should also include other unstructured data such as:

- **Email.** The email has become the mainstay of business communications. It forms a large part of unstructured data. A single email could cover a business transaction involving multiple employees, partners or other stakeholders. It is the document to show that a transaction has been received or confirmed. Emails are "unstructured data" because they are not part of a structured database, and their formats can vary. Companies like Google and Microsoft have solutions to address how to classify and analyse emails via workflow, collaboration tools and the intelligent management of subject, content and attachments. So emails are now increasingly being considered as "structured data".
- **CRM.** Customer relationship management is crucial for all companies. CRM helps you profile your customers. You can capture CRM data when your customers or prospects visit your websites or buy your products or services via e-commerce platforms. You can integrate the relevant information with your IT apps through CRM and web analytics. CRM data falls under "structured data". However, some components of CRM can be unstructured, such as complaints; the number of times customers called before a purchase, or for service. Incorporate all such feedback into your CRM system.
- **Audio and video.** Multimedia has become a key source of data for many companies. Data from video-conferencing, from security camera footage, from your prospect's visit to your retail shop, your online store, or reaction to your product advertisement, and others, can be insightful. Audio- or

video-based data can be searched, collated and analysed. Key behaviour insights can be gleaned from the raw video as well. You can use this information for advertising or campaign management, or to launch your next product or service.

▪ **Images and documents.** You need to preserve all documents, due to legal obligations like a minimum retention period. Legally significant clauses might exist in emails and other documents. For cost savings, convenience and cataloguing, you can scan and store all paper-based documents in electronic folders or data banks. An array of tools are available that allow you to handle these images beyond just cataloguing. You can also do data analytics of the content using OCR (Optical Character Recognition) if it is a typed document; if it is an image, software programs can recognise critical objects in the photo for characterisation and cataloguing.

▪ **Machine-generated.** There is an increasing slew of machines that generate electronic data that your organisation needs to collect, collate and analyse continuously. In manufacturing, you may have performance data that comes from your factory or shop floor. If you're handling logistics, the warehouse can generate a massive amount of data on product movements, supply shortages or shipments. Use all this information to perform real-time and postevent analytics and modelling to boost efficiencies and operations. You can also use data analytics to predict equipment failures or to project bottlenecks in your supply chain.

▪ **Social media.** Social media plays a significant role in corporate reputation and risk. Social media posts on platforms such as LinkedIn, Facebook, Twitter, Telegram, and WeChat reflect what others think of your company, your products and services. They are a mirror of your corporate reputation. You should leverage them and conduct surveys or solicit feedback through open contests on social media platforms. You should also plan on advertising campaigns on social media, search engines and e-commerce sites. As a CIO, you need to understand the power of social media and to leverage it effectively for your organisation.

DATA MANAGEMENT

Data management is an integral part of your role as a CIO. That includes audits, setting confidentiality policies, ensuring layers of automated security management, and delegation of authority. The CIO is the custodian of raw data, of where the data originated, how was it used, by whom, for what purpose, and what happened to it – was it archived, or deleted. The data lifecycle is part of data governance.

Managing data security just within your organisation is no longer adequate because the source of data could create legal liabilities in the future. As the CIO, you may need to work with your business owners or senior stakeholders to set data policies on the ownership and usage of data captured or created within your organisation. These policies could be subject to regular checks or audits to ensure compliance. Where does your organisation's data reside? Usually, in a DW (data warehouse).

Data Warehouse

Your corporate data assets need to be stored safely and securely. You can do so in either a "data lake" or a "data warehouse". What's the difference between the two? Gartner defines a data lake as a concept consisting of a collection of storage instances of various data assets. These assets are stored in a near-exact, or even exact, copy of the source format and are in addition to the originating data stores.

A DW, on the other hand, is storage designed to hold data extracted from transaction systems, operational data stores and external sources. The DW combines that data in an aggregated, summary form suitable for enterprise-wide data analysis and reporting for predefined business needs.

Forbes magazine defines a data lake as a repository that holds data in an unstructured way, and there is no hierarchy or organisation among the individual pieces of data. It contains data in its rawest form; it's not processed or analysed. A data lake accepts and retains all data from all data sources; it supports all data types and schemas (the way a database stores the data), which is applied when the data gets used.

However, a DW provides a snapshot in time through basic reporting of structured data – or clearly defined data types that are easily searchable. It's impossible to glean real-time insights from a DW; it can often take days to generate reports. The DW contains data arranged into logical or subject categories with time-variant versions of records. These might be differentiated with additional information to make it useful for analytics. That is where the concept of a "data mart" comes in.

A data mart is intended to retrieve client-facing data. It is usually a subset of the DW and is oriented to a specific business line or team. The DW may have an enterprise-wide depth, but data marts could pertain to a single department.

In some companies, each BU (business unit) is the owner of its data mart, including the hardware, software and data. That enables each BU to isolate the use, manipulation and development of its data.

Organisations build data marts and a DW because the information in the database is disorganised in the sense that it is not readily accessible. You need to query it using a database language, and it's tough to access or resource-consuming. Since data is a corporate asset that must be managed and used wisely for competitive advantage, many organisations have set up a DSS (Decision Support System) around a DW that integrates operational and archived data for manipulation and analysis from a business perspective.

The benefit? Having a DW will avoid having end-users query operational databases, which may have unverified fields or missing fields that may impact data integrity. Business managers may also have access to user-friendly GUI tools, so they can get the information they or their teams need, thereby increasing productivity all around.

Building a DW is easier said than done. Many DW projects get frequently side-tracked or derailed by nontechnical factors. Inherent in all DW failures is office politics and the exercise of power. That's because a DW is a crucial data consolidation and pumping station in a complex data distribution system that touches ITD teams, marketing and sales managers, business analysts, customer-relationship staff, and others. That cuts across the invisible boundaries within the organisation and overlaps domains of control.

Usually, power accrues to those who gather data and control access to it in the organisation. Hence one of the most challenging tasks in building the DW is to get data owners to open up their data for access by others. Sometimes, the data owners would not want to surrender control of their data, especially when some data is unclean or ambiguous. The fear? The data will be inspected by other groups that may have a vested interest, or blame them for data quality issues.

Reporting tools have evolved over the years and don't use computing resources extensively anymore. For business users, a new set of tools – called the EIS (executive information system) – has evolved that works with the DW. EIS tools use graphical displays and easy-to-use user interfaces. They facilitate and support senior executive information and decision-making needs.

The EIS offers robust reporting and drill-down capabilities. The EIS is an enterprise-wide DSS to help business executives analyse, compare and highlight trends in important variables so they can monitor performance and identify opportunities and problems. The EIS has now evolved to BI tools with reporting, analytics and digital dashboards.

Case Study

One of the first actions I took when I became CIO of HDB was to ask for an inventory of all the data in the organisation. I also wanted to see which applications were using or producing data. I set up a team to draw up the systems architecture of HDB and extract an MDM inventory. That included ownership, access rights and maintenance responsibilities. With this inventory, we could implement data administration and an enterprise data dictionary. From that point onwards, anyone in the organisation that wanted to create a new data field would need the approval of the EA (enterprise architecture) team.

The next stage was to identify the root databases that are central to all the applications running in the organisation. That meant that all the data in the organisation must have a relationship to the root databases. We identified the property database, the customer database, the employee database and the organisational asset database as the root databases.

Organisational data can be classified into three categories: operational data, tactical data and strategic data. Operational data is collected continuously at various customer and stakeholder touchpoints. The volatility of the operational data makes it unsuitable for creating management reports for decision-making purposes. So data must be collated at a certain point in time, for example, at the end of every month, quarterly and annually. At HDB, my team collected the relevant data, cleaned it and stored it in the DW so that useful intelligence could be mined. In this way, HDB built one of the first DWs in Singapore.

 TOP TIPS

To ensure the success of your DW project, you as the CIO must master politics as well. Here are nine tips:

1. **Understand.** Understand your role. As a DW designer, you play the role of a sociologist, marketer, diplomat and technologist, at various times or phases. Try to understand your users and their needs, know how you will market to them, and how you will establish working relationships with

them. Know what their risk/reward profiles are, what they have to give up for the project to succeed, and what will they gain if the project is successful.

2. **Inform.** Inform your dataset owners. Be frank with them. Tell them that you expect that you may find dirty, inconsistent or incomplete data. Help data owners get comfortable with this as something natural, rather than some failing on their part. Help them clean up the data, remove duplicates, check out missing fields. Point out to them that the DW project is an ideal opportunity to clean up the data.

3. **Develop.** Develop an internal marketing plan before you do the DW design. Know whom you have to sell the DW project to, what the value proposition for each target user group is, the obstacles you are likely to face, and how you will know when you have the support of the BU groups that you need.

4. **Establish.** Set specific agreements with all the data owner groups that are involved in the DW project before completing the design phase of the project. Spell out in a document which person gets what from whom, when, and under what circumstances.

5. **Spend.** Spend time during project meetings to discuss the political climate surrounding the project, changes in the user groups, status of internal marketing efforts, and late-breaking gossip and hearsay.

6. **Conduct.** Conduct regular meetings with project sponsors or management. Make sure they know, regularly, what the status of the project is, what the organisational roadblocks are, and what the project team can expect the sponsors to do about the roadblocks. Use your sponsors to break down resistance in the organisation that the project team cannot remove through diplomacy.

7. **Avoid.** Avoid pitfalls where possible. One error made by many DW managers, according to the Data Warehousing Institute, is promoting the value of the DW with arguments to the effect that "this will help managers make good decisions." When a self-respecting manager hears those words, the natural reaction would be, "Why do you think I have not been making good decisions?" and "Do you think your DW system is going to fix my faults?" From that point on, that manager will be tough to please.

8. **Manage.** Manage user expectations. Do not believe that once the DW is up and running, your problems are over. Every happy DW user will ask for new data and tell everyone about this "great new tool". They, in turn, will ask for more data to be added and will want it done immediately. That will put massive pressure on you and your ITD team.

9. **Note.** That DW is a journey, not a destination. Note that every delivery problem will result in a high-pressure search for additional technology or a new process. The DW project team will need to maintain high energy levels over long periods. A standard error is to place DW in the hands of project-oriented people who believe that they will be able to set it up once and have it run itself.

PART TWO

Information

4

How to Handle Info Overload

 INTRODUCTION

If information is the "new oil" as is often said, does too much information translate to an "oil wealth"? Not quite. Otherwise, most information-generating economies would be rolling in wealth by now.

Even the comparison seems flawed. For one, unlike oil, information is not a homogeneous product. We use oil in almost the same way worldwide – as an energy resource to power machinery and industry. Information, however, means different things to different people. If not processed and converted into intelligence or wisdom, it is of no use to anyone. At the core of all information is data.

Data is a set of raw, unorganised facts – or otherwise – that require to be processed to be useful. Data can be something simple and seemingly random and useless until it is processed or organised or collated. When data is processed, organised, structured or presented in a given context to make it useful, it becomes information.

When data storage became very cheap and accessible – especially with the arrival of cloud computing – organisations began to store lots of information. The overwhelming repositories of information led to what's commonly called "information overload". We have more information than we need; this has become a pervasive problem in most countries. Enhancements in technology such as the Internet has enabled an abundant source of information to access on demand.

The information deluge is not new. When I first became CIO of HDB in 1990, none of the staff had PCs, and there was no email. But I was given a task: to improve the productivity and efficiency of HDB. I had to set up an IT infrastructure and get all executives to be trained in the new technologies as soon as possible.

I developed what I called the OAM (Office Automation Masterplan). My aim was for HDB to issue PCs and email accounts to all executives. The only enterprise-grade messaging platform then was Lotus Notes. It's worthwhile to recount the rise of Lotus here briefly. Lotus was founded in April 1982 by the then-32-year-old Mitchell Kapor. It was well-known for the Lotus 1-2-3 spreadsheet, the first feature-heavy, user-friendly spreadsheet, to become widely available in the early days of the IBM PC.

Much later, together with Ray Ozzie's Iris Associates, Lotus released a workflow and email system, Lotus Notes. IBM bought the company in 1995 for US$3.5 billion, primarily to acquire Lotus Notes and to establish a presence in the rapidly growing client-server computing segment. In December 2018, IBM sold Lotus Software/Domino to India's HCL Group for US$1.8 billion.

I opted to introduce Lotus Notes into HDB as a workflow and messaging system. When all the key executives in HDB had a PC and an email account, information started to flow throughout the company. With the arrival of the Internet, data from outside the organisation started coming in, too. That was the beginning of the information deluge in HDB – and the start of information overload for me.

What exactly is information overload? It's a state in which a decision-maker faces a set of data points – as well as viewpoints – that may either be huge in terms of quantity or may comprise a level of complexity or inconsistency; all of which inhibit the user's ability to determine the best possible decision optimally. The limitation of scarce resources could cause this suboptimal use of information. A scarce resource can be limited individual characteristics (such as serial processing ability, little short-term memory) or limited task-related equipment (such as time to make a decision).

Overload occurs when there is too much information available, resulting in some people not being able to find the most relevant information, very much like the proverbial "looking for the needle in a haystack". A 1997 study of Fortune 1000 companies found that managers sent and received an average of 178 electronic documents a day. That figure would be exponentially higher today. According to the Radicati Group, the number of emails sent and received a day was 246.5 billion globally in 2019 and was growing at 5 per cent per annum.

Most organisations unknowingly pay a high price as individuals struggle to manage the information glut. For one, employees lose productive time to deal with information of limited value. Effective spam filters have subsequently reduced this problem with emails. A survey of 2,300 Intel employees in 2009 revealed that most considered about 33 per cent of all email they received as being irrelevant. Given that those very employees spent about two hours a day processing email (employees surveyed received an average of 350 messages a week; executives up to 300 a day), a considerable amount of time was wasted.

"Many companies are still in denial about the problem," Nathan Zeldes, a former Intel senior engineer, who oversaw the study, was quoted in an *HBR* (*Harvard Business Review*) article published in September 2009. "And though people suffer, they don't fight back, because communication is supposed to be good for you." Mr Zeldes took over as president of the Information Overload Research Group, a consortium of academics and executives, in 2008.[1]

Another set of problems could involve the constant interruptions employees face, whatever be the value of the content. When you respond to an email alert that pops up on your screen or to the vibration of your phone, or when you're "poked" by a Facebook friend, you do more than spend time reading the message. You also have to recover from the interruption and refocus your attention. A study by Microsoft tracking the email habits of co-workers found that once their work had been interrupted by an email notification, people took on average of 24 minutes to return to the interrupted task. The 2009 HBR article found that:

- Ringing phones and email alerts can lower your IQ by an average of 10 points.
- Knowledge workers spend an average of 20 hours a week managing email.
- Information overload costs the US economy US$900 billion a year.
- About 60 per cent of computer users check email in the bathroom.
- A typical knowledge worker turns to email 50 to 100 times a day.

---

[1] https://bit.ly/2BlGmeE.

▪ Up to 85 per cent of computer users say they would take a laptop on vacations.

▪ Employees consider one in three emails to be unnecessary or spam.

Most enterprises today have a massive repository of information. Some of it is valuable; most of it is not unless it is processed. Much information is regularly collected from customers in the form of purchases, creditworthiness, buying patterns and others. Data also gets collated from suppliers about their production capacity, logistics support, reliability, among others. There is also considerable information collected about employees, policies, procedures, practices and others. What happens to all this data?

Data Types

All information comes as data, digital and discrete. It has to be stored, cleaned, analysed and used. Not all data is the same. There are typically three kinds of data:

1. **Structured data.** Structured data is usually quantitative data and one that fits neatly within fixed fields and columns in relational databases and spreadsheets. Examples include names, dates, addresses, credit card numbers, stock information and geolocation. Structured data is highly organised and easily understood by the computer. Those working with RDBMS (Relational Database Management Systems) can provide input, search and manipulate structured data relatively quickly. That is the most attractive feature of structured data.

2. **Unstructured data.** Unstructured data is usually qualitative data. It cannot be processed and analysed using conventional tools and methods. Examples include text, video, audio, mobile activity, social media activity, satellite imagery and surveillance imagery. Unstructured data is difficult to define or deconstruct because it has no predefined structure, meaning it cannot get slotted in relational databases. Instead, nonrelational, or NoSQL, databases are ideal for managing it. More than 80 per cent of all data generated today is considered unstructured, and this number continues to rise.

3. **Semi-structured data.** Semi-structured data is like structured data but does not obey the formal structure of data models associated with RDBMS or other data tables. However, it contains tags or other markers to separate semantic elements. In semi-structured data, the entities belonging to the

same class may have different attributes even though they get grouped, and the attributes' order is not essential. Examples include XML, JSON and even HTML, which contains tags and elements with specific properties and hierarchies. However, the sequence and numbers of those tags vary from document to document, which is why it's called semi-structured.

 ## ROLE OF A CIO

A repository of information can become a rubbish heap if it is not analysed, sorted and transformed to become "knowledge". The dictionary defines knowledge as "the body of truths or facts or principles accumulated over time from study and investigation." Your job as a CIO is to help the enterprise distil knowledge from information.

In his 1995 book *The Politics of Information Management*, author Paul Strassman writes that information management is inseparable from politics. The management of information defines the patterns of organisations; the availability of information in the free market system determines the scope and availability of market power. Thus, organisations and their information resources are synonymous with power. Organisations and information systems management is also synonymous with politics.

That is why Mr Strassman suggests that a CIO must have sufficient authority to create, set and execute information systems management policies. Otherwise, IT and information will never become sufficiently crucial for organisations.

It is an age-old adage that information is power. Many managers hold firmly to this belief. If knowledge management is about sharing and making information available, then political boundaries must be broken, and nobody in the organisation should have a monopoly on any information. This mind-set is tough to change, and the innovative CIO will have to convince information owners that it is more beneficial for everyone to share information, instead of individuals or departments hoarding information.

Case Study A

When I was appointed to head the CSD (Computer Services Department) at HDB in 1989, my primary role was to support various functions of HDB. Since I was a non-IT executive who had become head of IT, I felt there must be something more that IT could do for HDB.

I started looking at information as a product of the tech – and my job was to develop information systems that produced the right insights for the various BUs (business units) so they could do their jobs efficiently. I changed the name of CSD to ISD (Information Services Department) to better reflect the work we did, which was to provide information. The CEO (chief executive officer) agreed when I suggested that my job title should be CIO. With that, the first CIO role in Singapore got created.

What's the difference between a CIO and a CSD head? In 1990, there was no difference because the CIO role was undefined. I had to invent the job, write my own JD (job description) and define the role as I saw fit. The first task of the day was to get the house in order.

So I set up teams to map out the enterprise systems architecture, the infra-structure and the information architecture. With these three teams and their inputs, I was able to understand which systems produced what information, how information was delivered, and where the disconnects and bottlenecks were across the three systems categories.

The next crucial task was to change the mind-set of the IT staff and the top management from being purely tech-focused to becoming more business-focused. For that, I deployed more than 10 teams to discuss with the BUs to understand what their critical business processes were, their KPIs (key performance indicators) and their business plans. I also tasked other teams to study the business environment, the profile of HDB's customers, what their concerns were, and how they interacted with HDB.

The last piece of the puzzle was the current and future tech landscape. Several teams went deep into technology issues. Everyone was out there gathering information. That had a tremendous effect: all IT staff at the ISD were engaged, involved and participated in what is now a buzzword, "digital transformation". At the same time, the team also learnt more about the business of HDB.

How did we leverage all this knowledge? All the information the staff gathered got distilled into what would become HDB's first strategic IT plan. Called Vision2000, it mapped out how HDB would use IT to deliver services to its customers. From Vision2000, several IT initiatives, projects and investments were launched, which together formed the foundation of the digital transformation of HDB. There were many subplans to support Vision2000, such as:

- The Office Automation Plan.
- The Network Infrastructure Plan.
- The Technology Roadmap.

- The Information Security Governance Plan.
- The End-user Computing Plan.
- The Quality Management Plan.
- The Data Governance Plan.
- The Staff IT Training and Proficiency Plan.

These series of corporate IT initiatives helped transform HDB's services to its customers and won HDB the National IT Award – as well as the National IT Training Award – in 1996.

KNOWLEDGE MANAGEMENT

Every organisation has two types of knowledge: explicit knowledge and tacit knowledge. Explicit knowledge, as the term implies, is one which is structured, documented, transferable and reproducible. It comprises manuals, rules, regulations, procedures, circulars, guides, structured databases and others.

The second type of knowledge is tacit or hidden, and therefore not easily captured and documented. Tacit knowledge includes hands-on skills, unique know-how, experience of key staff, and beliefs that the people in the organisation hold. It's akin to IP (intellectual property) but goes more in-depth. Since tacit knowledge resides in the brains of the employees, many companies with high staff turnover lose a lot of it.

A new buzzword has emerged in the ICT industry in the recent past: KM (knowledge management). KM promotes an integrated approach to the creation, capture, organisation, access and use of an enterprise's information assets, including explicit and tacit knowledge.

KM is touted as the antidote to the information overload syndrome because it is supposed to manage materials and information available throughout an organisation. Anyone should ideally be able to find the information they want or need, seamlessly and efficiently. KM would be the tool for employees to take intelligent and logical decisions and to leverage the repository of available expertise.

If KM were that simple, nobody would be complaining about information overload. Instead, employees would be very efficient and productive because they can easily find the information they require. It is not so because looking for the right information is not easy. That's because the data is improperly stored or kept by someone in their private storage and not made available to the organisation.

Most organisations did not have a formal infrastructure to handle KM in 2002. Even today, companies are struggling with the storage and retrieval of data. Some organisations have gone beyond KM and practice a more holistic approach to governing and managing data; the new buzzword is "data governance".

Case Study B

As CIO of HDB, I often thought about the best way to leverage technology to make HDB "a learning organisation". HDB was and continues to be a reasonably large enterprise with more than 5,000 staff and a long corporate history. HDB was set up on February 1, 1960, and tasked to solve Singapore's dire housing crisis. Many people were living in reasonably unhygienic slums and crowded squatter colonies. Only 9 per cent of Singaporeans lived in government flats, while others yearned for a place to call home.

HDB sprang into action, and in less than three years, it had built 21,000 flats. Two years after that, the number was 54,000. Within 10 years, HDB built a sufficient number of apartments for Singaporeans that helped resolve the housing crisis. HDB is now home to more than 80 per cent of Singapore's population. It spans 23 towns that house more than a million apartments.[2]

Even in the 1990s, HDB had accumulated a tonne of data, information and knowledge. One positive aspect was that HDB's staff turnover was low, with a majority of staff being with the organisation for a long time. Hence, a considerable amount of tacit knowledge resided in employees' minds.

To capture this tacit knowledge, we had to come up with a KMS (knowledge management system). Several projects were launched in the BUs, starting with an "expert system" to capture the tacit knowledge of the officers with expertise in housing policies. The KMS would help capture the decision-making processes of senior officers as they navigated problems associated with housing policies.

We also set up a DMS (document management system) to allow searches on unstructured data related to policies and guidelines. I used Microsoft Share-Point in ISD in 1996 to capture both structured and unstructured data and created an "Ask the Expert" search-bar in SharePoint. Staff would nominate and vote for SMEs (subject matter experts) in systems development, network, security, software and programming languages. We trained the SMEs to respond to staff queries.

---

[2] https://bit.ly/3ePDJiR.

There was an autonomous grading system for SMEs. Based on their responses, SMEs might get voted out every six months. Every quarter, the most active SME would receive a reward. The KMS, which we piloted in the ISD, was so successful that other departments began deploying similar systems. HDB's journey as a "learning organisation" had begun; this contributed to HDB winning the Singapore Quality Award in 1997.

There are five critical processes in a sound KMS:

1. **Create.** Creation is the process of discovering the information and its potential location.
2. **Capture.** Includes the process of digitising, documenting, extracting and storing information in corporate databases. It was called an "information warehouse"; now labelled as a "data warehouse".
3. **Organise.** The next process is to make the captured information useful. That is the process of organising the data, including cataloguing, categorising and analysing it.
4. **Access.** The processed information must now be made accessible to users. There are many tools to search and display data in the "information warehouse". Some companies created "portals" to make information more accessible and more user-friendly using Internet technologies.
5. **Share.** The final step is to share the information across the enterprise, with security, authorisation and authentication. That's because employees may benefit from the repository of both explicit and implicit knowledge in the enterprise.

Some Examples

Some examples of different KMS include:

- **Feedback database.** It is a good practice to set up a database consisting of feedback from customers and employees. Share this feedback with your organisation's design teams, R&D departments and other relevant BUs. Employees should be able to enter input into the database. The aim is to understand customer issues and preferences and translate them by tweaking products or services accordingly.
- **Shared files.** Organisations can set up a system of shared files so that employees or teams can work collaboratively on projects. Information should be accessible to everyone on the team; they should be able to upload and comment on the work done by others.

■ **Research files.** Most companies research their competitors – as well as hold focus groups – to find out how products or services can be improved, or new ones launched. The database should include this research data as well. The database should also contain objective reports on market sizes, sales potential, the assets and processes the company has in place to address marketing, sales, complaints and others.

■ **Cultural issues.** There is a need to change mind-sets and behaviours to be able to capture tacit knowledge from employees. The organisation must cultivate a culture of knowledge sharing. Many organisations have created successful ESSs (employee suggestion schemes), backed by incentives, to allow staff to articulate their ideas and to give feedback on organisational processes and services.

■ **ESS database.** The ESS database can be a rich repository of tacit knowledge. The ESS encourages employees to contribute constructive ideas for improving the organisation's workflows. The aim is to gather, analyse and implement ideas to create results that may have a positive impact on the business or deliver better value to customers. The ESS may generate ideas related to new products or services, improvement of current products or services, or improvement of business processes.

Given the importance of information and knowledge to boost efficiency and productivity, organisations must manage their knowledge repositories effectively. KMS could help people in an organisation share, access and update business knowledge and information. Here are some examples of such systems:

■ **Cross-train.** Mentoring, shadowing and other training programmes allow teams to gain business knowledge by observing how others do their work. For example, new hires at Toyota shadow experienced employees for months; new Toyota factories include experienced workers from existing factories working alongside new hires.

■ **DMS.** DMSs such as Google Drive and Box, help organisations store documents on the cloud, share files, and control access permissions at granular levels. These tools have systems for tagging files and adding metadata that makes information easier to find.

■ **CMS.** CMSs (content management systems), such as SharePoint and Bloomfire, allow teams and individuals to publish, update and access information on an organisation's intranet.

- **Social networking tools.** Private social networking tools, such as Facebook's Workplace and Slack, allow teams to communicate and collaborate on a shared space. These tools also double up as a KMS because they store archived conversations, allowing staff to search for previously discussed topics.
- **Chatbots.** Chatbots represent the natural evolution of a KMS. Chatbots like Spoke use AI (artificial intelligence) and ML (machine learning) tools to respond to staff requests for information. Employees don't have to go digging around in a CMS, DMS or chat history. Chatbots can respond to natural-language queries – for example, how do I add a new baby to my insurance plan? The chatbot can dig into the relevant databases, regardless of where that data resides in the organisation.

Case Study C

In HDB in 1998, I wanted to create a KMS for the ISD. I asked my head of Office Systems to double-hat as the KM manager. His job was to find and curate all the knowledge contained across HDB. In today's terms, this specific role has a name: CKO (chief knowledge officer).

What are the responsibilities of a modern CKO? Here's a sampling:

- Collecting relevant data that is useful for the organisation – and converting it to knowledge.
- Developing an overall framework that guides the KMS.
- Actively promoting the knowledge agenda within and beyond the organisation.
- Overseeing the development of the knowledge infrastructure across the enterprise.
- Facilitating connections, coordination and communications for knowledge sharing.
- Encouraging individual learning and innovative thinking as much as possible.
- Implementing reward plans and incentives so that more employees will share ideas.
- Determining the tech needed for the KMS and implementing the solutions.
- Putting processes in place to facilitate the creation of organisational learning.
- Measuring the impact of knowledge management on the business.

Why is a KM crucial for the organisation? Poor knowledge-sharing practices cost Fortune 500 companies US$31.5 billion annually. Up to 75 per cent of organisations estimated that practical KM disciplines boosted company productivity by 10 to 40 per cent.

The bottom line: KM already exists in many forms in most organisations. However, it is not well organised, centralised and given due recognition. Here's a classic closing line from Lewis Platt, former CEO of Hewlett-Packard: "If HP knew what HP knows, we would be three times more productive."

 TOP TIPS

Forbes staff writer Laura Shin references Daniel J Levitin's book, *The Organised Mind: Thinking Straight in the Age of Information Overload*. She lists 10 tips to overcome information overload.[3]

1. Information Dump. Get information out of your head. David Allen, the author of *Getting Things Done*, recommends what he calls "clearing the mind". That means creating a list of everything floating around your head. Immediately note down any thoughts that interrupt your work.

"Writing [these thoughts] down gets them out of your head, clearing your brain that is interfering with being able to focus on what you want to focus on," Mr Allen writes in his book. It also permits your mind to "relax its neural circuits so that we can focus on something else."

Once on paper, prioritise the items into four buckets: things to be done today, stuff to delegate, items to do this week, and things to drop. Mr Allen calls these categories: do it, delegate it, defer it, drop it. He writes that if you find something that keeps lingering on your list, it may be ill-defined, and not actionable. For example, you may write "decide whether or not to get a new car this year." That could be better broken down into sub-tasks such as: find out what your car is worth, ask the mechanic how much it would cost to keep your current vehicle on the road, among others.

2. Two Minutes. If you have to do a lot of little tasks, keep aside 45 minutes every day to plough through any items that will take you two minutes or less, like emails, phone calls, tidying up, and checking your accounts. If you're unsure how long tasks take you, follow time-tracking techniques from the most successful people.

---

[3] https://bit.ly/3fQlZoI.

3. Tag Tasks. If you have many bills, pay all of them at once. If you're planning to clean the house, don't get distracted by reorganising your closet. Completing each task once you begin is another way of being efficient with your mental resources; it compels you to keep attention on one item for some time. That allows you to get more done and finish up with more energy.

4. Don't Multitask. Multitasking may "costs" you by forcing you to decide whether to respond to or ignore a text, how you should answer if you should file this email, whether you should continue with what you're now doing, or attend to the minor interruption. All such little decisions "spend" oxygenated glucose, the very fuel you need to focus on a task. Switching between tasks will make you feel exhausted, disoriented and anxious. In contrast, once you engage the central executive mode, staying in that state uses less energy than multitasking and reduces the brain's need for glucose.

Multitasking trips you up in other ways. Russ Poldrack, a Stanford neuroscientist, found that students who study and watch TV simultaneously, the information that should reside in the part of the brain for facts and storage may instead end up in the region for learning new procedures and new skills. If you find it incredibly hard to disengage, try adopting this one habit.

5. Email Derail. Multitasking can be detrimental to your cognitive performance. Just having an unread email in your inbox while you're trying to complete a task can chop 10 points off your IQ, notes Glenn Wilson of Gresham College in London. Mr Wilson says multitasking is even more of a detriment to memory and our ability to concentrate, as compared to smoking pot. Emails coming in every few minutes is terrible for your decision-making skills and impairs judgment. Set aside 2-3 times a day for email. Just turn off notifications, so you're not constantly being interrupted.

6. Eat the Frog. You start every day with your energy for that day. As the day progresses, every decision, whether trivial or momentous, consumes a bit of your glucose. Questions like: "Should I use a red or blue pen?" draws from the same energy store as "I have been diagnosed with cancer. Should I opt for surgery or radiation?"

"The important decisions should be made at the beginning of the day when gumption and glucose are highest," says Daniel Levitin, Professor of Psychology at McGill University and author of *The Organised Mind: Thinking Straight in the Age of Information Overload*. Prof Levitin says that the Oscar-winning producer Jake Eberts had a dictum: "Eat the frog."

"If you eat a frog first thing in the morning, the rest of the day goes better," says Dr Levitin. "Whatever is the most unpleasant thing to do, do it first in the morning." Turn off all distractions by setting aside some time, focus on the task, which is the most significant thing you could work on at that time.

7. Conserve Energy. If you want to organise your bills and receipts, there's no need to run to the stationery shop, colour-code files and spend the next few weekends organising papers – unless you need to access those files many times. If you're planning about organising five-year-old bills and receipts, throw them in a box and when you need something, look for it, Dr Levitin advises.

8. Take Breaks. "People who take 15-minute breaks once every couple of hours are much more efficient in the long run," Dr Levitin says. It gives the brain an option to hit the reset button in a specific region of the brain, which is called the insula.

Taking a break, or taking a nap, or taking a walk around the block, or listening to music – these activities, which most bosses would think that they're a waste of time, they can be a significant adjunct to productivity and creativity. For instance, a 15-minute nap can increase your IQ by 10 points, though there are individual differences, he says. For most people, though, an hour or two is too long.

9. Do Daydream. The brain works in two oppositional modes: One is when you're directing the thoughts, and the other is when the ideas take over and run themselves, says Dr Levitin. Focusing allows you to get your work done, whether you're an office worker, chef or tile layer, but your mind can't stay in one gear all day long in daydreaming mode. "One thought may meld into another, and they may not particularly be related," he says.

The daydreaming mode acts as a neural reset button and replenishes some of the glucose we use up in doing a task. It also offers the great benefit of boosting creativity. The thoughts may meander from one to another, thereby creating links between things you might not have seen as being linked before, and from that may come the solutions to problems, Dr Levitin notes. Downtime is one of seven types of experiences your brain needs during the day.

10. Delegate Down. "Managers may tend to think of the workers below them as just doing the work for the pay-check," Dr Levitin notes. "But most workers reported they loved their jobs, even in jobs where you wouldn't think that's possible, such as working in city sewer systems, having to shovel manure out of the stable, or people doing heavy labour with jackhammers – things that might sound unpleasant."

That's why most workers like at least some autonomy, which is great for managers who could be suffering from information overload. Managers can then push down authority and empower people under them to exercise their good judgment.

For instance, General Stanley McChrystal told Dr Levitin about how soldiers used to phone him from Iraq in the middle of the night. "We've been watching this building for a while, and we think it might have some munitions in it," they would say. "We'd like your permission to bomb it." McCrystal would reply: "There's nothing you can tell me on the phone at 2 a.m. in five minutes that's going to make me more of an expert than you already are. You've been watching this building for six weeks. If you think we should bomb it, you should bomb it."

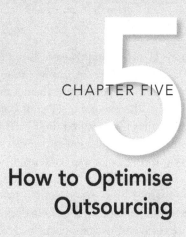

CHAPTER FIVE

How to Optimise Outsourcing

 INTRODUCTION

Outsourcing has been defined as the strategic use of external resources to perform activities traditionally handled by the company's internal staff and resources. Although outsourcing can apply to any function in the organisation, its use became commonplace in the IT world.

Companies can outsource fully, in which case the responsibility of running the entire ITD falls on an external service provider. In the early 1990s, the American giant Kodak Company shocked the IT industry when it outsourced almost its complete IT function to another American giant, EDS (which was later bought by Hewlett-Packard). The United States has seen many since mega-outsourcing deals since then.

Or it can be done selectively, in which a group of activities within the IT function gets outsourced. That is more palatable to companies that do not want to lose control of their ITD. The reasons for outsourcing are the same: lack of requisite talent at a reasonable cost. Many companies have been finding it hard to recruit IT professionals because of the global shortage of talent.

That was a significant issue during the 1990s with a boom in the "dot-com" companies. Retention of IT staff was a big problem as more and more IT professionals were lured by opportunities to make big bucks in the dot.com start-ups. Although many economic analysts then predicted that more than 90 per cent of the dot.com companies would not last beyond a few months, the exodus of IT staff continued unabated. Increasing demands by companies that wanted their ITDs to implement new systems to improve customer service and competitiveness exacerbated the situation. As a result, many organisations opted to outsource.

In Singapore, outsourcing did not take off in a big way. However, many companies have experimented by outsourcing some of their IT activities to external parties, such as help desk, data centre operations, programming services and end-user support.

The outsourcing model assumes that it is more profitable for companies to keep the most important people and activities within the organisation, and identify an external entity that can accomplish the rest of the jobs effectively and efficiently. Proponents of outsourcing have cited its many benefits, apart from overcoming the shortage of IT staff. These include reduction of operating costs, enhanced productivity, access to world-class capabilities, ability to free resources for other purposes, reduction of risk in implementing new systems, acceleration of reengineering benefits, and improvement of company focus.

Whether these benefits materialise is the subject of many studies by universities and research organisations. There are papers, articles and books written about the topic, debating the advantages and disadvantages of outsourcing. I am not going to contribute to the debate. Instead, I will touch on some issues you should consider if you choose to outsource some activities of your IT function.

Key Issues

- **Outsourcing versus contracting.** What's the difference between outsourcing and contractual work? Contract work is a clearly defined task, which the contracted party has to complete in a specific time frame, on negotiated terms and conditions, which may include financial terms as well. Once satisfactorily completed, the contractor gets paid, and the relationship gets terminated. The two parties have nothing to do with each other until another contract is negotiated and signed.

  Outsourcing, on the other hand, is a continuous process of updating and working in concert with the day-to-day operations of the business. An example of contracted work would be a contract to develop an e-commerce application for the company. Letting a vendor manage and deliver all systems development work for the company would, on the other hand, be an example of an outsourcing arrangement.

If you are going to let a vendor take over some of your IT activities, then you must first do a detailed requirements study. What do you expect the vendor to deliver? The scope, obligations of the vendor, responsibilities of the customer, acceptance criteria, payment schedules, delivery schedules, list of deliverables, change request process, among others.

▪ **The SLA.** You will also need to iron out an SLA (service level agreement) and performance indicators to measure the vendor's performance. The SLA should focus on measuring and managing productivity and service quality improvement. It is key to determining the actual value of an outsourcing engagement. To be clear, an SLA should validate the expectations of the respective parties and set parameters for measuring the project's success.

The SLA measures the status of an outsourcing project. It tracks the vendor's performance using measurable and enforceable metrics. An effective SLA can help to ensure that your outsourcing vendor is helping you meet or surpass business and technology service levels. That could lead to increased productivity and flexibility, as well as standardisation and capacity planning. An SLA brings accountability to the vendor–client relationship.

For a sound SLA, the outsourcing vendor will need to know the nature of your business. Please take time and effort to detail the business processes the vendor needs to manage, who the customers are, and what expectations the customers have. Note that there should not be any deterioration of customer service and staff productivity, as a result of outsourcing.

The assumption is that the outsourcer will do a better job than your internal staff. You also don't have to worry about IT staff turnover. However, how would you know if the outsourcing vendor has a team who are less qualified or experienced than your internal staff? What if the outsourced vendor also suffers from the same human resources problems that your organisation does? Safeguard the interests of your organisation, add penalty clauses in the SLA for instances when the outsourced vendor fails to meet agreed performance benchmarks and service levels.

INFRA OUTSOURCING

Increasing economic pressures continue to drive IT professionals to take a closer look at infrastructure outsourcing as an efficient solution to mitigate their resource gap and driving business transformation. As a result, there are a few best practices in IT infrastructure outsourcing that can help your organisation. Here are excerpts from "The Benefits of Infrastructure Outsourcing" written by Phil Sayer in *CIO* magazine:[1]

- **Focus on the Core.** The competitive business environment, coupled with a volatile economic climate, demands that companies invest time, talent and financial resources on their core competencies and activities that differentiate their businesses from competitors. Even if your organisation is tech-centric, the management and support of your IT infrastructure is unlikely to be a core competency or a key differentiator. Instead of deploying internal resources on routine activities, look at outsourcing your IT infrastructure management.

- **Commodity Elements.** It would be best if you focused on outsourcing the commodity elements of IT infrastructure on short-term contracts with standard SLAs. That's because your organisation should deploy resources on what you do best, and leave the rest to someone who specialises in it. The need to drive down costs, boost efficiency, and simplify IT operations has never been more vital. Now is not the appropriate time for major IT outsourcing initiatives. Such initiatives could take many months to plan and execute, and they only make sense in a stable economy. In today's uncertain times, you need immediate cost reductions combined with maximum flexibility.

- **Measurement Metrics.** The business case for infrastructure outsourcing may be sound, but organisations may still find cost savings lower than expected. That's because too many companies go after infrastructure outsourcing agreements based on short-term cost savings, with not enough consideration given to service quality, flexibility, and long-term needs. Moreover, organisations also neglect to measure infrastructure service levels and therefore don't know what SLAs they need from vendors.

---

[1] https://bit.ly/2ZG4XTt.

Infrastructure outsourcing contracts often fail to incorporate adequate provisions for innovation to ensure that businesses stay current with emerging best practices.

- **Cost vs Flexibility.** Forced to cut budgets and headcount, CIOs may turn to infrastructure outsourcing firms to maintain service levels while trying to reduce costs. Outsourcing may work best for well-defined commodity services that are delivered against standard service levels. The ITD must push back against an overemphasis on cost reduction and provide evidence of the problems that arise when a purely cost-driven approach rules the outsourcing decision. Aggressive demands to lower costs will force outsourced vendors to respond with proposals for long-term contracts with little flexibility. Rigid contracts may not be able to accommodate the dynamic nature of today's business environment. The result: organisations could end up buying services á la carte or growing internal staff or contractors to accommodate their urgent needs – an approach that often costs more in the long term.

- **Think Longer Term.** To be able to pay for transformation, vendors need long-term agreements to achieve the expected ROI (return on investment). Such agreements necessitate that the ITD plan for five or more years ahead. In today's environment, this is not realistic. Therefore, avoid the need for transformation by fixing your processes before you outsource. The adage is still true: If you outsource a mess, you will end up with a more expensive mess. Retain flexibility and plan for disruption, such as rapid changes in external business conditions and organisational changes resulting from divestiture or through a merger or an acquisition.

Forrester's Advice

It would be wise to plan the size of the organisation and the skillsets that need to be retained, as an integral part of the outsourcing project, not as an afterthought. My experience is that most firms underestimate both the size as well as the skillsets to manage an outsourced contract.

Why? Usually, due to a combination of overoptimism coupled with a view that the outsourced vendor will deliver what you need without being actively managed. You need to define the look and feel of the retained organisation. While some roles could become redundant during an outsourcing engagement, new positions may be required to ensure smooth contract management. Here are six critical tips from Forrester Research:

1. **Retain.** Retain knowledge and expertise. Consider business, technical and governance criteria when identifying essential skills and resources required for rapid response to unplanned business needs, as well as control over future strategy and architecture.

2. **Manage.** Manage the outsourcing relationship. Precise, continuous communication of business needs and expectations between the internal IT staff and the external provider helps establish and manage realistic expectations all around. Regular service and contract reviews are a vital part of this process.

3. **Monitor.** Monitor and manage the supplier. IT organisations need dedicated internal resources to monitor service levels, manage change, escalate late trouble tickets, and hold regular service meetings. Attention to detail is essential to obtain good service from the supplier.

4. **Maintain.** Maintain a balance of control and initiative. An adequately staffed and knowledgeable internal IT organisation signals independence and helps drive, external providers, to deliver service to the contracted quality level and to demonstrate value.

5. **Virtualise.** Hardware platform trends and emerging technologies help enable the commoditisation of IT. The key to this is virtualisation. The virtualisation of servers and storage within the data centre improves internal efficiency and flexibility. The next step is to add self-service to the process and turn the data centre into an internal cloud. That will enable the pool of available resources to be extended seamlessly outside the organisation to resources in outsourcers hosting centres, or hosted clouds.

6. **Consolidate.** This on-demand approach to computing gives organisations the flexibility to add processing and storage resources dynamically and to cope with temporary increased requirements. Consolidation and centralisation of servers into a single data centre reduces the total physical server resource required and simplifies management and security. You can access the cloud for SaaS (Software as a Service) delivery of applications that allow you to reduce the number of servers you need. If you can eliminate some of your servers, you are already simplifying your infrastructure and reducing the cost of your IT operations.

The flip side of outsourcing? The need to safeguard critical data. One of the most crucial issues revolving around outsourcing is the safeguarding of uniquely confidential information. "I consider it unwise for management to let someone else manage all of their information systems processes," writes Paul Strassman in *The Squandered Computer.* "Information management and information systems (whether computerised or not) are indeed the core competence of almost every business in the information age. With the increasing embodiment of information management into software, the control over information systems remains one of the essential managerial functions that an organisation should not entirely abdicate."

The bottom-line: To outsource or not? The answer to that question depends on you, your organisation, your needs and your options. If you have to do it, ensure that you let the vendor know what you precisely expect from them.

 ## CASE STUDIES

Some Success Stories

Here are seven examples of companies that benefited hugely from outsourcing, compiled by writer Natalia Myakinkaya in a blog post published on July 11, 2019, on Israeli company MWDN's website.[2]

1. **WhatsApp.** WhatsApp was founded in 2009 by Brian Acton and Jan Koum, former employees of Yahoo. They quit Yahoo in September 2007. Facebook even rejected their application for a job at the company. They outsourced the iOS development on the app to others who later joined the team. Almost all of the core development was entrusted to professional teams from Eastern Europe. WhatsApp took off to the top in rankings on Google Play and App Store, sounding a tech death knell to SMS. In February 2014, Facebook acquired WhatsApp for about US$19.3 billion. WhatsApp became the world's most popular messaging app by 2015 and now has more than 2 billion users worldwide.

2. **Alibaba.** This e-commerce conglomerate is now arguably as well known as the Great Wall of China. Alibaba was founded in 1999 in Hangzhou, Zhejiang, in an era when companies were using websites for customer relations. The founder, Jack Ma Yun, outsourced website development to the United States to create a website that would appeal to audiences in China and across the English-speaking world. The rest, as they say, is history. On September 19, 2014, its IPO (initial public offering) at US$25 billion was the world's biggest, and its market value was US$231 billion.

---

[2]https://bit.ly/3e1xlVs.

The outsourcing game has since reversed, with American and European companies increasingly drawing on Asian expertise in several fields.

3. **Slack.** Slack Technologies was founded in 2009 in Vancouver, British Columbia, Canada. The core team comes from the founders of Ludicorp, the company that created Flickr. Slack started operations in August 2013. It was more like an IRC (Internet relay chat) inside a browser, of which there were many in the marketplace. However, Slack aced the market. The secret? Slack had a different and friendly look-and-feel to it that differentiated it from its competitors. That happened thanks to outsourcing the general design concept, which helped revamp the app, the logo and the website. In 2017, Slack's valuation stood at US$5 billion.

4. **GitHub.** Software developers worldwide would know about Git, and 40 million developers use GitHub for version control, source code management, bug tracking and task management. GitHub is the hosting provider that also adds valuable features. Its founders, initially based in San Francisco, started by writing in the Ruby on Rails framework. At one point, it became apparent that their solution required people proficient in Git itself. A specialist, Scott Chacon, was found and was engaged as an outsourced presence behind the project. That made GitHub perfect for Git, and Microsoft acquired the firm for US$7.5 billion in 2018.

5. **Unilever.** About 15 years ago, in 2005, the British–Dutch consumer goods giant could quickly have hired a development team for its ERP (enterprise resource planning) systems integration project. But it decided instead to outsource it. Unilever then had about 200,000 employees worldwide with extensive operations in dozens of countries. But it had a fundamental IT problem to solve: merge different ERP systems. It made a master move by outsourcing the required talent. Doing otherwise might have been detrimental to the focus of the company since IT was not its core business. Following Unilever's example, scores of companies began to outsource their noncore activities. In 2019, Unilever reported revenues of €51.98 billion.

6. **Google.** It is tough to estimate how extensively Google may have outsourced IT tasks because of Google's sheer scale. Here's one that made it to the headlines in 2011: Google AdWords, which covers almost 90 per cent of Internet users worldwide who use it as a marketing tool for goods and services. Google outsourced client support for AdWords to 1,000 representatives globally, who helped customers via phone and email support. This experience proved so successful that in 2016 Google outsourced software development and IT infrastructure management as

well so that Google's staff engineers could focus on software development and innovation.

7. **Skype.** To Skype someone is now a dictionary entry; this speaks volumes about this revolutionary communications platform. First launched in August 2003, Skype was created by Swedish national Niklas Zennström and Danish national Janus Friis, in cooperation with three Estonians, Ahti Heinla, Priit Kasesalu, and Jaan Tallinn. The Estonians developed the backend, which was also used in the music-sharing application Kazaa. The features like video chat, instant messaging and file transmission have made it indispensable. In 2005, Skype was acquired by eBay for US$2.5 billion, and in 2011, by Microsoft for US$8.5 billion. That is one story that drew attention to the IT outsourcing potential of Eastern Europe. Following Skype, dozens of companies outsourced software development and IT infrastructure projects to Estonia, Ukraine, Poland, and Russia.

Lessons from Failures

Here are five examples of companies that did not entirely benefit from outsourcing, compiled by writer Anna Garland, published in a blog post on December 19, 2015, on ITProPortal.com.[3]

1. IBM and Queensland. In December 2007, the State of Queensland in Australia awarded a contract to IBM Corp to develop an application to administer payroll for Queensland's Health Department. IBM proposed to complete the project by mid-2008 for US$6 million. Shortly after beginning the project, IBM realised that it faced numerous and unforeseen technical challenges and raised the project cost to US$27 million.

The project dragged on for several years, and the payroll platform never functioned as planned. In the interim, thousands of staff failed to receive payslips, while some others were allegedly overpaid. Eventually, the project cost ballooned to US$1.2 billion. The State of Queensland sued IBM and banned it from working on other government projects. In the end, IBM and the state agreed that both had to share the blame.

A report from the Queensland Health Payroll System Commission of Inquiry indicated that IBM staff had used unethical tactics to gain favourable consideration over competitors and that Queensland officials had neither communicated their full expectations to IBM nor vetted contractors properly.[4]

---

[3] https://bit.ly/2Ay9HlJ.
[4] https://bit.ly/31MVfRZ.

2. IBM and JP Morgan. In 2004, JP Morgan Chase cancelled the remainder of its seven-year, US$5 billion IT contract with IBM and opted to bring its own IT talent back in-house. The bank decided to terminate the agreement, initiated in 2004, following its acquisition of Bank One Corp. JP Morgan stated that, with its merger with Bank One, it would have the ability to manage its IT infrastructure internally and more efficiently than through outsourcing.

"We believe managing our technology infrastructure is best for the long-term growth and success of our company," said JP Morgan CEO Austin Adams. Although JP Morgan did not accuse IBM of failing to meet its contractual obligations, IBM lost money on it, and the decision to dismantle and later reassemble its IT team cost JP Morgan a considerable chunk as well.[5]

3. EDS and US Navy. Sometimes, it is a total breakdown in communications that causes an outsourcing disaster. Such was the case between IT contractor Electronic Data Systems (EDS) and the US Navy. In 2000, the US Navy and Marine Corps contracted EDS to provide voice, video, network, desktops and systems training for their staff. By 2004, EDS had to write off more than US$500 million in lost assets because it was unable to fulfil its obligations.

In its enthusiasm to win the contract, EDS had failed to grasp the project's full scope. Only after starting work on the project did EDS realise that the Navy and Marine Corps expected EDS to integrate or replace tens of thousands of legacy applications; EDS had planned on only 10,000. The Navy claimed its share of responsibility, admitting that indecision among its staff led to EDS receiving poor direction.

The contract obligated EDS to absorb the costs for hardware changes, and there was plenty of that. EDS was also contractually bound to perform unplanned customisation of legacy software before installing new PCs. Loose contract language had left EDS vulnerable to costly and unforeseen obligations. Finally, EDS closed Q3 2004 with a loss of US$153 million.[6]

4. Navitaire and Virgin Atlantic. Sometimes, it's not the problem that creates an outsourcing disaster; it's the vendor's inability to correct it. In September 2010, Virgin's Internet booking, reservations, check-in and boarding system – among others – suddenly crashed. That was the second instance in three months. Navitaire, a subsidiary of Amadeus, was the outsourced vendor. The cause of failure was due to a failed disk drive.

---

[5] https://bit.ly/2Z2naeN.
[6] https://bit.ly/31Q7xZM.

Under its contract with Virgin Air, Navitaire had to resolve mission-critical system failures within a "short period". It took nearly 24 hours, during which time the US FAA grounded all Virgin flights, leaving more than 50,000 passengers stranded and frustrated. In hindsight, Navitaire's decision to attempt repairs on the lousy unit – instead of switching to a backup – was not wise.

The Virgin–Navitaire crisis highlights one of the key risk factors when using a SaaS vendor: your workloads become dependent on issues occurring on the vendor's hardware at remote locations. With cloud-based outsourcing, a failure in one part of the world could impact your services in another region.[7]

5. Royal Bank of Scotland. If there's one thing worse than leaving customers stranded at an airport, it is to deny them access to their money. In June 2012, a failed software update left millions of customers of RBS (Royal Bank of Scotland) unable to access their bank accounts. The bank was also unable to conduct transactions for its customers.

About 30,000 social welfare recipients did not receive their payments, despite the funds being transferred from government accounts. Also affected were customers of Britain's NatWest Bank and Ireland's Ulster Bank. It had a severe ripple effect on local businesses that created a backlog that took several days to clear.

While RBS did not disclose details about the IT vendor responsible for the software update that initiated the shutdown, it was clear that a backup plan for such contingencies was either insufficient or absent. As companies continue to focus on their core capabilities, in the face of looming competition, they need to begin to determine where to place their people and resources. Outsourcing seems an easy solution in such cases, but constant diligence is a must.[8]

6. IBM & DBS Bank. DBS signed a 10-year outsourcing deal valued at S$1.2 billion with IBM in November 2002. The deal included the transfer to IBM of 500 IT staff from DBS based in Singapore and Hong Kong. The agreement scope was broad, with IBM agreeing to "provide an integrated 24/7 customer helpdesk support, manage many of DBS's current applications, and provide systems management disciplines across the bank," stated a press release about the announcement.

As part of the deal, IBM also built new IT facilities in Hong Kong and Singapore, which used "the latest computer technologies to improve the processing

---

[7] https://zd.net/3e6C9sl.
[8] https://bbc.in/2NVaikx.

power further, security and backup capability of DBS' IT operations," the statement said. DBS retained direct control over many essential IT functions, including IT strategy and architecture, IT security and strategic projects.

On Monday, July 5, 2010, DBS suffered a major IT outage that lasted seven hours. The blackout caused DBS Bank's backend computer systems to go offline, leaving its customers unable to withdraw cash from ATMs. The root cause of the outage was uncertain, and DBS began investigating the system failure with help from IBM.

The Monetary Authority of Singapore (MAS) criticised DBS and IBM over the outage. MAS ordered the bank to redesign its online and branch technology and reduce its reliance on outsourced partners. MAS said the problem arose partly because the bank failed to put in place a robust technology risk management framework. DBS had to "diversify and reduce its material outsourcing risks" so that it does not rely on a single provider. MAS also asked DBS to review outsourcing vendors' processes and functions to ensure that its maintenance and support teams were up to scratch.[9]

 ## TOP TIPS

Here are 10 tips for setting up an effective IT outsourcing policy (Source: *InformationWeek* January 2009):

1. **Perform.** Perform due diligence to determine whether outsourcing is appropriate for your company. Tie your outsourcing strategy to your corporate business strategy. Make sure your ITD has a sourcing plan.
2. **Understand.** Understand how outsourcing is likely to impact your current ITD's staff morale and productivity. Check whether a potential outsourcing relationship is likely to impact existing customer relationships?
3. **Obtain.** Obtain top management support by creating a decision-making framework based on your outsourcing strategy. You can do this by determining the components of your ITD's costs, your IT service levels as per the SLAs (Service Level Agreements), and which IT functional areas might be ideal for outsourcing.
4. **Conduct.** Conduct a full-scale RFP (Request for Proposals) process to select an IT outsourcing provider. If your organisation has BUs units

---

[9] https://bit.ly/2Ay87Aj; https://bit.ly/3fftCoJ.

that also provide IT services, insist that these BUs participate in the RFP process, just like an external supplier would. This exercise will help you understand comparative costing.

5. **Ensure.** Ensure a detailed understanding is documented between your company and the IT outsourcing supplier. Document the responsibilities of each party in the relationship. Clearly define the duties of each party in the SLA governing the IT outsourcing relationship.

6. **Maintain.** Maintain a slate of internal IT leaders who must take responsibility for setting up IT strategy and managing the routine activities of the IT outsourcing relationships. IT leaders should report to the CIO.

7. **Identify.** Identify and document it the deal involves the transfer of internal employees to the IT outsourcing provider. If crucial staff terminate their employment with the IT outsourcing partner, clearly lay out the steps required to replace these vital staff – and timelines – with the IT outsourcing partner.

8. **Define.** Clearly define and document your security and IP (intellectual property) protection requirements with your IT outsourcing partner.

9. **Specify.** Specify that your internal ITD is responsible for the management of all services provided by your IT outsourcing provider. You, as the CIO should be the primary point of contact for all current and future activities of the IT outsourcing partner.

10. **Monitor.** Continuously monitor the performance of your IT outsourcing partner once the SLAs are signed. Ensure that the SLAs are being achieved. Insist that the provider submits improvement plans for service levels that are not being met.

CHAPTER SIX

How to Plan for Effective BC-DR

 INTRODUCTION

I first heard the term disaster recovery, or DR, when I started my career as a CIO. My colleagues urged me to plan for outages at my organisation's mainframe computer system. Planning for systems disruptions or outages was mandatory as much work in the company depended on computer systems being available. However, in those early days, such planning was limited to a straightforward method of providing redundancy with systems, applications and data backup.

Colleagues and friends warned me to prepare for outages caused by natural disasters such as fires or floods. However, in more than 30 years of working in the ICT (info-communications technology) world, fire or floods never occurred. We were planning our disruptions based on a low-probability event. We could have analysed other scenarios that could have caused an outage and measured their impact and probability. Using the Pareto principle, we could then concentrate our efforts on treating the 20 per cent of scenarios that would have caused 80 per cent of impact.

Partial or Total?

Organisations usually have SLAs (service level agreements) with vendors or service providers. The SLAs promise systems or applications uptime ranging from 95 to 99.99 per cent. The higher the uptime, the more intensive measures the IT department will need to employ to mitigate against outages. Usually, the actions will involve building system redundancy like a standby site from where the ITD can operate in case the primary system suffers an outage.

The secondary site can be a "warm site" or a "hot site". A warm site is a secondary facility an organisation uses to recover its technology infrastructure when its primary DC (data centre) goes down. A warm site features an equipped DC but no customer data. The warm site has some – or all – of the IT equipment found in a typical primary DC, including software and hardware. If a disaster strikes the primary site, an organisation can introduce customer data and may install additional equipment at the warm site. A hot site is fully functional and can enable immediate recovery from a disaster. A "cold site" would only include infrastructure but no technology until a disaster hits.

Organisations with a relatively short RTO (recovery time objective) will prefer a warm site or even a hot site. A hot site is ideal for organisations that need almost instant failovers to the secondary site in case the primary site suffers brownouts or blackouts. For banks, where the system availability must be 100 per cent, a duplicate set of equipment will operate the same system simultaneously. In case of an outage, the ITD will immediately switch applications to the hot site. Having a 100 per cent redundant system like this is very expensive.

Providing for systems availability is expensive but is it essential or necessary? In most organisations and businesses, the dependency on IT systems is so high that an outage could lead to a massive loss of revenue or reputation. So, preventing an outage is of paramount importance.

One such event that impacted all organisations worldwide was the year 2000 (Y2K) rollover event. That was as a result of the way systems were programmed to handle dates. The year field was limited to two digits; 1995 would be captured as "95" in the system. At the turn of the millennium, the year would have rolled back to 1900. That would stop all applications and databases unless companies fixed the Y2K Bug.

Although the Y2K Bug upset many ITDs, there was at least one positive outcome. The Y2K Bug made organisations realise how much they depended on IT and how badly impacted their businesses would be if any component in their IT broke down.

BUSINESS DISRUPTION PLAN

By end-1999, many organisations, whether they were well-prepared for the Y2K rollover or not, began drawing up contingency plans to cater for the possibility of a breakdown in their ICT infrastructure. These plans mapped the procedures that staff had to undertake to handle business transactions manually if there was a continuous outage in the ICT. This method was called the business resumption plan (BRP).

BRP was not only useful for the Y2K rollover but was also essential during regular times for businesses that are highly dependent on information systems. In the current competitive environment where companies need to respond to customer needs at all times, the organisation should be able to resume regular business activity quickly after a disaster.

Why Plan?

A University of Texas study shows that 93 per cent of companies without access to their ICT for 10 days failed within a year. Another study by the University of Minnesota indicated that on average, a business that suffers an ICT outage exceeding 4.5 days would find its operation capabilities diminished by more than 50 per cent. Many enterprises went bust during disasters like floods, earthquakes, terrorist attacks and other disasters simply because they did not have a BRP.

What is the possible effect on business when there is an information system outage? The initial impact is a break in the business momentum, affecting the company's ability to serve its stakeholders. Customer satisfaction levels will fall, and the reputation of the company may be damaged. In the process, whatever competitive edge the company has over its competitors may be lost.

A prolonged outage may impact the company's cash flow, especially when financial systems are down. The company will have to rely on manual teams to take orders from customers and process them at slower speeds compared to computer-assisted automation. Not only will customers be unhappy, but staff morale will also be affected. It will be worse if the breakdown impacts the company's ability to pay its employees.

Business Resumption Plan

The BRP is a process that provides safeguards to a company to help it overcome a systems outage. It helps to protect the company's assets and resources, reduces the risks associated with disasters, provides the capability to continue operating during a disaster, and helps plan a return to normal operations. The BRP provides for the development and testing of recovery procedures and standards to provide for an effective and efficient continuation of business following a disaster.

Three components make up a sound BRP: the DRP (disaster recovery plan); the BCP (business continuity plan); and the data backup plan. The DRP describes actions to be taken by the ITD to move staff, data and equipment to another site or facility to restart the computer systems. The BCP describes the activities to be undertaken by users to continue operating and serve customers manually while the ITD is busy restoring systems and backed-up data. The data backup plan describes how data should be backed up, preferably in a remote location.

The steps in developing a BRP include:

1. Determine the activities essential to continue functioning after a disaster.
2. Rank them by urgency and importance.
3. Perform a business impact analysis report to quantify the impact on the organisation.
4. Involve managers of user departments and critical team members to develop the BRP.
5. Develop a recovery strategy by determining the resources needed, the cost and location.
6. Plan for accommodations, furniture, ICT equipment, power, essential records and staff.
7. Plan for resources (such as staff) that may not be available locally.
8. Communicate the BRP to employees to assure them that such a plan exists.
9. Store copies of the plan in a secure off-site location.
10. Realistically test the BRP with ample warning to all employees about the testing process.
11. Review the BRP regularly to keep it up-to-date.
12. Identify key business dependent processes that are critical to your business operations.
13. Quantify all the risks of processes if a disruption occurs.
14. Form a BRP working team with all significant stakeholders, apart from the ITD.
15. Set up a technology architecture map that integrates with external systems.
16. Implement governance controls and backup processes for all identified critical processes.

17. Ensure there is an escalation process within the BRP, and all parties have a contact list.
18. Ensure that you should conduct regular "fire drills" to keep the BRP in top form.

The list of actions is not exhaustive. A detailed study needs to be carried out, preferably by a team trained to carry out DR and contingency planning. Hire external consultants to advise on drawing up the BRP. Whatever the case, it is essential to bear in mind that the BRP is a company activity, not an ITD project, and the executive management should support it. It is, ultimately, the management's responsibility to ensure that it is "business as usual" when a disaster strikes.

In the traditional world, the BRP may sit between the ITD and the BUs (business units). As IT services are now extended to vendors or third parties, as well as with business partners, you will need an EBRP, or extended BRP. The approach and the processes to develop a typical BRP would become the foundation to create an EBRP.

 ## MANAGING PROJECTS

At a more advanced level, a competent project manager should demonstrate several critical skills. Under the IT Project Management Certification Programme in Singapore, essential project management skills include the following: project integration, scope and time management; managing project costs, quality, procurement, communications and risk; and managing human resources, interpersonal skills, clients and project complexity. On-the-job training and experience help hone many of these skills.

Project Failures

Project failures are costly, affect morale, and are bad for business. With competent people equipped with good project management skills and techniques, you can reduce the risk of project failures and use our resources more effectively.

Only 16.2 per cent of projects are completed on time and budget, and with all the promised functionality. That's the verdict from a study conducted by Standish International, an independent IT research advisory founded in 1985. More than half of all projects – 52.7 per cent, to be precise – are overcost, overtime, and lack promised functionality. That leaves 31.1 per cent to be classified as failed, which means they were abandoned or cancelled. What causes these projects to fail?

- **Poor project management.** The leading cause of project failures is the lack of good project management. Project management is the application of processes, methods, skills, knowledge and experience to achieve specific project objectives according to the project acceptance criteria. Project management may have deliverables that must be done within a finite timeline and budget. Project management principles apply to all kinds of projects, including IT projects.
- **Poor scoping.** Many projects fail due to poor scoping at the initial stages. That includes inadequate planning and incomplete requirements, an ambiguous listing of project scope, and poor management of expectations, roles and responsibilities. Other reasons: ineffective resource management, lack of authority to overcome impediments and poor estimating practices.
- **Frequent changes.** Changes in scope or timeline or budget, especially when the project is underway, is a significant contributor to project failures. The project plan may have been well-constructed at the start of the project. Frequent changes of project managers, responsibilities and relationships of contractors and in-house staff may add to the problem. Poor change management practices, changes in technology when the project is underway, and insufficient or inappropriate skills being available are other contributors.
- **Poor management.** With many things that could go wrong, isn't it wise to have competent and experienced project managers to take charge of large projects? Unfortunately, many IT project managers are not equipped with the right skills to do their jobs, and, sadly, many of them do not even realise that their skills are inadequate.

Project Management

Here are some essential project management tips and techniques for project managers:

- **Project plan.** First and foremost, the project manager must have a project plan. It defines a project from the start through completion. The goal should be realistic, up-to-date and reviewed frequently. Break work into manageable chunks to facilitate monitoring and adjustments. Identify critical milestones and monitor them carefully. Often, many activities are interdependent, and the project manager should be aware of their inter-relationship to avoid delays.

■ **Chain of communications.** The project manager should establish short and straightforward chains of communications with the project team. Electronic means of communication is acceptable, but there should be frequent face-to-face communications to develop a better rapport with project members and have a better feel of the morale of the project team. Face-to-face communications are also more effective for problem-solving. The lack of structured communication often lets small problems create considerable delays during the project.

■ **Document changes.** Set up change control procedures to document changes made to the project requirements and the resultant changes in systems development. Change control procedures should specify how to handle changes and to charge the relevant BUs for changes. Changes are often unavoidable in a project, and the project manager should be flexible enough to accommodate changes in the project's scope and requirements. A good project manager should not be emotionally involved in a perfectly designed project plan, but in keeping the project's scope manageable and in tune with the business.

■ **Define deliverables.** Deliverables should be well-defined. The BUs and the ITD should understand and agree on the deliverables and the benefits of the project. Set up lines of communication with the key stakeholders. These would include business sponsors, executive management, users and IT professionals. Regular discussion forums should be convened to air concerns from all parties, revisit project priorities, define action items and make decisions on urgent matters.

 TOP TIPS

Here are six real-life business continuity examples compiled by author Tracy Rock for InvenioIT:[1]

1. Ransomware. Ransomware hobbled the City of Atlanta in March 2018. The SamSam ransomware attack devastated the city government's computer systems, disrupting numerous city services, including police records, courts, utilities, parking services and others. Computer systems were down for five days. That forced many departments to complete the essential paperwork

---

[1] http://bit.ly/38fZ1Fb.

by hand. The services were slowly brought back online over a period, but the full recovery took months. The attackers demanded a US$52,000 ransom payment; the maximum impact of the attack probably cost about US$17 million; US$3 million went to contracts for emergency IT consultants and crisis management firms.

The attack was a lesson in inadequate BCP. The incident revealed that the city's IT was woefully unprepared for such an attack. Just two months before the attack, an audit found 1,500 to 2,000 vulnerabilities in its IT systems, which were compounded by "obsolete software and an IT culture driven by ad-hoc or undocumented processes," according to StateScoop.

Which vulnerabilities allowed the attack to happen? Weak passwords, most likely. That was a common entry point for the SamSam attackers, who used brute-force software programs to guess thousands of password combinations in just a few seconds. It was an unsophisticated method that could have been prevented with more robust password management protocols.

Despite the BC-DR missteps, credit should still be given to the IT professionals (both internal and external) who worked to restore critical city services as quickly as they could. In effect, the city had some DR procedures in place that allowed it to restore essential services; if it hadn't, the consequences likely would have been much worse.

2. Lightning. In 2013, a fire broke out when an office building in Mount Pleasant, South Carolina, was struck by lightning. The building housed the offices of Cantey Technology, an ICT company that hosts servers for more than 200 customers. The fire burnt Cantey's network infrastructure, including cables and servers. The equipment was destroyed beyond repair; the office was ruined. For a company whose core service was hosting servers for other organisations, the situation looked bleak. However, Cantey's clients never knew the difference.

As part of its BCP, Cantey had already moved its client servers to a remote DC (data centre), where it stored continual data backups. Even though Cantey's employees were forced to move to a temporary office, Cantey's clients never experienced service interruptions.

It was an outcome that could easily have turned out differently. Only five years earlier, the company had kept all of its client servers onsite. But founder Willis Cantey thought that this setup created too many risks. All it would take is one significant onsite adverse event to wipe out his entire business, as well as his clients' businesses. It would potentially leave him exposed to legal liabilities. Cantey thus implemented a more comprehensive BCP and moved his clients' servers offsite. In doing so, he averted disaster.

3. Virus. In November 2016, a computer virus infected a network of hospitals at the Northern Lincolnshire and Goole NHS Foundation Trust in the UK. The virus crashed its systems and halted operations at three separate hospitals for five days. Patients were turned away at the door and sent to other hospitals, even in cases of significant trauma or childbirth. Only critical trauma patients, such as those suffering from severe accidents, were admitted. About 3,000 patient procedures and appointments were cancelled.

A report published in Computing.co.uk speculated that there had been no BCP in place. Even if there had been, there were failures. Disaster scenarios can be life-or-death issues at healthcare facilities. The hospital executives were initially tight-lipped about the incident. But in the year following the attack, it became clear that ransomware was the culprit – specifically, the Globe2 variant.

It was interesting to note that the hospital executives did not say the ransomware attack was because an infected email was opened (which is what leads to most malware infections). Instead, the hospital said that a misconfigured firewall was the cause. It's unclear precisely how the ransomware passed through the firewall – it may have come through email after all. Unfortunately, officials knew about the firewall misconfiguration before the attack occurred. They had plans to fix the problem, but they were too late. The attack happened before the necessary work on weakest parts of the system had been completed.

4. Network. A major electric company in Georgia suffered a failure on one of its data lines. Following that incident, it took several proactive steps to ensure its critical systems would not experience service interruptions. The company deployed a FatPipe WARP at its primary site, bonding two connections to achieve redundancy; it also planned for a third data line. Additionally, the company replicated its mission-critical servers offsite, incorporating its site-failover WARP. (FatPipe WARP combines multiple WAN connections over multiple backbones and ISPs or on the same ISP with different POPs to provide a very high level of reliability and redundancy for inbound and outbound IP traffic).

"Each office has a WARP, which bonds or collates lines from different ISPs connected by a fibre loop," according to Disasterrecovery.org. "They effectively established data line failover at both offices by installing a single WARP at each location. They also accomplished a total site failover solution by implementing the site failover between the disaster recovery and main office locations."

The initial network problem was minimal; this is an excellent example of a company that planned to prevent a worst-case scenario.

5. Fire. A German telecom company discovered a dangerous fire that was encroaching on a crucial company facility. The facility was a central switching centre, which housed vital telecom wiring and equipment that were essential to providing service to millions.

The company used an incident management system from Simba. The system alerted staff to the fire, evaluated the impact it would have, automatically activated incident management response teams and also sent emergency auto-alerts to Simba's 1,600 Germany-based employees. The fire reached the building, ultimately knocking out the entire switching centre. However, with an effective incident management system in place, combined with redundant network design, the company was able to restore service within six hours fully.

6. Hurricane. In August 2017, Southeast Texas was hit by Hurricane Harvey which uprooted homes and businesses across the region. Over four days, some places received more than 40 inches of rain. By the time the storm died down, it had caused damage worth more than US$125 billion.

The hurricane impacted numerous small businesses. A small Internet marketing agency, Gaille Media, was almost a victim. Despite being located on the second floor of an office building, Gaille's offices got flooded when Lake Houston overflowed. The flooding was severe; staff could not enter the building for three months. When Gaille's employees were finally able to enter the building after water levels receded, any hopes for recovering the area were quickly crushed: the office was destroyed, and mould was everywhere. The company never returned. However, its operations were hardly impacted.

That's because Gaille stored the bulk of its data in the cloud; this allowed staff to work remotely during the storm and later. Even with the office building shuttered, they never lost access to their critical documents and records. When a decision had to be made on relocation, the owner decided to keep the company decentralised, allowing staff to continue working remotely. Had the company kept all its data stored at the office, the business may never have recovered.

PART THREE

Motivation

CHAPTER SEVEN

How to Motivate and Mentor Your Staff

 ## INTRODUCTION

Two sides define a CIO's roles and responsibilities: On the one side are technical and organisational skills, including time and project management, planning and budgeting, and helping the enterprise "keep the lights on". On the other side are soft managerial skills, of which finding, motivating and retaining a good pool of talent should take the prime role.

With a tight labour market within the IT industry, and with more non-IT companies seeking IT staff, employers would always be chasing after a limited number of IT talent. In some companies, IT staff turnover could reach as high as 25 per cent a year.

Before we get to the task of managing IT talent, let us first define what or who constitute IT talent. Is it programmers and software developers? Or systems analysts and systems integrators? Or support and maintenance personnel? The simple answer is that it depends. It depends on the organisation and its core business. It depends whether IT is done in-house or contracted out or outsourced,

For the last two decades, IT talent meant trained staff who had specialised in technical skills in data security, systems architecture, systems engineering, or related areas. These were silo skillsets that took time to get trained and often included domain knowledge in specific areas like banking, insurance, healthcare and logistics. For example, there was specialised IT talent in ERP (enterprise resource planning) or software developers with domain knowledge of public housing or hospital management. Today, such skillsets should include "horizontal soft-skills" such as social skills, interpersonal communication skills and agile development.

In technology terms, in the early days of "big iron" computing, IT talent resided within the data centre (or server rooms). The DCs (data centres) housed mainframes, typically made by IBM or Digital Equipment Corp. Later, as client-server architecture took off, IT talent with distributed computing skill-sets were in demand. And now, IT talent must be proficient in Internet and mobile technologies, depending, of course, if the organisation or the business it is in requires such skills.

Technology gallops at a fast clip. For CIOs to be successful, they will have to be able to hire, motivate and retain their experienced staff while providing a work environment that encourages teamwork and innovation. At the same time, the IT staff should take time to understand the business of the company, and be able to hire and train new IT hires. Missing any part of this equation can make your IT – or IT talent – unstable or ineffective.

Value Good Talent

"It doesn't make sense to hire good people and tell them what to do; we hire good people so they can tell us what to do." The quote comes from Steve Jobs. The right talent, like good china, must be nurtured, appreciated and showcased.

The hiring of IT talent depends on the health of the economy, or the company. In a strong economy, there is a general overall demand for talent. But there are also other periods when IT skill is suddenly required in good numbers. That was the case when there were sudden surges in demand during the Y2K (Year 2000) rollover, cyberattacks, and during the SARS situation in 2003. I'm writing this book in 2020 at the peak of the Covid-19 pandemic, during a sudden demand for IT talent with highly specialised skill-sets in videoconferencing, remote security management, and others.

For millennial readers, here's a brief history: The Y2K problem arose because many software programmes listed years with only the final two digits; it thus made the year 2000 indistinguishable from 1900. That caused severe errors, such as the incorrect display of dates and the inaccurate ordering of automated dated records or real-time events.

These demand peaks require specific skillsets that attract a high premium. It is also during these periods that companies lose IT talent that the organisation has trained, nurtured, and is now leaving. When this talent quits, companies need to replace their expertise, which takes time and effort. Often at this point, the hiring process is rushed, compromises made, and less skilled or inexperienced talent gets hired. The direct and indirect costs of replacing the right talent are enormous. New hires need to not only know their IT but also be an excellent cultural fit and get along with the team.

It is at these periods that the IT leader needs to become a tech beacon, a leader that existing employees want to work for, and where talent in the industry would love to join the team. Retaining or recruiting IT talent should not be about meeting headcounts; it is to build a well-oiled team with shared goals and that celebrates success together. Such high-performance teams will keep the existing staff motivated and encourage external talent to join.

The value of keeping the right talent motivated cannot be understated. All organisations, whether SMBs (small and medium businesses) or LBs (large business) or GLCs (government-linked companies) run on IT. When a new player, or a new subsector, or an existing company that's expanding in other markets starts to flourish, they need talent and are willing to pay "big bucks" to get them.

The only way to get talent quickly is to poach. That's because educational institutions can't keep up with the rapid pace of technological change. Moreover, tech development and deployment involve a complex integration of technologies and a good knowledge of business processes. Therefore, when a new player in the industry, such as logistics, wants talent, they will poach IT talent from existing logistics players with domain knowledge to complement their development teams and ramp up innovation rapidly.

This practice is not limited to start-ups; it involves traditional players as well. Many large players set up "skunkworks" outside their ITDs (IT Departments). The skunkworks recruit outside their organisations to infuse new ideas and prevent any disruption to their current operations. The irony is that if you as the CIO are doing a great job, the success of your team will be a target for others to poach your talent. Your challenge then is to ensure that your "pull factor" is much stronger than the poacher's "pull gravity".

Value Good Managers

A manager's core skillset should be people management. They should be skilled in managing people and their expectations. If your managers can't keep their staff motivated, you are likely to lose staff quickly. Send your managers for training in HR management and institute a 360-degree review process for your managers, so that they know how employees and peers perceive them. Another good feedback could come from staff satisfaction surveys conducted either annually or semi-annually.

What skills do good IT managers need? Over the years, I have seen both the definitions and the expectations change as technology, business and culture evolves. Recognising these changes is an essential first step to define the CIO's expectations from the managers directly reporting to the CIO. There are three core skillsets that IT managers must have to perform their roles responsibly:

1. People management skills.
2. Stakeholder management skills.
3. Technology integration/innovation skills.

For example, if you need to set up a mobile apps development team, your manager needs to be able to handle a reasonably young, inexperienced bunch of software developers. The manager needs the skills to also work with other stakeholders, both internal and external, as well as organise teams to develop, test and implement programs that could range from ERP to IoT. How should the manager go about this task?

Here are is a short list of critical actions that every CIO should take right away:

- **Purpose.** Give employees a sense of purpose, an understanding of the "big picture" and how they fit in it. Equip them with the required training, provide them with exposure to multiple technical and project management roles, and recognise and appreciate their contributions. Recognition could be monetary rewards in due course, but a more satisfying and sustainable reward would be technical leadership and peer recognition.

- **Rotate.** Another incentive could be to offer IT staff a job rotation option. That could provide staff with greater exposure to different types of work, gain insights into various aspects of the organisation, and make their job more interesting. I don't think many people will relish the thought of spending 5 to 10 years doing the same kind of work in the same department, with the same set of colleagues. Giving staff avenues to express themselves and to contribute to the well-being of the company is an excellent way to help retain staff.

▪ **Train.** Statistics have shown that employers who do not invest in staff training suffer a high rate of attrition. That's because technology is changing rapidly, and unless staff have regular training opportunities, neither they nor the company can keep up. Training, mentoring and appropriately defining job roles are ways to get your IT talent up-to-date, relevant and willing to go the extra mile when a crisis occurs.

Be prepared that despite your best efforts, people will still leave. Some people will leave because of lack of acknowledgment or recognition of their actions and capabilities. Others may leave because of perceived inequities in salary compared to their peers. Still, others will quit because the firm does not have a clear vision and direction, or does not give enough opportunities for professional and career development.

COSTING OF TALENT

It is quite challenging to estimate the cost of losing vital talent. Some studies have reported that the actual price of losing highly talented or valued IT staff could be as high as 250 per cent of the departing person's salary. How come? The burden of finding, training and retaining a similar hire could be higher than most employers – or their HR departments – care to consider.

As discussed earlier, IT skills have evolved from being highly specialised (such as Cobol programming) to having more horizontal knowledge of other business functions. The new hire may need to know about programming and tools and be able to create value propositions of efficiencies, optimisation or new ways of doing business.

Currently, IT has become a highway that cuts across the organisations. IT aims to personalise the experience of every customer or stakeholder that interacts with it. Therefore, unlike other corporate functions, hiring IT talent is getting increasingly complex. It goes beyond basic qualifications, it seeks experience in a similar industry, it requires knowledge of other processes, and it requires that the hire can work across functional departments.

Very often, this makes the hiring process lengthy and complicated, because scouting for and finding such talent is tough. This long and tedious process is expensive and exposes the organisation to IT risk as CIOs try to recruit, onboard and train new hires. Sometimes, it takes a year to get the right candidate. Note that many professionals place great emphasis on continual education and appreciate employers who provide training and learning opportunities.

Hidden Costs

When key IT staff quit or become disgruntled, the organisation incurs various costs, most of them hidden. For example, your IT staff may have insights on which software worked, which upgrades failed, what the system weaknesses are, and where temporary patches are applied.

These oversights – and the ultimate loss of knowledge – can cause your systems to fail, as many did during the Y2K transition period, or the prolonged downtime that some companies suffered and could not figure out why. Of course, teams could have mitigated these risks through proper documentation and a thorough handover from the exiting staff to the incoming team. However, in a complex IT system – such as an EMR (electronic medical record) in healthcare, there are far too many issues that need attention.

When an IT staff member quits, her work and responsibilities have to be temporarily shouldered by others in the ITD until the ITD recruits a new hire. Sometimes the replacement may take more than six months to be hired and trained. It is not surprising, therefore, that morale among the remaining staff suffers a dip.

Staff morale makes a big chunk of hidden costs. Confidence dips further when a second staff member from the ITD resigns even before finding the replacement for the first vacancy. If the situation continues like this, the remaining team will begin wondering why they should not also be looking outside the company.

The problem is that new hires are not productive from day one. They often need to be trained. There is usually a learning curve of between three and six months (depending on the type and complexity of job role), and during this time, the new staff can only be partly as productive or effective as existing staff.

One other cost that's hidden, but significant, is the cost of the manager's time in finding and interviewing candidates, onboarding and training and them, and getting them to be a "cultural fit".

Open Costs

Unlike hidden costs, open or apparent ones are measurable. Some examples: hiring talent to fill temporary positions, paying recruitment agencies to find the right candidates and the opportunity cost of missing some milestones.

What about other open costs? One high expense is the loss in training costs of the employee who has quit. Training typically accounts for 2 to 10 per cent of a company's IT budget. In actual terms, that can translate to a few thousand dollars spent in training for staff to acquire or update technical skills to carry out their work. There are often new skills to be learnt because of the rapid advances in technology. It is therefore now not uncommon to find employers who are reluctant to send staff for training so as not to incur significant losses in training costs.

On the other hand, not providing adequate training or updating can be disastrous. For example, when CIOs want to deploy a new system, they will often budget for the implementation cost, but forget to add training cost for their staff to learn best practices in the latest technology. When an unbudgeted situation occurs, CIOs are often reluctant to send their team for training; they rely instead on project-based training. A typical example is when a new employee is thrown into the project to learn "on the fly".

During my career, I have learned that the only constant is change and that CIOs, as well as managers, need to keep themselves updated on new techniques and processes continuously. That is a real cost, as it takes time, effort and funds to give managers – including the CIO – time off to study or attend conferences.

With this knowledge, we might not be able to recruit new talent to replace the lost skillsets, but we will help boost the core skills of the team. It would also help if we took the trouble to know the real reasons why staff are leaving. Some common reasons could be higher pay, or a bigger brand, or a promotion.

But often it's because the current organisation seems stagnant and complacent. We all know how quickly new skills evolve in the IT industry, and IT professionals who have acquired new skills are often in high demand. They naturally command a premium in remuneration. They are also aware that they only have about three years to exploit their knowledge before having to learn or upgrade their skills again. Getting a better paying job may serve a dual purpose: get more money and learn new skills.

Managers need to note that IT professionals today are far more mobile and more willing to jump to another job. Many are eager to trade job security for time and money. They look for flexible working hours and good pay and benefits. Many also look for employers who are generous in providing training.

Jobs that offer frequent travel opportunities are also high on the shopping list. Managers need to understand that many young IT professionals are sensitive to compensation because of the higher living costs and higher aspirations. Some also need to repay debts incurred during their college years.

Case Study A

During June 2018 to July 2018, a cyberattack of unprecedented scale and sophistication occurred on Singapore Health Services (SingHealth). In what was until then Singapore's worst ever cyber data breach, hackers downloaded personal data and medication records of 1.5 million citizens, including that of Prime Minister Lee Hsien Loong. A Committee of Inquiry (COI), formed to investigate the cyberattack released a 454-page report that detailed its findings and recommendations. Here's a summary – compiled by PwC – of the key lessons from the COI's report:

- Employees did not have adequate levels of cybersecurity awareness, training, and resources to appreciate the security implications of their findings and to respond effectively to the attack.
- Employees holding key roles in IT security incident response and reporting failed to take appropriate, effective, or timely action, resulting in missed opportunities to prevent the stealing and exfiltrating of data in the attack.
- Network and systems had several vulnerabilities and misconfigurations. That made it easy for hackers to gain access to the data. All of this could have been remedied if identified earlier.
- The attacker was a skilled and sophisticated actor with the characteristics of an APT (advanced persistent threat) group.
- Cyber-defences will never be impregnable. It may be tough to prevent an APT from breaching the perimeter of the network. However, the success of the attackers in obtaining and exfiltrating the data was not inevitable.

 ## MENTORING METRICS

Motivation, or the willingness to get the job done by starting – rather than procrastinating, persisting in the face of distractions and investing enough mental effort to succeed – accounts for 40 per cent of the success of team projects, noted an *HBR* (*Harvard Business Review*) article published on March 13, 2019.[1]

"Yet, managers are often at a loss as to how to motivate uninspired employees effectively. Our review of research on motivation indicates that the key is for managers to first accurately identify the reason for an employee's lack of motivation and then apply a targeted strategy," the article authors Richard E Clark and Bror Saxberg wrote. "Carefully assessing the nature of the motivational failure – before taking action – is crucial. Applying the wrong strategy

---

[1] https://bit.ly/2ZGwsMQ.

(say, urging an employee to work harder, when they are convinced they can't do it) can backfire, causing motivation to falter further."

From A to F

Here's a checklist of activities – from A to F – that organisations should have in place already:

Amenable. Set up an amenable work environment. Organisations should strive to provide a comfortable working environment for their staff because this impacts staff morale. Ensure that staff take vacations, get time off and enjoy flexible working hours as far as feasible.

Bonus. Offer performance- and skills-based rewards to staff. Instituting a staff retention programme is a proactive step a CIO can take to minimise turnover. This programme should examine, first and foremost, the compensation of the IT staff. A competitive compensation package could include skill-based bonuses, market adjustment allowances, stock options, and others. Reward good work. Recognise good staff.

Communicate. Keep an open channel of communication between staff and management. Staff who are frequently kept in the dark about what is going on in the company will find it hard to be loyal and motivated. Raising employees' self-esteem will also help increase productivity and breed loyalty.

Direction. An IT organisation should have a clear sense of direction. Having a plan will help to focus the energy of the staff and foster a greater understanding of belonging. ITD staff will be excited about the direction the organisation is going to take, and the resultant projects it is going to implement. They would then be more likely to stick around. People are excited by challenges and exciting dreams.

Envision. It is not just the organisation, but also the ITD that should have a vision. As technology becomes commoditised, you can set up a cascading mission through the ITD that will allow teams to strive to achieve the overall goals. With achievable subvisions, your team can celebrate success in achieving each goal. You, as the CIO, can then mark the success of the entire ITD, which has been able to make a difference to the whole organisation. For example, a software team that develops an excellent AI-based logistics algorithm to support the ERP system, which makes the company's logistics to be the most efficient in the industry.

Focus. Focus on continual training for staff. Due to the high turnover of IT staff, many organisations are reluctant to invest in training their staff, especially new hires. Some companies do not allow their new hires to attend any external paid training courses until they have stayed more than six months on the job. Often, expectations are that the new hires will learn how to do their job through on-the-job training. Most of the time, such on-the-job training is unstructured, unplanned and more like learning by trial and error. The recruits would not be happy with this arrangement and would not want to stay long in such an organisation.

Indeed, the pervasiveness of technology to drive modern business has created a need to find better ways to manage IT talent. It is no longer enough to hire, pay and reward employees. High-performing IT teams are expected to be driven, collaborative, integrated and with strong business process knowledge. It is in such a culture that CIOs can guide their team to be innovative and provide disruptive business solutions to benefit the organisation.

Despite all these efforts, you may still experience high turnover because of the tight labour market in the IT sector. In my career, IT talent is always scarce. But be assured that as long as the employees are with you, they will do their very best.

Mentoring Schemes

As far back as 2004, Gartner noted that low integration processes and ill-defined mentoring processes would cause 30 per cent of newly hired employees to leave within 18 months of being hired. Enterprises that fail to provide influential mentors, strong sponsors and meaningful work will see their investments in recruitment become investments in turnover.

In 2016, Gartner again advised companies to start mentoring schemes, especially in the ITDs where talent is hard to come by, and skills take time to learn. "To help enterprise architecture members enhance their soft skills, EA leaders must implement a mentoring and coaching program. That will help develop the soft skills of the participants as they work with a wide range of stakeholders to deliver the required business outcomes," Gartner reported.[2]

It makes logical sense. Since companies spend so much time, effort and money to hire people, they should ensure that the new hire feels welcome in the organisation and starts being productive as soon as possible. During the first few weeks, the recruit has to get adjusted to his new environment, his

---

[2] https://gtnr.it/3gyR7Jz.

peers, his boss (or bosses) and his work. It can be quite a harrowing experience. That's where mentoring can help.

In the induction programme, each recruit could be assigned a mentor for the first few months in the organisation. Mentors could act as an advisor, teacher, counsellor and a positive role model. They would help the recruit adapt to the new environment in a one-to-one relationship that is nonthreatening for both parties.

During the mentoring period, mentors guide mentees and facilitate their transition from the university or another organisation. The mentor provides counsel on topics of concern and offers insight and perspectives in work, relationships and any other issues of interest to the mentee.

- **Induction programme.** A well-planned and structured induction programme gives sufficient time for the recruit to get familiar with the workplace, the organisation structure and culture. The recruit also learns the rules, regulations, standards and procedures; meets colleagues, peers and superiors; understands the nature of the work and his role; the facilities and resources available for staff use; and the people who will affect their career.
- **Mentoring programme.** Compared to an induction programme, the mentoring programme will be unstructured and personal. The induction programme is on a group basis (several recruits together), the mentoring programme is more flexible and is available when someone joins the company. The induction programme is to enable the recruit to know the company, department, role and technologies. The mentoring programme is to get an experienced employee to start working with the recruit. Or it can even be for an employees who are promoted; they will have a mentor assigned to ensure adequate hand-holding through change management, identifying and addressing gaps, among others.
- **Who Can mentor?** The quality of the mentors is vital. Provide formal training for mentors. Mentoring skills include effective communication, patience and listening, counselling, team building, and coaching. The mentor must also possess relevant technical skills to help the mentee with work problems. Not all staff in the company are suitable to be mentors. Since they have to be a role model for the mentee, they should be a person of good standing in the organisation, with proven integrity and well-respected. Also, they need to be diplomatic, team-oriented, insightful, have strong ethics and empathy for others. It would be good if the mentor is trained in storytelling because stories are acceptable means of sharing

knowledge and values. The mentor must be willing to sacrifice time and effort for the mentee, especially for meetings outside of office hours. The mentor can also share a meal with the mentee occasionally.

▪ **The rationale.** A successful mentoring scheme cannot be an ad hoc one. The organisation has to be clear about the rationale for implementing a mentoring system. Management needs to invest in the programme and give full support. An example would be to send selected mentors for training and to monitor the progress of the mentees carefully by requiring all mentors to submit progress reports. Provide a small expense account for mentors for them to have occasional meals with their mentees. Closely monitor the performance of the mentors; replace those who are found not to be diligently doing their mentoring duties. Note this: Having a lousy mentor is worse than having none.

Case Study B

Throughout my career, I have mentored both new hires and many experienced professionals who moved up the ranks. I would choose to have frank "coffee talks" with my mentees where we could both exchange views about issues related to the organisation or society. It was during these "coffee talks" that I began to see the deficits within my organisation from a fresh pair of eyes.

At the same time, when the mentees opened up, my experience and advice helped them to overcome their challenges. I found that effective mentoring can build successful employees who can contribute hugely to the organisation. The time sacrificed – and the patience needed to observe and listen to your mentee – brings tremendous benefits to both the mentor and the mentee. It builds a more trusting relationship, boosts team spirit and ensures success for both the mentor and the mentee.

I began mentoring in all the organisations in which I worked. Over time, it became a part of the evaluation of each employee's performance. As CIO, I had the responsibility of match-making the mentor and the mentee. This match-making goes above the conventional manager–employee relationship. Mentors get a chance to hone their skills to teach, disciple, manage and build talent. Often the mentors, in turn, were mentees of another mentor. That helped create a sustainable flow of constant learning and teaching. It helped me boost teamwork, inculcate a trusting culture and build high-performance teams.

 **TOP TIPS**

When properly implemented, the mentoring scheme will benefit the mentees in the following ways:

- Individual recognition and encouragement.
- Increased self-esteem and confidence when dealing with other professionals.
- A realistic perspective of the workplace.
- Ability to balance work and other responsibilities.
- Learning to set priorities.
- Knowledge of what to do – and not do –in the workplace.
- Learning how to network with colleagues.
- Understanding of career and workplace politics.

When properly implemented, the mentoring scheme will benefit the mentors in the following ways:

- Satisfaction in helping a recruit adapt to the organisation's culture and values.
- Recognition by peers for being entrusted to mentor new colleagues.
- Increased self-confidence and enhanced self-esteem.
- An affirmation of professional competence.
- Recognition for service to the community.
- Contribution to increasing productivity and reducing turnover.
- Learning new soft skills such as teaching, listening, and learning from the mentee.

CHAPTER EIGHT

How to Train and Certify Your Staff

INTRODUCTION

Over the last couple of decades, there has been an explosive growth in the digital economy globally, and more so in Singapore. That has created a strong demand for IT workers. At the beginning of the decade, few people had training in computer science or engineering. But the field was booming. So a large number of people, most of whom had trained in other disciplines, entered the IT workforce.

Some people described the IT sector as a "porous industry" because anyone could join the IT workforce, even without formal qualifications. There were few barriers to entry. There was also very little reason to bar anyone from entering the industry because it was very short of IT workers. There was one catch: Apart from the formal universities and IHLs (institutes of higher learning), there were no certification or short-term courses for people to get upskilled quickly and at little cost. This paradigm had to change.

FORMAL SKILLSETS

From the 1980s to the 2000s, Singapore has seen a continuous boom in the ICT (info-communications technology) industry. Starting from the NCB (National Computer Board) kick-starting the civil service computerisation, all sectors of the industry began to computerise their operations and networking.

Getting qualified and trained human resources to implement and support all of this was a problem. There was one other issue: IT professionals were building and supporting systems that impacted people's lives. So it was assumed the IT professionals would be suitably qualified to do their job. However, just how can anyone be sure whether someone who identifies as an IT professional is qualified?

When the IT industry started to take off, most companies hired people based on their educational qualifications and their working experience. Over time, the qualifications criteria included vertical skills such as programming languages. But with the coming of the Internet, mobile apps and cloud computing, new tools and management software had to be quickly learnt and deployed. The IHLs couldn't keep up.

To be sure, the necessary academic qualifications are still vital, they count as the entrance criteria, but such basic qualifications are not enough. Over time, new skillsets got added, with the advent of e-commerce, business models disruptions, big data analytics, virtualisation and containerisation. And now, there's more to learn and deploy, such as ML (machine learning), DL (deep learning), AI (artificial intelligence), IoT (Internet of Things), blockchains, and coming next, quantum computing.

Into this volatile mix, you have to add soft-skills, as well as skills related to innovation, creativity, resourcefulness and ability to disrupt by thinking out-of-the-box. Singapore has done well so far. We struggled when the Internet era began; and with the mobility era, both of which required a dash of innovation and e-commerce. And now, the struggle may become a bit harder with AI in the mix.

▣ **Apprenticeships.** Many countries have been debating for a long time about the professional status of IT workers. The idea was to take a page from other professions and accord IT workers a professional status like those enjoyed by engineers, chartered accountants, lawyers and medical doctors. The ICT industry wanted to find a way to ensure that these workers adhered to a "code of practice" or a "code of ethics". A certification scheme was needed to admit suitably qualified people of good standing into the ranks of ICT professionals. However, this was easier said than done, mainly because changes in the ICT world were far more rapid as compared to the world of lawyers, accountants or physicians.

There were two options to consider: An apprentice scheme and an internship programme. What's the difference between the two?

- **Apprenticeship scheme.** The trainee undergoes training in the skills required for a particular occupation or trade. The trainee can get hands-on experience while working with a skilled and experienced worker.

- **Internship programme.** The recruit gets on-the-job training at the actual work location. These may include orientation, coaching, job instruction, and completion of one part of the internship to be raised to the next level of competence. The training is usually for undergraduate students where they learn specific skills and work experience for which they may or may not get paid.

- **IT skills.** There were various initiatives to upgrade skillsets of IT professionals over the decades. In 1980, the DPMA (Data Processing Management Association) of Singapore was founded, since data processing equated to computing in that decade. In 1986, the SIM (Singapore Information Management) chapter of the SCS (Singapore Computer Society) was set up. Both DPMA and SIM overlapped each other.

Therefore, I began the process to merge the DPMA and SIM into a new body called ITMA (Information Technology Management Association), which was formally born on March 28, 1998. The ITMA thus becomes the sole authority to represent the IT managers in Singapore, and I was its first president. It has since inherited an impressive history created by the combination of two organisations.

Right from the 1980s, the DPMA and the SCS came together to develop a framework to train or upgrade professionals on new IT skillsets. But it was a constant catch-up game since the technology was advancing so rapidly. That's when the idea of taking a leaf from the apprenticeship scheme of the engineering industry took root. The goal was to have independent or third parties evaluate and certify skill levels and competencies of candidates.

The IT industry is still finding its way on how to address the current ICT needs of Singapore. We have always been one of the leaders in Asia to define the role of IT talent. Could we also lead in coming up with a professional status certification such as with engineering, for IT? It may be necessary for two reasons: One, the current legacy of IT organisations and role definition are old and need constant revamping. Two, we need to address soft skills, an increasing need in IT. For example, for the role of a CTO (Chief Technology Officer), even though the person may be qualified, the part calls for innovation, people- and cross-technology skills, which may be lacking. The jury is out on this one.

 ## CERTIFICATION

In 1965, an engineer named Gordon Moore, then age 36, wrote a paper stating that the number of components per IC (integrated circuit) would double every year for the next decade. In 1975, he revised the forecast to doubling every two years, at a CAGR (compound annual growth rate) of 40 per cent. Gordon Moore was the co-founder and chairman emeritus of Intel Corp; as of October 2019, his net worth was reported to be US$11.9 billion.

What has Moore's Law got to do with us? It has become an obstacle to the implementation of a certification scheme for IT professionals due to the rapid advancement of IT. With every doubling of the speed of the microprocessor, new systems get launched, which are more powerful compared to the previous ones. Hence, more complex and powerful software is possible.

The introduction of new systems and software every 18 months would necessarily mean that a lot of IT knowledge has a shelf life of only two years. Since the body of experience in the IT profession keeps changing every couple of years, to which standard should we then certify the professionals?

The issue is that the IT industry is riding on two highways of change: The first is a change in technological prowess every two years. The second is a high velocity of change in the business environment. Therefore, should the certification measure a candidate's depth of technical skills, or should it also include business process knowledge? It is akin to judging the skills of a carpenter against his ability to use a saw to cut a perfectly straight line – versus measuring him on his ability to build a sturdy and beautiful chair.

Despite all that, there was yet another issue: Which educational institution to trust? There are many educational institutions – ranging from private schools to polytechnics to universities – which offer computer or IT training. How can companies be sure whether the qualifications obtained from one institution is of an acceptable standard versus another?

Certifying Bodies

The only way to be sure is if there is an external, independent accreditation body that accredits all these institutions and their educational qualifications against a standard benchmark. Here is a list of organisations that are trying to standardise the certification process:

- **IFIP.** At a global level, the IFIP (International Federation of Information Processing) has been working to harmonise IT qualifications for many years. IFIP is a worldwide entity for researchers and professionals working in the ICT sector. Founded in 1960 under UNESCO, it links 50 societies and academies of science with a membership of more than 500,000 professionals. IFIP is headquartered in Austria; it is a nongovernmental, non-profit organisation.[1]
- **SEARCC.** Closer to home, the SEARCC (South East Asian Regional Computer Confederation) has also been working on a project to harmonise professional standards in the IT profession. SEARCC is a confederation of IT and technology professional associations. Headquartered in Sydney, its members represent more than 200,000 ICT professionals across South-East Asia.[2]
- **SFIA.** Certification is a complex problem to solve if we want to align it with the current developments in the IT industry and the professional competencies that are required to use technology effectively. SFIA (Skills Framework for the Information Age) developed one such model. This London-headquartered not-for-profit entity is a model for describing and managing skills and competencies for professionals in the ICT industry. Set up in 2000, SFIA is a consortium of many organisations, spearheaded by the British Computer Society.[3] (SFIA table on page 110).
- **SCS.** For more than a decade, the (SFIA). SCS (Singapore Computer Society) has been trying to implement a certification scheme for IT professionals in Singapore. In early 1998, the SCS decided to try a new approach to the problem of trying to certify entry-level candidates. The SCS agreed that this was the job best left to educational institutions. Those who earned a

---

[1] https://www.ifip.org.
[2] https://searcc.org/about-us.
[3] https://www.sfia-online.org/en.

diploma or a degree from these accredited institutions would be qualified. What was needed was a certification scheme for professionals at higher levels. The SCS, with support from the NCB (National Computer Board), implemented CITPM (Certification for IT Project Managers) from November 1998. That was the first certification scheme for the IT professionals in the region; maybe one of the first in the world.[4]

Certification at the higher levels of the IT profession is ideal for four reasons:

1. At higher levels where people-management skillsets are critical, soft skills have more weightage than technical skills. In any case, technical knowledge remains as the baseline.
2. Experience and expertise add to managers acquiring soft skills. Therefore, there is very little need for any harmonisation of skillsets for technical skills.
3. Certification at higher levels of the profession does not create barriers to entry. It instead serves to honour and recognise practising ICT professionals.
4. The certification scheme has support from the ICT industry and has received appreciation from the world community, including the distinguished PMI (Project Management Institute) in the United States.

Project Management

Project management is defined as the practice of initiating, planning, executing, controlling, and closing the work of a team to achieve specific goals and meet specific success criteria at the specified time. The critical challenge of project management is to accomplish all of the project goals within the given constraints. Project management is a very crucial component of the ICT industry.

Why certify project managers? Because all ICT systems that have been deployed, either involving hardware or software, were all implemented as projects. That is the crucial reason why the work done by IT professionals is comparable with the work done by engineers. The success of any IT deployment depends on proper project management. A skilled IT project manager would have the requisite technical knowledge and leadership skills to plan, execute, and deliver an IT project within budget and on schedule. For this to happen, not just technical expertise, but soft skills would also come into play.

---

[4]https://www.scs.org.sg.

Therefore, a certification scheme for IT project managers provides employers with a yardstick to measure the capability and suitability of a potential candidate to manage IT projects. It also provides a means for experienced IT professionals to distinguish themselves and for their abilities to be recognised.

At a macro level, having a pool of certified IT project managers helps position Singapore excellently well to be able to attract investors. In the digital age, no company can survive without the use of IT. Implementing strategic IS (information systems) projects is the key to competitiveness, and having the right IT expertise in-house is, therefore, a necessity. What then are vital project management skills? How can the team contribute to the success of a project? Here are four attributes of a good project manager:

1. **Entrepreneurial.** A good project manager should be like an entrepreneur setting up a technology company. That's because running a project is like running a company. Both require not only tech knowledge, but also financial, contractual, crisis and stakeholders' management. The soft skills of the manager are fundamental to the success of the project. Poor project management can lead to an array of issues, such as cost overruns, user rebellion, delayed implementation and team turnover.

2. **Certification.** Certification is one dimension to mitigate the risk of having insufficient project managers. The training, as well as the methodologies involved in passing these certifications, will equip the project manager in the core skills required. As a CIO, you need to access and train the project manager in additional skills like people management, presentation and negotiation.

3. **Multifaceted.** The project manager needs to be multifaceted to succeed in completing projects on time and budget. Often the scope of a project may be more comprehensive and stretch beyond the boundaries of your company. It may include multiple technologies, multiple teams, including remote teams. It may need regulatory compliance so as not to violate local or international regulations such as PDPA (Personal Data Protection Act) in Singapore, and GDPR (General Data Protection Regulation) in the EU.

4. **Challenges.** A good project manager should anticipate and prepare for challenges, very much like a good entrepreneur will do. That may not be just in managing people, but also against evolving challenges in people, process, technology and budget. Very often, a multimillion-dollar investment on a project's success rests on the quality of good project

Project Management	Level 4 description	Level 5 description	Level 6 description	Level 7 description
Deals with the management of projects.	L4 defines, documents & implements small projects or sub-projects (usually less than six months).	L5 defines, facilitates & completes medium-scale projects or ones with direct business impact & firm deadlines.	L6 defines, facilitates & completes medium-scale complex projects or ones with direct business impact & firm deadlines.	L7 defines & facilitates organisational strategy to govern the direction & conduct of complex projects.
Focuses on the development/ implementation of processes to meet business needs.	Constraints include limited budgets, limited interdependencies with other projects, & no significant strategic impact.	Adopts appropriate project management methods & tools: predictive (plan-driven), or adaptive (iterative/agile).	Adopts appropriate project management methods & tools: predictive (plan-driven), or adaptive (iterative/agile).	Sets corporate or organisational strategy governing the initiation, conduct & monitoring of all project management.
Involves acquiring & utilising the necessary resources & skills within cost, quality & time parameters.	Involves identification, assessment & management of risks that might impact the success of the project.	Ensures project plans are maintained, quality reviews are regularly done & updates to stakeholders is regularly given.	Ensures effective project control, change control, risk management & testing processes are deployed/ maintained.	Determines the application of appropriate methodologies for medium, large, complex, medium- & long-term projects.
Project management methodologies can differ based on project needs & context.	Gets agreement on project approach with stakeholders; prepares & monitors quality, risk & communications plans.	Manages change control procedures so that the deliverables are completed within agreed cost, timelines & quality.	Monitors & controls scarce resources, especially revenue & capital costs vis-à-vis project budget guidelines.	Authorises large projects for the organisation & leads project planning, scheduling, controlling & monitoring parameters.
Approaches can be predictive (plan-driven) or adaptive (iterative/ agile) based on project parameters.	Ensures that projects are completed, signed off, closed, reviewed & lessons documented to be learned.	Provides effective leadership to project teams; takes appropriate action where team performance deviates widely.	Manages expectations of project stakeholders; arranges for regular project updates to be provided to stakeholders.	Sets strategies & methodologies to manage risk & take mitigation measures to ensure risks are within agreed tolerances.

(Source: https://bit.ly/3gyubd9).

management. In accounting, what's required are not "bean counters", but financial controllers. In project management, be cautioned that you do not need "spreadsheet timekeepers", but a well-grounded producer of a product or service that complies with the intended quality, delivered on time and at the budgeted cost.

 ## TRAINING ROADMAP

Rapid advances in IT make skills and knowledge get obsolete quickly. For the ITD to continue to meet the demands for better, innovative services as well as cope with technological changes, IT staff need to be trained and equipped with current and relevant skills.

Therefore, pay special attention to training; it should be proactive. Tutoring has to be on-demand because it is now a strategic tool to ensure the competitiveness of the IT workforce. Training needs to be a professional function in the IT department. For this, I employ a training roadmap.

A training roadmap is a document that spells out the skills and competencies required for specific job roles and from which individuals need which specific training. For example, there could be a roadmap for application development analysts, another for programmers, a third for end-user support teams, and others.

Draw up a Map

The process of drawing up the training roadmap starts with examining the organisation's mission and objectives. If training is to be a strategic tool, link the training offered to staff to future business needs and the strategic direction of the organisation. Proactive training helps to provide the organisation with appropriately skilled resources to develop the business continually. For example, if the strategic direction of the organisation is to offer more electronic services to customers in the future, then the training function needs to identify what the staff require and provide the relevant training in e-commerce skills.

▪ **For groups.** The next step in drawing up a training roadmap is to identify the various job groups in the ITD. Categorising staff into job roles facilitates their identification of skills and training needs. Specific job groups in an ITD include business and systems analysts, webmasters, programmers, communications specialists, end-user support specialists, quality analysts, data administrators and subproject managers. After this, as a CIO, you need to decide which skills and competencies are required to carry out the specific job functions and tasks. The goal is to determine the knowledge and practical skills required for the specific roles to perform their jobs. For example, to estimate project cost and time, the systems analyst must know the systems development lifecycle of an application development project and be able to chart function point analysis, critical path analysis, among others.

▪ **For individuals.** Draw up an individual training roadmap for each member of your staff based on the job role or group. Drawing up a personalised training roadmap should be a joint effort between the staff member and the supervisor. It should take into account the current skillsets and knowledge of the staff member and address gaps with additional training or certification. This individual training roadmap can help with the career development of the staff member as well since long-term training needs can be identified. Collating all the personal training roadmaps can enable the organisation to chart an effective training programme to equip it with the right skillsets and knowledge at the right time. A bonus: Trained staff are usually highly motivated and effective, and they will ensure that the organisation will be able to meet the challenges of new business initiatives powered by advances in technology.

▪ **For the company.** The training roadmap can provide a systematic and well-managed approach to upgrading the skillsets and knowledge of individuals and teams. Ensure that staff don't get sent for training that they do not require, and are instead equipped with the right skillsets to perform their jobs. Investment in T&D (training and development) will then be focused and supported by top management. Collating all the training roadmaps will also enable the organisation to allocate sufficient training budget. Identify training priorities. Training roadmaps provide the organisation with an accurate inventory of the skills and competencies of its staff.

▪ **External training.** With the availability of outsourced services, companies have an option to hire temporary resources from companies such as Wipro, Infosys, TCS, and Cognizant. There are pros and cons. On the negative side, you as the CIO will feel that you can procure technical talent from these companies. That could make you complacent because you don't need to hire more staff or invest in their training. On the positive side, you can use these companies to bring new talent that can upskill your teams. Some of these outsourced companies also provide certified training courses. For example, vendors like Cisco Systems, Oracle Corp, IBM Academy, Microsoft, AWS and Google offer professional training courses. The training and certification that are provided by these companies will build the competencies and skills that are required.

The critical question: Do certifications lead to building a competent core ITD team? I don't think so. That's because you need to create a team with competencies that your company needs. Most certification is very generic. So you may need to add to it by providing training tailored to your organisation's needs. Augmenting training gaps through contracted resources should be temporary or opportunistic. It will offer opportunities to upgrade – or check new technologies and skills. Exposing your team to these courses will be the right motivation, and this can be part of the individual's training roadmap.

Many companies have some form of the manager–employee evaluation process. These processes can motivate, train and provide feedback on the employee's performance to incorporate a training roadmap with agreed programmes to achieve these goals. A departmental training roadmap could be an aggregation of these individual training plans.

Case Study

Ever since I became CIO in 1990, maintaining and upgrading the skills of ITD staff in my team has always been one of my top priorities. At the training roadmap level, my team and I begin to plan based on goals attuned to fit the corporate agenda. For example, we may have five developers going for advanced programming training in ABAP or Python. The training roadmap had to plan for time off for these staff to attend training.

Most companies have an excuse that they have planned for their staff to attend training; they are so short of staff that training had to be postponed or cancelled. I realised early on that training was an essential part of my role as CIO to ensure that my team stayed competent, updated and motivated. I also decided that we were not training for certification alone, but to build a talented team.

Within each job group, my team and I would then identify the specific functions and tasks required of that role. For example, a project manager should know about budget control, quality management, risks management, resources management, among others. A systems analyst would need to know requirement analysis, data analysis, risk analysis, time estimation, negotiation, and others.

 **TOP TIPS**

Here's a list of what to do – and not do – for staff training. These tips are from US-based RTO (Ready Training Online). The company offers web-based training for employees and training administrators.[5]

Do:
- Provide consistent training to all staff. If one employee is given a certain level of training and another is offered a lower level of training – or not offered at all – you could face failures in customer service failures and/or non-compliance.
- Set individual and company-wide goals. Align staff training goals with your corporate core values and sales objectives. Document goals, so they're clear to everyone.
- Celebrate staff successes. Reward employees who complete their staff training quotas. Offer incentives, rewards, recognition to employees who implement critical concepts on the job.
- Track staff training for assessment. Deploy an automated system of assessing and monitoring the training courses. This will help you identify who needs to follow up, when, and in which BU.
- Use tech to streamline training. Online staff training programmes take the pain out of administering physical training. Take advantage of an LMS (learning management system) to help you reach your corporate training goals.

Don't:
- Do not set a bad example. You and your senior management set the tone for how well training is implemented and received. Aim to always set a good example for your employees.
- Do not put off training. Many managers procrastinate by thinking they can cover important training topics "later" or "when things slow down". Training is an essential component and must continue.
- Do not abandon training. All training programmes require proper follow-ups. Schedule refresher courses for all staff, especially related to customer service, safety, and compliance topics.
- Do not rely on only one form of training. Blended learning strategies – with case-studies – provide the most comprehensive and practical training.

[5] https://bit.ly/2YZ1Mau.

CHAPTER NINE

How to Resolve
Conflicts Amicably

 INTRODUCTION

According to many managers, one of their most difficult tasks is managing people. These may include their subordinates, their peers, and sometimes even their superiors. In many cases, it may also have people from other teams tasked to work together to achieve common corporate goals.

Some managers, faced with staff problems, prefer to look the other way or bury themselves in more technical work, rather than tackle the issues head-on. Part of the reason for this is because managers may not have adequate training in HRM (human resources management). Having worked for many years in management positions, I strongly feel that all managers must go through intensive short-term, scenario-based, mandatory courses in HRM, preferably once every half-year, if not quarterly.

That's because, in HRM, the essential skill that all managers need to learn is how to handle conflicts. Managers may spend almost half of their time on resolving HRM issues. As far back as 1998, a survey conducted by Grant and Zerbes Management Consultants found that managers spent about 40 per cent of their time resolving disputes among team members.

It is therefore not uncommon in every office to hear employees complain about the "office politics" at their workplaces with a fervent wish that it would stop, or someone higher up would put a stop to it. Such office politics are problems caused by some staff members pursuing their private agendas, resulting in conflicts. No office is immune to office politics. Managers need to recognise its existence and take proactive steps to deal with it, preferably nip it in the bud before it causes severe damage.

Causes of Conflict

Conflicts are situations where two or more people do not agree with a specific point of view. That could be either defining a problem, or the process of solving it, or the intended outcome. When such disagreements occur, emotions come into play, and this can cloud the judgment of the staff in finding solutions. If parties involved don't arrive at a comprised solution in time, it could develop into a crisis.

Organisational conflict, or workplace conflict, is a state of disagreement or discord due to actual or perceived opposition of issues, needs, and interests between people working together. Confrontations take many forms in organisations, including:

- The disputes that occur between those in authority and individuals or groups.
- Disputes that arise from the distribution of revenues, profits or workloads.
- Disputes about how long or how hard should staff work.
- Disagreements between labour unions and management.
- Subtler forms of conflict due to rivalries, jealousies, personality clashes, role definitions.
- Overt or covert struggles for power and favour.
- The conflict between individuals – if there are competing needs and demands.

As a CIO, you need to be aware of the following factors to be able to resolve conflicts:

- **Manage issues.** Managing issues of contention begin by first clarifying and agreeing to the definition of the problems. If you spend time and effort to get this step right, you will avoid many situations later that are fuelled by emotions. Break down the issue into smaller components. The clarity should not be limited to the precision of the language that you use to document the problem; it should instead focus on understanding and agreement of each of the smaller components.

Whether it is an existing application or a new implementation, every situation needs to have a clear understanding of whether they have an agreement in defining the problem or solution, such as a conflict between a manager and her staff, for example. If a staff member is not happy with how the manager treats him, the CIO needs to drill down as to what was explicitly not well handled. It could be a simple issue such as the manager not giving enough notice for a solution to get implemented, or a more difficult situation of insubordination. Therefore, talk to both parties, come to a clear understanding and get started on working with a renewed, clarified focus.

▪ **Manage emotions.** Managing emotions is a tricky part of conflict resolution. "When your heart goes into your brain, your ears become shut," according to an old Chinese proverb. As a CIO or people manager, you will come across emotional outbursts in your line of duty. You should try to understand the underlying causes of such explosions, and not jump into the fray with an emotional outburst (such as anger or frustration) of your own.

You should avoid using emotional words or adjectives in your conversation to resolve such conflicts. Use terms such as "I understand your frustration" or "you could help me understand your concerns better" or "it would be helpful if you could hear me out as well".

Your role as a manager is to provide solutions and resolutions. By consciously concentrating on the end goals (such as implementing an IT solution or starting an IT project), it will help you avoid the emotional language that may escalate the conflict. Over the years, I have learned that I needed to suppress my emotions while working on projects, no matter how angry I got. Instead, I would calmly ask probing questions to clarify the issues or problem statements. There were compromises that I had to make, but my job as the ITD head was to steer my staff or customers (as the case may be) towards an acceptable solution. As CIO, the buck stops with you; you must find the right way to get the problem solved on time.

Case Study A

During the COVID-19 outbreak, every hospital required – in a great hurry – expensive laboratory equipment and specialised healthcare personnel. If you're a leader tasked with "making miracles happen", how do you address such emergencies? The problems are immense: multiple hospitals are calling on you; you have to procure various sets of expensive lab equipment that's currently not in any supply chain; scarce healthcare personnel need to be pulled out from current tasks and rescheduled.

It's a logistical nightmare. But you need to find a solution. Here's a suggested plan of action:

- Use a structured methodology.
- Break down the problem into its components.
- Involve all stakeholders.
- Charge up your team.
- Leverage digital technology.
- Co-create a solution with your team and other teams.
- Brainstorm ideas to implement the solution.

It is a challenging task, but that's where your leadership and problem-solving skills come into play. That's the reason you're the CIO. You realise that many assumptions that you initially made were wrong. But working on the project with other teams, you overcame each variation and problem together, and jointly find solutions. You execute the project as one team, you achieve a breakthrough, and you celebrate it together.

ANALYSING CONFLICTS

Not all conflicts are severe or need the same amount of attention. It would be good to categorise conflicts by their severity or emotional involvement. Understanding the cause of disagreement can help you decide on the best approach to take to resolve it.

Individuals make up an organisation, all with their own needs, interests, goals and desires. Since everyone is different, the differences in the background (values, upbringing, culture, religion, education, race, gender, personality) can become potential causes of conflict if not handled appropriately. Jealousy and aggressive competitiveness are sometimes the catalysts for disputes. In the corporate world, it is common to find staff problems caused by promotions and bonus payments.

As the CIO, you must treat office politics differently from office interaction. Here are some salient points:

■ **Office politics.** During my career, I often found that many of the conflicts that I needed to resolve were more about office politics. Here's an example of how it works in a typical organisation large enough to have an ITD:

The organisation is keen to implement a new IT technology or solution. This solution requires significant changes to the organisation structure or specific departments. These changes may threaten an employee or a manager or even the HOD (head of department). Employees may be worried about their jobs getting obsolete; managers may be worried that their department will be merged or cut.

These threatened actors will raise walls of objections or create obstacles; some may even sabotage the implementation. On the surface, their actions may look like conflicts with the IT team. But the underlying cause is fear. When you try to resolve these conflicts – which may also become emotional – you need to identify, and, if required, isolate these actors.

You may also need to work with your HRD to consider skills upgrading or job rotation for employees. As for the managers, HR may need to discuss their roles with the C-suite or top management. It would be good to carry out a "situational analysis" exercise initially. That could be a critical step for the CIO as it will save you a considerable amount of time addressing people with a political agenda in the future.

■ **Internal conflicts.** Internal conflicts are those that occur within teams or departments, such as conflicts within the ITD. If left unchecked, such conflicts among staff can lead to low morale, reduced productivity, higher staff turnover, anger, frustration, antagonism, misunderstandings, and hurt feelings.

You will waste valuable resources when there are duplicated activities, which happens when staff do not share information. There will also be resentment against management for allowing conflicts to thrive, and for not creating a conducive environment for work. In the end, nobody wins; everybody loses, including the organisation.

From experience, you know that where there are people, conflicts will occur. That's because each one of us is different and thinks differently. Can conflicts be avoided in a company or a department? Not if employees have a point of view and want everyone to follow their own way. The best scenario then is for you to foster an environment of trust, fairness, objectivity and teamwork. Only then, conflicts can quickly get identified, resolved, and the team can jointly celebrate success.

▪ **Management.** As a manager, you need to manage conflicts. Managed effectively, they can have a positive effect on the entire organisation. Understanding and appreciating individual differences in vision, ideas, passions and capabilities is the starting point in the management of conflicts.

Much like an orchestra, each member of the department has a role to play and possesses the skillsets that complement other staff members. Smart managers are ones that harness the differences in people and use them to create synergy. When conflicts get handled well, there will be a more productive workforce, less stress, and higher morale. The management's image as a caring employer will be enhanced, and the organisation can serve its customers – and meet its challenges – better prepared.

▪ **Mediation.** Organisations can minimise conflicts but not eliminate them. If your staff members are unable to resolve their disputes, then you, as a manager, must be prepared to mediate between the disputing staff.

Your role as a mediator is to provide an avenue for the disputing parties to air their points of view, and you help them come to a mutually acceptable agreement. Make use of such mediation opportunities to create a better working relationship between the two parties and achieve a "win-win" solution.

Mediation is part of the problem-solving skills portfolio. It's an essential soft skill for the IT professional because, in the process of developing a system, several problems may occur. The key to effective conflict management is having the right mind-set towards conflict management and the right set of conflict management skills.

Case Study B

My department had to develop a customer information database shared across business units (BUs). Customers were becoming irritated when asked to provide personal information repeatedly to different BUs of the same company. So we decided to develop a shared database. Several questions cropped up:

▪ Which department would "own" the database?
▪ How do we map out the business processes?
▪ On which platform should we install the database?
▪ Should we do the project in-house or outsource it?
▪ How do we find the resources required?
▪ Who's going to fund the project?
▪ What would be the security requirements?

We had to address each issue before the project began. While I'm not going to answer each of the earlier questions, I'm going to discuss the thought process that needs to go into project management. That's the best way to hone your problem-solving skills. Problem-solving must be a systematic process so that you don't jump too quickly into conclusions and make the wrong decision.

One effective method that I employed involved the following steps:

1. Define the problem. Put down on paper what you are trying to solve.
2. Ascertain the limits. Where are the boundaries and what are the assumptions?
3. Generate possibilities, using your team's creative thinking skills as much as possible.
4. Evaluate alternative solutions and choose the best course of action.
5. Implement and follow-up with the plan of action.

The CIO can help to minimise the occurrence of conflicts through seven steps:

1. **Vision.** Set a clear vision and direction for the organisation. The CIO should spare no effort in driving everyone towards a common goal. When everyone puts aside their private agendas and works towards a common goal, there will be more cooperation and synergy.
2. **Consistency.** Be consistent when dealing with staff. Do not be indecisive and keep changing direction. That will confuse the team and cause misunderstandings, miscommunication, and lead to conflict.
3. **Favouritism.** Do not practise favouritism. It is quite natural for us to favour some staff over others, but we should be careful not to cause a split in the cohesiveness of the team. Avoid giving some staff privileges that they have not earned or do not deserve.
4. **Communications.** Promote communication among staff. When staff are not well informed about the goings-on in the organisation, gossip and rumours will fill the information gaps. Ensure there are open lines of communication vertically (top to the bottom of the organisation) and horizontally (within teams).
5. **Rapport.** Build rapport and esprit-de-corps. Organise social and recreational activities for the staff and make time to join them in these activities. When the esprit-de-corps is strong, there is less likelihood of disputes and conflicts.

6. **Training.** Provide training in HR management. Train middle managers to handle conflicts, motivate staff and address personnel problems. Understanding salient points about HR issues is vital for senior, middle and junior management because all managers have to deal with subordinates.

7. **Capability.** Bring out the best in your staff. Work should be allocated based on the ability of the staff member. Everybody has their strengths and weaknesses. Look for strengths to complement weaknesses, and you can build a stronger team. If you allocate work to people who do not have the skill and capability to carry it out, it will affect their self-confidence and productivity. If mistakes get made, others may have to be called upon to provide recovery, and there will be plenty of opportunities for conflicts to arise.

 ## SOLVING PROBLEMS

Is problem-solving a soft skill? Yes. Hard skills are technical skills that one learns through an education process. You don't learn soft skills in the same manner. You can learn the methodology involved and gain experience as you interact with people or manage people. One effective way to learn soft skills is to learn from case studies. You study from the experience of others and try to avoid making the same mistakes that others did.

Often, the most straightforward soft skill is common sense. You will discover that most situations are not clear-cut and don't have a binary solution. There will be a lot of grey areas and overlapping conditions, and sometimes you have to use your judgement to decide on the right course of action. That's where experience counts; the way to gain experience is to regularly keep practising the art of solving simple and complex issues.

One problem-solving model comes from an excellent book published in 2001: *The McKinsey Mind: Understanding and Implementing the Problem-Solving Tools and Management Techniques of the World's Top Strategic Consulting Firm* by Ethan M Rasiel and Dr Paul N Friga. That was Mr Rasiel's second book. His first, published in 1999, was a bestseller: *The McKinsey Way: Using the Techniques of the World's Top Strategic Consultants to Help You and Your Business.*

The McKinsey Mind presents the first step-by-step manual for achieving McKinsey-style solutions and success. The book reveals the hands-on secrets behind the firm's success and discusses how executives can use some of those tactics to be more proactive and effective in their day-to-day decision-making.

Solving problems is both a science and an art because most issues can be addressed differently under different environments, groups, teams, or stakeholders. The positive news is that digitalisation has become a railway track for all stakeholders to be aligned and move in the same direction.

In October 2020, Chuck Kosal, CIO for Deloitte Tax LLP, led interviews with 600 tax executives on what they would want from the ITD or the CIO. The top four themes that could be of relevance, not just for tax leaders, but all others across the enterprise:[1]

1. **Transparency.** In virtually every interview, the survey respondents mentioned that word. At every stage of their business, they want to be able to see where things stand – the status, who's working on it, next steps, and so forth. They're tired of the walls separating teams or processes that have traditionally made that kind of insight hard to find.

2. **Integration.** Leaders want an end-to-end digital view globally – a single user experience offering a window into all the different parts of their work. If enterprise resource planning (ERP) systems aren't configured for the tax department's needs and integrated with its other systems, for example, it can be difficult to find and incorporate the insights they contain. In global organisations, leaders are looking for simplicity and a user experience that brings together the information they need to know about their compliance activities, and the content or knowledge to help them think about compliance data, proactively.

3. **Personalisation.** A contextualised and personalised experience. The dashboards in many tax tools, for example, are effectively one-size-fits-all, delivering essentially the same information to all users. What tax professionals need, however, is a personalised strategic view, with content customised to the user's role in the organisation, geographic location, practice area, and other factors.

4. **Streamlining.** A more streamlined workflow. There's a lot of redundancy in many processes. AI capabilities such as automation and machine learning are among the tools that can be used to help reduce that, freeing up human professionals to focus on higher-value tasks such as finding new insights.

---

[1] https://bit.ly/3lfXnIJ.

THE AIKIDO WAY

The ideal situation to minimise conflicts would be to help your staff learn to resolve personal disputes on their own. In August 1999, Dr Marilyn Barrick wrote an article, "Handling Conflict in Relationships the Aikido Way", in *Spiritual Psychology* magazine. In Aikido, which is a self-defence style in martial arts, practitioners attempt to channel their energy to disarm their opponents without hurting them.[2]

Dr Marilyn Barrick specialises in spiritual-transformational work for the healing of soul and spirit. She's author of multiple books: *Sacred Psychology of Love; Sacred Psychology of Change; Dreams: Exploring the Secrets of Your Soul; Emotions: Transforming Anger, Fear and Pain; Soul Reflections: Many Lives, Many Journeys; A Spiritual Approach to Parenting: Secrets of Raising the 21st Century Child;* and *Everything Is Energy: New Ways to Heal Your Body, Mind & Spirit.*

Here are her nine rules for handling conflict using the Aikido way:

1. Choose your words carefully. Your words should express your conviction in a positive manner that encourages communication and could lead to resolution.
2. Indulge in interactive sharing. The aim is to take you "out of the box" of your original position. You can the be open to new ideas and concepts that neither of you may have ever thought of before.
3. Keep your emotional balance by staying heart-centred and being true to your higher principles and moral values.
4. Whenever you get stuck, feel hurt or draw a blank, pause and take three slow deep breaths. Try to focus on your heart and convey your truth gently as well as firmly.
5. Attempt to be a good listener. Try to listen with your heart - and your mind. Be appreciative of the effort and courage it takes to be authentic, especially when you have differing points of view.
6. Be open to understanding the other person in the same way that you want to be understood.
7. Try to bring to the surface the more profound message of the soul. That may often be hidden in words that seem inadequate or clumsy when spoken.
8. When you do not understand, ask the other person questions - and listen carefully to their answers. Repeat what you do know until both of you know you've "got it".

---

[2]https://bit.ly/31zQ2N9.

9. Keep trying for a win-win resolution that allows both of you to be true to the best in each other. When you handle conflict the Aikido way, you can generate exciting, creative solutions beyond any simple sum of your separate points of view. By intertwining your insights, hopes and dreams, you bring gifts of joy and enlightenment to your hearts and souls - and peace in your relationships.

IV

Change

CHAPTER TEN

How to Ensure Good Governance

 INTRODUCTION

The IS (information systems) organisation, which usually is a part of the IT department needs to consistently deliver software and services of acceptable quality to its users. Unfortunately, for the past two decades, many IS organisations were unable to provide reliable, usable software within budget and schedule. That was mainly due to an inability to manage the software development process.

Changing the mind-set of the IS staff to be quality-conscious is a significant hurdle. That can be a slow process, especially if there is resistance at the ground level. The organisation must raise quality awareness among both management and staff by conducting in-house training and seminars. Senior management should support the team in the quality improvement process because it's a stringent process, and problems will crop up during the journey.

The first hurdle is to identify all the essential processes that need improvement within the organisation. Considering that quality goods get produced from quality processes, new guidelines must get developed for operations that need to be updated. Draw up standards, protocols or procedures for each of the processes in the value chain (preferably according to specific globally recognised standards).

It is always good to adopt best practices from other organisations. These organisations can provide a benchmark for you to challenge your staff. Study especially the benefits that accrue from acceptable quality practices in these organisations because they can help you to justify the efforts and resources that you need to invest in getting your team and processes trained. Note that enhancing standards and procedures and putting them into practice would be an additional workload on staff. Senior management must, therefore, set realistic deadlines and expectations without adversely affecting staff morale.

Quality Policy

A quality policy is a statement of direction in an organisation's quest for quality. The quality policy must include a "quality goal" with a realistic timeframe to achieve it. Having a goal helps to challenge and motivate staff to attain set targets in quality improvement; it's a valuable tool to revitalise the team.

Many organisations have quality policies that govern operations, back-office processes, sales, distribution and human resources. An IT quality policy should not be a standalone item in the organisation; it must be in sync with the company's corporate quality policies and mission. It is easy to develop an IT quality policy that revolves around the ITD (Information Technology Department). But this will isolate the ITD from the rest of the organisation, which is not ideal.

The most sustainable and effective way is to integrate the IT quality policies and processes with the rest of the quality processes in the company. For example, you may have a quality process that defines the accuracy of accounting reports at the month's end. The accounting department will activate a few stages of checks using relevant software. If there is an error, they will send a request to the ITD. An investigation will start. Having a quality policy that's in tune between the two departments will help solve such issues without having to waste time and effort in setting up complex procedures, forms and escalations.

Project Management

Whether the ITD is managing an ERP (enterprise resource planning) project or a software development project, your team is involved in the planning, deploying, testing and support functions. Project management is a complex discipline involving people, resources, solutions and customer requirements.

In the past, we relied on project managers with experience and expertise to deliver projects on time and budget. We often read about project failures. We cannot prevent failures from happening, but we can institute processes and controls to ensure a higher chance of success.

The PMI (Project Management Institute) has developed a set of practice standards and guidelines – called PMBOK (Project Management Body of Knowledge) – to help project managers in their tasks. It's worthwhile checking the treasury of information on the PMI website, including risk management. All projects come with risks, whether expected or not, that may occur with impacts on the portfolio, programme and project objectives. The effect can be positive or negative and may cause deviation from the intended goals. Risk management processes allow for proactively planning to capture opportunities and limit threats.[1]

I have used PMBOK to run large projects successfully. You don't need to follow all the guidelines in the PMBOK, because each project is unique. But the PMBOK framework provides you with a structured checklist to ensure that you consider as many factors as possible. The PMI also offers professional certifications, like the PMP (Project Management Professional), which assures that project managers have the competencies to follow the framework.

As a CIO, your success will depend on the delivery of successful projects. Enterprise-wide implementation involves different parts of your organisation and many users. Therefore, any failures in these projects will be highly visible. Organising and managing a good project delivery organisation within the ITD is an excellent strategy to ensure a CIO's success.

Case Study

In 1990, after becoming CIO of HDB (Housing and Development Board), I reorganised the ITD and renamed it as the ISD (Information Services Department). I created several IS units that were responsible for creating and maintaining various applications that served the town councils and the administration teams. These units got support from the infrastructure, operations, security and administration BUs.

---

[1] https://bit.ly/384xhCZ.

However, I did not feel that this was good enough to ensure that we delivered quality services that meet end-user expectations. I created a QAU (Quality Assurance Unit) to administer and enforce our QMS (Quality Management System). To ensure consistent quality practices throughout the ISD, we produced a quality manual and disseminated to all ISD staff. The next step was to adopt an international QMS standard. We decided that the ISD will opt for the ISO9001 Certification; we got certified in 1994.

I felt we needed to go one more step further to strengthen our QMS. My goal was to go for the CMM L3 (Capability Maturity Model Level 3) Certification created by the CMU (Carnegie-Mellon University), based in Pittsburgh, Pennsylvania. Getting ISO9001 certified was tough; preparing for CMM was torture.

It took the ISD about three years to obtain the CMM Certification. Meanwhile, CMU replaced the CMM with CMMI (Capability Maturity Model Integration). CMMI was a more comprehensive standard and addressed the shortcomings of process integration and critical performance areas.

Together with the ISO9001 standard, the CMMI model helped us to ensure that all systems produced and maintained by the ISD met international QMS standards. That was critical in assisting the transformation of HDB into an information-centric organisation.

QMS

A QMS is a formal methodology to document processes, procedures and responsibilities to achieve quality policies and objectives. A QMS helps coordinate and direct an organisation's activities to meet customer and regulatory requirements, as well as improve its effectiveness and efficiency continuously.

A comprehensive QMS would be essential to help the IS or ITD manage and control the quality of its project management, software development and support processes. A QMS equips the ITD with standard governance controls, work processes and measurement tools. Every CIO organisation is unique and has inherent legacies and setup.

Ideally, the QMS should not be an ITD project but also involves your customers and senior management. The ITD is the underlying utility of any large organisation. Hence, engaging senior and top management to define the governance and process to support the ITD implement the QMS will ensure its success.

QMS Principles

Implemented correctly, the QMS helps ensure projects and work functions proceed under set practices. It also ensures that products and services satisfy customer expectations. The QMS is proactive – not passive – because it emphasises the importance of prevention over cure. The benefits are many: increase in product or service quality and reliability, lower cost of remediation, reduction of wastage, and increase in productivity and efficiency.

The QMS must include the processes in the value chain, and have applications development, operation support, development and end-user support, security and control, and maintenance. Before launching the QMS, senior management must demonstrate a strong commitment to quality. One way is to form a steering committee to direct and coordinate the efforts to boost quality. Without strong endorsement and support from top management, the QMS is unlikely to survive beyond its infancy.

From a CIO's viewpoint, there are many reasons why many QMS projects fail. Here are some pointers to make them work:

- **Objectivity.** Quantify project or software deliverables and technical specifications. That is the main reason for the success or failure of a project. Be objective and impartial, quantify the measurement criteria and hold everyone responsible for delivering to specification and duration. Not quantifying each process or milestone can give rise to grey areas or gaps between customer expectations and ITD capabilities or considerations.
- **Subjectivity.** Project management is also about people management. That's where subjectivity comes in. In a new project or software, people, including IT teams, could tread on new grounds or step on personal egos or opinions. That could result in a tug of war between users and developers. It can result in multiple rounds of discussions and meetings to resolve project issues. Angry customers or ITD teams can lead to irrational decisions that threaten projects or milestones. Avoid mixing emotions into a project or software development – document the technical specifications, minutes of meetings, compromises, or points of disagreements.
- **Implementation.** There are various stages of implementation and testing. In the alpha and beta stages, there will be software bugs or broken links. The rapport built initially between teams could resolve such issues quickly. But miscommunication can occur when teams understand the requirements differently. On the other hand, users or

customers may not comprehend the problems accurately. Users may miss out on steps or checks during implementation, and these missing steps become bugs.

▪ **Standardisation.** Keeping to industry standards is an excellent discipline to ensure quality. It is not acceptable to just ensure that the project completed on schedule and cost, but also that there is a high degree of quality during implementing and testing. Adhering to standards enables future upgrades and maintenance with fewer errors and bugs.

▪ **Integration.** Enforce a robust governance process. Some of the projects that your team will manage may involve a few hundred users or stakeholders. In more complex projects, you might have multiple subprojects that are running simultaneously and may have to get integrated as the final deliverable. It will be impossible to run such projects without the help of a QMS methodology.

QMS Standards

The next step in the QMS journey is to implement the improved standards and procedures in all projects progressively. Encourage staff to give feedback on the criteria and be ready to adjust them if necessary. Urge the staff to form teams to develop new methods or enhance existing ones so that they can take ownership of the improved processes. There are many tools within the QMS community that your team can use, including Continuous Quality Improvement, Quality Circles, Fishbone Root Cause Analysis.

To help management verify that the team is adhering to QMS standards and procedures, suitably qualified staff should conduct internal quality audits on QMS projects. Regular dialogues with end-users and business partners will be useful to provide feedback on whether the QMS needs improvement. There are five areas for an ITD to consider for the QMS:

1. Software or application development.
2. Project management.
3. IT services delivery.
4. Service level agreements.
5. IT management and governance.

The complexity of managing a large ITD is akin to running a company. Over the years, many CIOs have learnt to run the ITD as a business. The ITD has moved from the backroom to the front aisle of corporate operations. Similar to running a business, the ITD has to manage the following functions efficiently:

▪ **The bottom line.** The ITD is no longer a mere cost centre. It is a part of the core operations of all organisations, whether they are in the IT industry or not. Almost all companies have some e-commerce activities, and the ITD is the one that keeps the e-commerce engine running. Even in logistics where everything is automated, the ITD is at the forefront. The CIO is responsible for the cost of running the ITD. The ITD is accountable for achieving cost efficiencies in the use of technology. The ITD must know about finance, accounting, contract laws and its limitations,

▪ **CRM.** Customer relationship management is central to the functioning of the ITD. The ITD delivers value to its internal and external customers. That is because all customers present themselves online. Therefore, the ITD needs to provide better customer experience, offer services to agreed SLAs, ensure privacy and confidentiality, and be accountable for the IT services being available 24/7.

▪ **ITaaS.** IT as a Service. To meet the demand of being an "always-on" operation, the ITD is like a utility company. In an ideal situation, the ITD will have the latest technology to offer the best services to its stakeholders. In reality, capital and investments are limited; the CIO must use all the instruments at his or her disposal. That includes using leases or rentals to book IaaS (Infrastructure as a Service) or PaaS (Platform as a Service) with CSPs (cloud service providers) at peak load periods. The ITD will otherwise get blamed for any drop in the quality or availability of IT services.

CERTIFICATIONS

Certifications issued by reputed institutions offer a stamp of approval for staff who have gone through the training, testing and examination. Here is a list of top certifications that the ITD staff are encouraged to obtain to boost the quality and governance standards in the team:

▪ **ISO 9001.** The ISO (International Standards Organisation) 9000 family of QMS is a set of standards that helps companies ensure they meet stakeholder needs within regulatory requirements related to a product or service. ISO 9000 deals with the fundamentals of QMS, including the seven quality management principles. ISO 9001 deals with the conditions that companies must fulfil.

ISO 9001 provides a checklist for the development, supply and maintenance of computer software. The recently updated version combines the proven benefits of ISO 9001 with some of the world's most essential support documents in software engineering, allowing an organisation to benefit from best practices to improve quality at every step of the lifecycle. That includes everything from the supply, acquisition, operation and maintenance, to the circular process of continuous improvement, according to the ISO.[2]

Third-party certification agencies provide independent confirmation that companies meet the requirements of ISO 9001. More than a million companies worldwide have been certified, making ISO 9001 one of the most widely used management tools.

- **CMM.** Another type of certification, which is not so common, but is perceived to be more prestigious, is the CMM (Capability Maturity Model). The model describes a five-level evolutionary path of increasingly organised and systematically more mature processes. CMM was developed by the Software Engineering Institute (SEI), an R&D entity sponsored by the US Department of Defense.

SEI was set up in 1984 to address software engineering issues and advance appropriate methodologies. The CMM has five maturity levels of software processes:[3]

- **Initial.** At this level, processes may be disorganised or seem chaotic. Success may likely depend on individual efforts, and may not be repeatable. That's because processes may not be sufficiently defined and documented for them to be replicated.
- **Repeatable.** At this level, basic project management techniques may be established. Successes could be repeated. That's because the requisite processes would have been established, defined, and documented.
- **Defined.** At this level, an organisation would have developed its standard software process through greater attention to documentation, standardisation, and integration.
- **Managed.** At this level, an organisation may monitor and control its processes through data collection and analysis.
- **Optimum.** At this level, processes would continuously be improved through monitoring feedback coming from current processes. Innovative processes to better serve the organisation's particular needs would be introduced.

---

[2] https://bit.ly/3eEtBdj.
[3] https://bit.ly/3g4dNAY.

▪ **COBIT.** COBIT is short for Control Objectives for Information and Related Technology. It is a framework that was created by the ISACA (Information Systems Audit and Control Association) for IT governance and management. Designed to be a supportive tool for managers, it bridges the gap between technical issues, business risks and control requirements. COBIT is a recognised guideline that applies to any organisation in any vertical sector.

COBIT is used by IT business process managers to equip them with a model to deliver value to the organisation and practise better risk management practices related to IT processes. The COBIT model assures the integrity of the information system. The latest COBIT 5.0 certification not only prepares professionals for the global challenges to the business IT process but also delivers information on:

▪ IT issues and how they can affect organisations.
▪ Principles of IT governance and enterprise IT.
▪ Determine the differences between management and administration.
▪ Accessing how COBIT 5.0 processes can help the establishment of the five basic principles along with other enablers.
▪ Discussing COBIT 5.0 concerning its process reference model and goal cascade.

ITIL and ITSM

ITIL (IT Infrastructure Library) refers to a set of detailed practices for ITSM (IT Service Management), which focuses on aligning IT services with the needs of the business. In other words, ITIL is a set of best practices to guide ITSM, while ITSM is the actual practice, or professional discipline, of managing IT operations as a service.

ITSM is all the activities involved in designing, creating, delivering, supporting and managing the lifecycle of IT services. It is a set of policies, processes and procedures for managing the implementation, improvement and support of customer-oriented IT services. ITSM is about delivering and improving the delivery of IT services to users.

The ITIL framework of five core publications has best practices for each primary phase of the ITSM lifecycle. Their core concepts are:

- **Service strategy.** Describes business goals and customer requirements and how to align the objectives of both entities.
- **Service design.** Outlines practices for the production of IT policies, architectures and documentation.
- **Service transition.** Advises on change management and release practices; guides administrators through environmental interruptions and changes.
- **Service operation.** Offers ways to manage IT services on a daily, monthly and yearly basis.
- **Continual service improvement.** Covers how to introduce improvements and policy updates within the ITIL process framework.

ITIL adoption and maintenance requires trained and certified experts to guide the ITD staff. Businesses such as Microsoft, IBM and Hewlett Packard Enterprise use ITIL as a foundation for their internal operating guidelines.[4]

IT Governance

IT governance is a framework that provides a structure for organisations to ensure that IT investments support business objectives. The enactment of laws and regulations fueled the need for standard corporate and IT governance practices across US organisations. These included the Gramm–Leach–Bliley Act and the Sarbanes-Oxley Act, in the 1990 and early 2000s that resulted from the fallout from several high-profile corporate fraud and deception cases.

It's best to start with a framework that's created by industry experts and used by thousands of organisations. Many frameworks include implementation guides to help organisations phase in an IT governance programme with fewer speedbumps.[5]

The most commonly used frameworks are:

- **COBIT.** COBIT has its antecedents in IT auditing and is published by ISACA. COBIT comprises a comprehensive framework of globally-accepted best practices, sets of analytical tools and models designed for governance

---

[4] https://bit.ly/3eF1bA9.
[5] https://bit.ly/385guj7.

and management of enterprise IT. ISACA has expanded COBIT's scope over the years to support IT governance. The latest version is COBIT 5, used by companies focused on risk management and mitigation.

- **ITIL.** ITIL focuses on ITSM. ITIL aims to ensure that IT services support the core processes of the business. The framework comprises five sets of management best practices for service strategy, design, transition such as change management, operation and continual service improvement.
- **COSO.** This model for evaluating internal controls is from the Committee of Sponsoring Organisations of the Treadway Commission. COSO's focus is a little less IT-specific than the other frameworks; it concentrates more on enterprise risk management and fraud deterrence.
- **CMMI.** The CMMI (Capability Maturity Model Integration) method was developed by the Software Engineering Institute. It aims to boost performance by using a scale of 1 to 5 to gauge an organisation's quality, profitability, and performance levels of maturity.
- **FAIR.** FAIR is short for Factor Analysis of Information Risk. It is a relatively new model. It helps organisations quantify risk. The focus is on cybersecurity and operational risk to make more well-informed decisions. Although it's more modern than other frameworks, it's already gained much traction with Fortune 500 companies.

CHAPTER ELEVEN

How to Help
Your End Users

 INTRODUCTION

A common complaint in many large organisations is that the BUs (business units) are not well-supported by the ITD (Information Technology Department). Complaints range from the inability of the ITD to deliver systems on time, within budget and according to specifications. Some of these issues could be due to poor project management. However, many are because of poor communications between the BUs and the ITD.

Being a service organisation, the ITD has to balance aligning customer expectations with IT regulations, especially when it comes to deliverables. Customers always demand a higher standard of service than what the ITD may be capable of delivering. A mismatch between delivery and expectation often leads to miscommunications and unhappiness.

The ITD's task is to set up, monitor and maintain ICT (info-communication technology) systems and services. It is also responsible for strategic planning to ensure that all IT initiatives support business goals – and in some cases, innovation. ITD structures can be centralised or decentralised depending on the needs of the company. In large organisations, the CIO may head the ITD. Smaller companies may have an IT director or operations head. Figure 11.1 shows the traditional and current structure of an ITD.

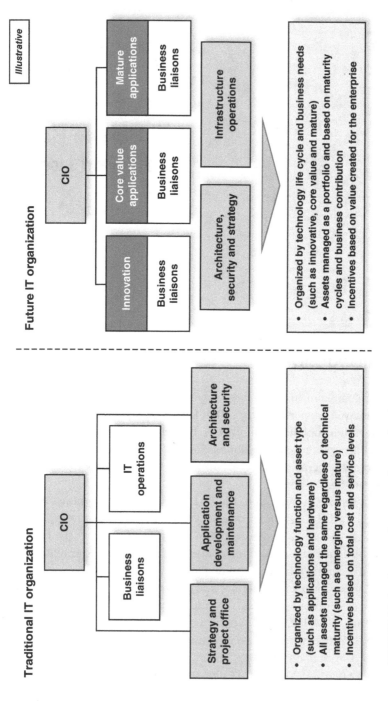

FIGURE 11.1   A strategic approach to technology management for tomorrow's IT organization

Source: A. T. Kearney.

Encourage Feedback

Getting feedback should be a continuous process and is part of the quality improvement process. If the ITD demonstrates its sincerity to improve systems and services, then the BUs will offer regular and crucial feedback. Not doing so would put the ITD at grave risk. That's because the BUs won't hesitate to push out system development projects or ITD functions to external outsourced vendors. The ITD has not only to offer BUs value for money but also change the end-user perceptions about the value of the ITD.

When I first began work as a CIO, I inherited much unhappiness with the ITD. It was up to me to turn things around. One of the first things I did was to ferret out the causes of complaints from both sides – the ITD and the BUs. I had long conversations with the ITD teams. We devised the following mechanisms to maintain a constant flow of communications between the ITD and the BUs:

- **Questionnaire.** We sent questionnaires to the BUs to get their points of view. When you ask for feedback, be prepared to get much flak. The truth may hurt, but it is better to face it and examine the negative comments, instead of sidestepping them. The goal, after all, is to improve ITD service to the end-users. Every criticism should be viewed as a useful pointer for improvement, even if the complaint sounds like it's wrapped around emotional baggage. Strip away the emotions, focus on the meat.
- **PIR.** You can't be sending questionnaires very often; otherwise, responders may develop "survey fatigue". To get feedback from end-users after deploying a system, we set up a Post Implementation Review (PIR). We conducted the PIR regularly to get feedback about the system's performance, ease of use, features that worked well, and what could be improved. Since the PIR results got reviewed by senior management, the system developers put in extra effort to ensure users were satisfied.
- **ERT.** End users were encouraged to report any shortcomings through an error reporting tool (ERT). They did not need to wait for the PIR to give feedback. Submit suggestions for enhancements and improvements through "change requests", which is also a feedback mechanism. An ERT is crucial because errors must be reported and fixed as soon as possible. Errors tend to escalate and clog up the system; it's better to correct the mistakes as soon as they get reported.

- **SSS.** The staff suggestion scheme (SSS) is another excellent tool for users and ITD teams to give feedback. Change requests are more formal and are usually submitted through the department's system administrators. But the SSS is more informal and can be submitted by any staff. Evaluate all SSS inputs on their merits and viability, and implement useful suggestions.
- **SM.** In the early days of the Internet, we introduced BBs (bulletin boards) or electronic discussion forums on our intranet. Users could post comments, share ideas, and get answers to FAQs (frequently asked questions). The BB can also be used by the ITD to offer tips on using IT systems more effectively. An administrator should manage the BB, and regularly provide responses to feedback received. If there is consistently no response to issues raised, then people will stop using the BB to provide feedback. With the introduction of social media (SM) platforms, we can now gather feedback not only from users but directly from customers on our website, Facebook page, LinkedIn, Instagram and Twitter.
- **PMM.** Conduct regular PMMs (project management meetings) with end-users. Such face-to-face meetings can be beneficial to build rapport and strengthen the partnership between BUs and the ITD. Besides obtaining feedback, areas of misunderstandings must be discussed and resolved. The PMMs take up time, so it's ideal for organising these once every quarter.
- **Workflows.** These would include customer feedback systems, which are built into workflows like Lotus Notes (in the old days), emails and project management tools today. That could have email systems with macros to channel feedback to the right process owners and to track the stages of responses. Use tools such as Microsoft SharePoint to integrate workflows.

▦ SUPPORT YOUR USERS

An effective ITD must be strong on all fronts. It is not enough just to be able to manage projects, deliver sound IT systems and provide good IT infrastructure for the BUs. It's also essential that a team offers reliable support, including maintenance of existing systems, making modifications and enhancements to procedures, troubleshooting of technical problems, upgrading of software and hardware. A help desk has to be set up for users to call when they encounter problems.

ITIL

A well-run IT organisation should be able to manage risk and keep the "lights on" so that the BUs can do their jobs more effectively. It is good to certify the ITD team in technical and operational best practices. One of the ideal certifications comes from ITIL, which is short for the IT Infrastructure Library.

ITIL is a framework of best practices for delivering IT services. It has gone through several revisions currently comprising five books, each covering various processes and stages of the IT service lifecycle. ITIL's systematic approach to IT service management can help businesses manage risk, strengthen customer relations, establish cost-effective practices, and build a stable IT environment.

ITIL focuses on automating processes, improving service management and integrating the ITD into the business. In large companies, the ITD has become an integral part of the organisation. ITIL encourages the ITD to use modern technology, tools and software to help the business become more agile, flexible and collaborative.

ITIL 4, which was released in 2019, contains nine guiding principles and covers organisational change management, communication and measurement and metrics. These principles include:

1. Focus on value.
2. Design for the experience.
3. Start from where you are.
4. Work holistically.
5. Progress iteratively.
6. Observe directly.
7. Be transparent.
8. Collaborate.
9. Keep it simple.

ITIL 4 also emphasises customer feedback, since it's easier than ever for businesses to understand their public perception, customer satisfaction and dissatisfaction. ITIL provides a systematic and professional approach to the management of IT service provision, and offers the following benefits:

▪ Reduced IT costs.
▪ Improved IT services through the use of proven best practice processes.
▪ Improved customer satisfaction.

- More professional approach to services delivery.
- Standards and guidance.
- Improved productivity.
- Improved use of skills and experience.
- Improved delivery of third-party services.[1]

Tips for Small Business

Small businesses face many challenges, such as insufficient staff, client dependence, and balancing a desire to create quality products with volume. The biggest challenge small businesses face is getting revenue and generating profit. Unfortunately, many small businesses tend to neglect technical support. The Acme Group listed the reasons why tech support is essential for small businesses in a blog post on their website.[2]

- **Implement.** Implement appropriate solutions. Whether you need new hardware, data processing software, computer security or network management solutions, either your tech support team or external consulting companies could be of help. Find solutions that might make the most sense for your operation, balancing your needs and your budget. That is vital for a couple of reasons.

First, the average owner of a small business, there is little awareness of the kind of hardware and software options that might be available, and which ones might be suitable for their needs. An IT consultant could help to put the right pieces in place, thereby ensuring efficiency for operations.

Second, good tech support services can manage and add to existing infrastructure as needed, keeping hardware and software updated and implementing upgrades as required. Having the right technology components in place is crucial for stability and growth today.

- **Maintain.** Maintain your systems. It's not sufficient to have an IT professional install your infrastructure; you also need to continue to maintain the systems. While business owners or their staff can take over the responsibility to update systems and software regularly (or automate updates), as well upgrading when necessary, it's better to have a qualified IT professional manage and maintain your computer networks.

---

[1] *CIO*, https://bit.ly/2YYs6QR.
[2] https://bit.ly/3f61Cnf.

▦ **Monitor.** Monitor the usage. Having the right structure can go a long way to ensure efficiency and security computer and network operations. However, it would be ideal if you did not forget the potential element of human error. That is where monitoring services and specialists come into play. Whether you're worried about employees misusing resources or you want to be vigilant where possible data breaches are concerned, proper monitoring by technical support staff is an essential element of protection.

▦ **Educate.** Educate your staff. You want to trust your team in passwords creation and management. You also want them to keep the company's best interest in mind when utilising technological resources; there may be sound policies in place to ensure this. With proper and available technical support, you can keep your staff educated on how to behave while working on the computer and network resources. Hackers are always planning new ways to trick employees into letting their guard down. A tech support consultant can stay on top of security trends and keep your staff informed and updated.

▦ **Prevent.** Prevent breaches – this the prime reason for tech support to be on hand. It's not a question of if – a but when – hackers will target your business. Without tech support, your small business can be highly vulnerable to breaches, as well as data loss, legal issues, and possible reputational damage.

▦ **Maximise.** Maximise profit. You'll indeed have to pay for tech support, whether you hire professionals in-house or work with outside consultants or firms. However, you'll gain many benefits in the process, one of which is addressing waste and maximising efficiency and profit.

You may end up paying professionals for tech support eventually. You might consider having dedicated staff in-house or sub-contract to consultants. In either case, you should get support services, ideally ones that are familiar with your area of operations. When computers don't function, or a hacker gets into your system, you'll be glad you invested in reliable tech support specialists to address the issue, minimise damage, and get your computer systems back and running.

 ## HELP DESK ISSUES

Setting up a help desk is the ITD's responsibility. The ITD must first list the roles and responsibilities for the help desk. It's necessary to set clear boundaries: Will the help desk cover all software, hardware and operating systems issues? Will it only handle problems related to specific applications? Will the help desk be outsourced or manned by internal staff?

Service desk outsourcing, as help desk outsourcing was previously called, started in the US in 1998 and was introduced to Singapore in the early 2000s. Companies like IBM, Hewlett-Packard, Computer Sciences Corp and Atos were the first few ones providing such services.

Even if internal teams handle the help desk, some issues can be outsourced to vendors or contractors rather than done in-house. The ITD needs to understand that it may not have answers to all problems, or all solutions may not come from a single source. It requires, therefore, to have a strategy to escalate issues to technical experts from relevant vendor organisations.

Helpless Desk

The help desk is often the point of contact between the ITD and your end-users, especially when end-users run into IT problems they can't solve. Unfortunately, many ITDs don't pay much attention to setting up and managing a practical help desk, prompting some users to call it the "Helpless Desk" derisively. ITIL describes a "service desk" or a "help desk" as the single point of contact between the end-user and the ITD. The service desk typically manages incidents, resolves L1 (Level 1) issues, and handles communications with users.

Rod Christensen, Service Delivery Manager at Nordic Consulting Partners, published a blog post on October 10, 2017, "Why do they call it the 'Helpless Desk'?"[3]

Here are some excerpts:

▨ The "Helpless Desk" is more interested in moving along to the next call. It will, at best, collect demographic details and promise to let someone know; at worse, they may disavow responsibility for a situation or blame the user's lack of knowledge. Rarely will the "Helpless Desk" offer real help or even an estimated time for recovery. It is clear why my physician friend chose to rename our service desk; they were providing no service.
▨ In contrast, a top-performing help desk will collect information from a user about an incident and immediately begin work to mitigate the impact, providing updates as they work. First Level Resolution (FLR) is a primary

---

[3] https://bit.ly/2zZWGRC.

goal of the help desk. For example, a user whose incident was resolved by the help desk agent is more satisfied and is back to work quickly. That improves employee satisfaction and operational efficiency. Also, because the help desk agent performs recovery, other members of the tech team can focus on critical tasks assigned to them.

▪ A practical help desk is one that focuses on the quality of information and assistance provided to callers. Staff it with qualified personnel with good communication, problem-solving and interpersonal skills. When users call the help desk, they would expect to speak to someone who is technically competent and who can understand their problems and recommend a solution. It will be a real shame if the caller feels that he or she is more proficient than the person staffing the help desk.

Help Desk

The help desk is only as good as the surrounding support systems. End-users or others who call or email the help desk must get a quick response. Set up procedures for handling calls, including guidelines for logging calls, handling simple problems, escalating to higher levels for technical help, and for referring issues to vendors or maintenance contractors when required.

Log every call to analyse trends or detect recurring problems. Help desk staff should be required to close loops by recording the time taken to resolve problems, who's handling which issues, and whether escalation is required. If the help desk gets outsourced, analyse the SLA (service level agreement) records to identify trends, including organisation-wide problems or questions, FAQs, among others.

Place FAQs in a database in the organisation's intranet for all staff to access. That will cut down the number of calls about common problems, thereby freeing the help desk staff to focus on more crucial issues. A discussion group could also be created for the help desk staff to post topics or offer solutions to problems they have encountered and solved. That would be invaluable.

The top skillsets for help desk staff should be technical competence, communications, interpersonal and problem-solving skills, ability to learn quickly, work in teams and under pressure. The ITD should conduct periodic reviews of the help desk's performance.

Measure success by speed or how fast problems get identified and resolved. Classify issues based on their severity and set performance standards for each classification. Matters related to mission-critical systems must be resolved immediately, for instance. Train help desk teams to classify problems correctly and to escalate issues to the appropriate technical personnel supporting the help desk.

Another performance measure is the rate of abandoned calls. If it's high, it means many users are frustrated because they can't get through to the helpline to report their problems. Or that the help desk staff are unable to cope with the call loads or are taking too long to resolve each case.

An exceptionally high number of calls may be received when there is an organisation-wide problem. Play a prerecorded message informing anyone who calls that the help desk is aware of the problem and it is currently being resolved. It is a simple and effective way to communicate with users.

Case Study

In my career as CIO of HDB (Housing and Development Board) and later CIO of StarHub, I experienced running both an in-house IT help desk, as well as an outsourced IT help desk. In HDB, the ITD provided IT support services; the IT support was divided into mainframe systems support and office systems support. In the early days, when the number of office systems users were few, the ITD had no problem supporting the users directly. With the advent of client-server systems and increasing implementation of office automation, it became untenable for a small ITD team to support 17 end-user departments and more than 5,000 office system users.

HDB's CEO approved our setting up PC support units in all the BUs. Most of these units consisted of two to three technical staff who reported to a senior officer, called the PC officer. The PC support unit was the first line of support when end-users in their BUs encountered problems. All complicated issues got escalated to the ITD. We held regular meetings and training sessions to ensure that the PC support units got upskilled.

It was a tale of two cities when I took over as the CIO in StarHub. The ITD did not believe that IT support was a core competency; it outsourced the function to an external vendor. Since StarHub was a relatively young company, it made sense to devote IT resources to in-house applications and infrastructure development. Non-core activities like IT support was best outsourced.

It was essential to have a strict SLA with the outsourced vendor. We also kept the SLA flexible, to leave room for negotiation if the complexity of the applications increased. StarHub was expanding rapidly with the acquisition of an Internet company and a cable TV provider. With additional staff and more office systems, the SLA had to be renegotiated.

IT support is not a core IT competency in most ITDs, but if support services are not up to standard, then there will be a tremendous impact on staff productivity and morale. At StarHub, I learnt that when the organisation scales, it is imperative to keep a small group of IT support staff in-house to support critical systems and not rely entirely on a vendor to solve all problems. So unless you are prepared to pay a hefty amount for a very high SLA, it would be wise to have your support staff to handle critical problems.

 ## TOP TIPS

Here are six tips – from Zendesk – on setting up an ideal help desk in your organisation:[4]

1. **Create.** Create a service catalogue. Agreeing upon and defining your services internally and externally will improve customer service and is, ultimately, a better way to manage expectations. Once you decide as a team and an organisation on what you're providing your customers, you can then forge ahead with setting expectations. Help desk software that includes an SLA solution makes it easy to incorporate them into the workflow.
2. **Develop.** Develop a culture of helping out within the help desk. If help desk management is too focused on minimising costs, then you end up delivering subpar assistance to your users. On the other hand, if you focus on giving the users everything they need to do their jobs, then you win, twice. How? First, your team becomes more proactive and looks for opportunities to help users before waiting for them to report issues. Second, your users will then view the help desk as a partner that fixes problems and issues, rather than people to blame at when things go wrong.
3. **Hire.** Hire good employees to retain good employees. When your company has stellar help desk management, it often means your best hires stick around. The support organisation wins with less turnover, and agents can become more skilled over time, able and willing to solve more complicated issues. Equip your employees with the tools – and the training – to succeed in their jobs.
4. **Build.** Build a workflow that tracks issues end-to-end. Both the help desk and the users should be able to identify the status of the case at a glance.

---

[4] Source: https://www.zendesk.com/blog/5-tips-for-setting-expectations-around-in-house-help-desks.

Such transparency reduces frustration and anxiety for all parties, and it, from a metrics perspective, it speeds resolution. Any employee should be able to jump in at any time, knowing where exactly the previous person left off, as well as the next step that needs to get done. The user should have updates regularly, with the option of tracking their issue online or by email.

5. **Remember.** Remember that the help desk is a partner. The help desk does not exist to mop up mistakes, a cultural message that should permeate throughout the company. The help desk is a valued partner for every department. Think of it this way: Where would Star Trek`s Captain Kirk be without Scotty in the engine room? If Kirk needs warp speed to get the job done, Scotty uses his technical prowess to find a way to give it to him and save the day. As a result, Scotty – our help desk – is hailed, and not cursed, by the rest of the crew. The help desk's mission, similarly, is to make every user as successful as possible, Monahan says.

6. **Offer.** Offer a knowledge base or self-service portal. Help desk software should also come with an option for a knowledge base. Often, end-users are just looking for a quick solution to a simple issue. Rather than submitting another ticket, a knowledge base allows employees to search for and solve their problems. That reduces the strain on the ITSM team so they can solve more complicated issues requiring 1:1 support.

It's possible to be overwhelmed by all the facets of help desk management: help desk software, knowledge management, ITIL; not to mention ticket queues and the always-on nature of customer support. But a good strategy, great talent, and the right help desk software can help ensure you provide quick and efficient customer support for your employees.

CHAPTER TWELVE

How to Handle Change

 INTRODUCTION

Roughly 500 years before the birth of Jesus Christ, a Greek philosopher, Heraclitus of Ephesus, said something that resonates even today and is part of twenty-first-century management theory: Change is the only constant in life. Heraclitus (born in 535 BC) lived in the ancient city of Ephesus, in modern-day Turkey, and influenced philosophy giants like Socrates (born in 470 BC) and Plato (born in 424 BC).

It took 62 years for 50 million automobiles to be sold, and 28 years for the 50 millionth TV set to be shipped. It took seven years for the Internet to reach 50 million users, and three years for Facebook to get to 50 million users. WeChat took one year, PokemonGo took just 19 days, and Zoom seven days. Following the Covid-19 lockdown, Zoom's daily users ballooned to more than 200 million users in March, from just 10 million in December 2019, Zoom's CEO Eric Yuan told the media on April 2, 2020.

As the CIO of a large ITD, I often worried about how to help my staff cope with the rapid changes in ICT. It is easy to draw up bold plans to adopt new technologies and to carry out scenario planning to prepare for the future.

However, the best dreams will come to nought if your staff do not buy-in and are not prepared to change their mind-sets.

Change Mind-sets

Mind-set is a state of mind that affects the way people think, feel and act when faced with specific situations. We often hear about the difficulty of training older workers to be computer literate. Even among IT professionals, it's challenging to get the more senior staff to accept new ways of doing things, like using object-oriented technology, creating more friendly user-interfaces, and using the latest programming languages.

The ITD often needs to restructure and reinvent itself to survive in the whirlpool of technological changes, such as handling e-commerce, knowledge management, web standards, or rapid application development. Making all these changes are tough when there is resistance to change. There are many reasons for resisting change within the ITD:

- **Fear.** Fear of losing dominance. It took several years for some of the older professionals to master the system development methodology, and that leverage would be lost.
- **Expertise.** Older ITD staff may have expertise in older operating systems, databases, applications and methodologies. That expertise would be almost redundant when new tech gets introduced.
- **Apathy.** There's a general apathy, complacency or resistance to learning anything new; it takes time, effort and patience, as well as a change in attitude.
- **Ability.** Some staff would be genuinely concerned with their lack of skills and their ability to cope with the change.
- **Benefits.** Teams will resist change when they do not understand its implications and perceive that change to be likely to cost them more than they might gain.
- **Trust.** In many cases, there is a strong resistance to change because of a lack of trust in senior management. More transparent communications could solve this issue.

Case Study

In 1990, after having been the CIO of HDB for a few months, I held regular breakfast meetings with the BU (business unit) heads. The BU heads complained that the ITD was declining many of their requests. I took the feedback very seriously. If the ITD turns away jobs and assignments, then very soon the BUs will form their own "shadow IT" units.

At my next quarterly ITD staff forum, I gave a talk titled "The Answer is Yes; What is the Question?" I said the ITD exists to serve the organisation, to enable business processes and facilitate the business. If the BUs have a problem that requires the ITD's help, it is our duty to help, no matter how difficult. By doing so, we will build up users' trust and prevent them from seeking outside help.

For a large organisation like the HDB, allowing shadow IT units to exist would be disastrous for IT governance due to data duplication. My mission, therefore, was for the ITD to accept all requests for help. If some queries or projects required skills beyond our capabilities, we could seek external help or consultancy. I wanted to change the ITD's mind-set.

Two issues needed change: One, the inertia of technical staff to stay in their comfort zone and try not to interact with end-users: two, a severe lack of interpersonal or inter-BU communications. I scheduled regular informal interactions with the BU heads over breakfast, lunch or coffee. It was when they were relaxed that I could gather frank feedback about the ITD's use and worth to them. I urged my staff to do likewise with their BU counterparts.

I also organised quarterly coffee sessions for the management and the BUs to build rapport and to brief them on the projects we were doing for them. We also highlighted any obstacles the project teams faced and how we proposed to overcome them. To build better rapport, we also organised interdepartmental games between the BUs and the ITD.

The most significant mind-set change I instilled in my staff was not to treat the end-users as our customers but as business partners. My motto: "Together with business partners, we serve HDB's customers." That means that we would feel the pain of the BUs when they faced customer issues and problems. With this mind-set change, a strong bond of comradeship began between the BUs and the ITD, which enabled HDB to be one of the leading IT-enabled organisations in Singapore.

 ## AGENT OF CHANGE

You must be the change you wish to see in the world. That quote comes from Mahatma Gandhi. Here is the story as narrated in a blog by New York author and executive coach Dolly Daskal:

Among the hundreds of people who were waiting to meet Mahatma Gandhi were a mother and her young son. When it was their turn, the woman asked Gandhi to get her son to consume less sugar. Gandhi asked her to come back in two weeks and said he would talk to the boy then. She wondered why he didn't just speak to her son when he was already there, but she complied with his request.

In two weeks, they returned, and after waiting for a couple of hours, she was able to approach Gandhi again. Gandhi immediately spoke with the boy, who agreed to begin working to eliminate sweets. After thanking Gandhi for his wise and compassionate words, the mother asked him why he wanted them to return instead of offering his advice the first time.

"Upon your visit two weeks ago, I too was eating sugar," Gandhi replied. "I could not teach your son not to eat sugar if I had not taken that journey myself."

Moral of the story: change in the ITD begins with the CIO. We are wary of change because we do not know if we can cope with the change. We are afraid of the consequences if we cannot adapt to the change. Yet change is part of nature. We grow older every day, and we consume new knowledge daily. We must, therefore, learn to thrive on change, harness this dynamic and enjoy the opportunities that change offers.

Change Metrics

What can the CIO do to get his staff to change? Australia-based Total Learning Company lists seven possible reactions people may exhibit when faced with change:

1. In the early stage, most people feel uncomfortable and self-conscious.
2. Some tend to think first about what they will have to give up.
3. Others feel alone, even if everyone is going through the change.
4. Many can only handle so much change at one time.
5. Some people are at different levels of readiness for change.
6. Others will be concerned that they don't have enough resources.
7. Most will revert to old behaviour when the pressure is off.

To implement change, take steps to address those reactions to change mind-sets and minimise the resistance to change. Here are seven steps that the CIO, as a change agent, should take:

1. **Communicate the change.** Prepare your staff for change. Clarify the scope, timing and reason for the change. Establish a common understanding of the intended outcome of the change. Set measurable goals. Explain what rewards the staff can expect when they meet performance targets. An effective communications plan can reduce the resistance to change.

2. **Get involvement.** Get affected by the change to provide feedback, suggestions, recommendations, if possible, before implementing the changes. The leadership team must engage in more active listening to find out the feelings of your staff. Help those who are psychologically affected by the change.

3. **Provide adequate training.** Adequate training is essential to help IT professionals get a handle on new technologies and survive the change. Equip ICT professionals with new skills and knowledge. That will ensure that your team will not feel helpless when they begin implementing the changes.

4. **Support change leaders.** Management support for those helping implement changes is essential. Use mistakes made as learning points. Reprimanding those who made mistakes would make others afraid to try. Reward improvements your staff makes with tokens of appreciation.

5. **Encourage learning.** Promote continuous learning. Faced with rapid changes in technology, many organisations, unfortunately, opt to outsource what they feel they can't handle. It is much better to encourage staff to strive to be learning continuously, to stay ahead of changes in ICT. Inculcate the habit of reading magazines, news, technology updates – and discussing them – in your team.

6. **Be an initiator.** Be the initiator of change, not merely a follower. As the CIO, you must lead the change in ICT in ITD by updating top management about new tools and solutions that can help grow the business or business operations. The rapid pace of change in the ICT world should always keep you on your toes. The ICT updates are like arrows that are moving towards you; you have to triage, prioritise or choose to ignore, considering the limited resources at your disposal.

7. **Discuss and decide.** There is a window for you to discuss with your team, to ponder, evaluate and decide whether to go for change, keep the status quo, or make smaller tweaks. Base your decisions on a variety of questions: Is there a need for change? What would the company gain by going ahead with the change? What would the company lose if it decides to keep the status quo? Is there a middle path?

Invent the Future

Is there is a way out of the change quandary? Since it is so difficult to predict the future, why not try and invent it? When I first proposed this to my team, the reactions I received ranged from amusement to anger. I explained to them that creating the future is not as tough as it seems. I initiated a process called "Creative Futuring" in my ITD when I first took over as a CIO. I realised that we needed a strategic plan to exploit ICT and to chart a path suited to our needs. Creative Futuring involved the following five steps:

1. **Scanning.** The ICT planning process starts by scanning the environment, both internally and externally. Make your team aware of technology trends: What direction is the technology going? Which technology is likely to dominate the market? How will users perceive and receive new solutions? Who else is using it? You can get this information from research reports from market research agencies like Gartner, Meta Group, IDC Corp, Forrester, and Frost & Sullivan. Not every prediction by these researchers is accurate, but they indicate how ICT may evolve.

2. **Planning.** Some likely questions to ask: What are the changes in your business environment? How would that impact demand for your goods or services? Do we have sufficient demographic data on our users? Since more people are using online services, are our products or services fully e-enabled? Is the organisation ready to embrace new technology? Do we have any legacy yet to be fully depreciated? What resources – capital, talent, infrastructure – do we need to prepare for change?

3. **Collaborating.** Bring people together. Deliver a standard message and goal. Allay concerns. Get the buy-in from other teams and stakeholders. Elevate enthusiastic people to lead the change. The downside of this approach is that you give a room to nay-sayers and "prophets of doom"; these people need to be appropriately managed, or they may spread negative energy across the organisation. There's an old corporate saying: Let people burn off steam in the classroom, instead of burning the backroom.

4. **Training.** Training should focus more on scenario planning. That is the process of imagining different ways in which the future might turn out and how it may impact the organisation. Plan a course that makes sense today; be flexible and alert when the unexpected occurs. Scenarios should be plausible or possible but need not be logical. For example, it may seem illogical to think that a mainframe computer could someday shrink to the

size of a mobile phone that everyone in the world could afford. Yet it was plausible, and it has been a reality for many years now.

5. **Implementing.** You can do all the planning you want, but the reality is when the rubber hits the road. Problems that didn't surface earlier will occur during implementation. Document every issue – and attempted solution. For example, which components in the new service or solution didn't work well, didn't work intermittently, or didn't work at all? Which users had trouble with the interface and why? Which issues were anticipated during the planning stage – and which unexpected problems surfaced?

 ## THE JOURNEY

CIOs face a myriad of issues in their roles, including dealing with technology changes, human resources and inadequate budgets. Prime among them are versioning issues. As updates and patches get applied, some solutions may not function properly. But the ITD is responsible for ensuring that the old applications (which many users are familiar with) continue to work with the new.

The technical issues combined with the new business processes that you create during the Creative Futuring process will form your ITD's strategic IT plan. That plan is not about how ICT will be implemented in the organisation, but about the ITD that can exploit ICT to improve products and services. Do not implement technologies that do not benefit the business.

Your strategic IT plan provides you with a vision for the future and gives staff a sense of direction and confidence. The programme offers the ITD a systematic way in analysing, adopting and deploying the new technology. You can evolve other related strategies based on the overall plan. That includes the infrastructure strategy, the ITD training strategy, the knowledge management strategy, and others.

Align with Business

As a CIO, you must be on a constant journey to acquire and understand new technologies and processes. You should participate in industries forums and contribute articles to journals. Your vendors are your partners; they could offer you technical resources, whitepapers, articles, reports that you could digest and refer to in discussions and articles.

Complacency can result in your getting labelled as "Career Is Over." As a CIO, you cannot afford to stand still. As soon as you implement your latest project, continue to educate yourself on what the ITD should do next. It will energise your staff and get them to think what improvements are possible to boost the value to the business. Your role as a CIO is to ensure that your team is vested in the project and its success. Being aligned with the company – or the BUs – is critical to ensuring the change goes well.

CIOs today are a vital part of the company since almost all business gets done online. The ITD is as much a contributor to the organisation's success as are sales or marketing or business development. Therefore your staff has to build presentation skills, understanding contract laws, create trust and confidence and ensure sensitive data is protected. During the later years of my career, I spent half of my time developing this extended network of collaborators, and the other half doing a typical CIO's work.

Remember that other organisations and your business partners have innovative ideas to offer. If you are invited as a trusted partner to be part of their processes, you will gain tremendously as ideas and strategies get cross-pollinated, resulting in very innovative business models that you can utilise.

 ## TOP TIPS

What can leaders and employees do to commit to changing themselves? "Our journey has led us to the deep conviction that off-site, workshop-based learning journeys of small groups of 20 to 30 employees are the most powerful intervention," authors Scott Keller and Bill Schaninger state in their book *Beyond Performance 2.0: A Proven Approach to Leading Large-Scale Change*. "These are typically centred on in-person working sessions, over two days, led by facilitators experienced in the principles of adult learning and knowledgeable in techniques developed in the field of human potential."[1]

The workshop methodology is based on the "U-Process". That's a social technology methodology developed during a decade-long partnership between four parties: Otto Scharmer and Peter Senge from MIT (Massachusetts Institute of Technology), Generon International, and the Society for Organisational Learning. The U-process has three phases:

---

[1] https://mck.co/2O8nF0R.

1. **Sensing.** Sensing typically involves a senior leader who has already been through the workshop and shares the company's change story, describes her or his change journey, and answers questions from participants.
2. **Presencing.** Presencing involves participants exploring their personal "iceberg" of behaviour. It includes working with modular, discussion-based material and questions that equip leaders to achieve higher levels of both, self-awareness and self-control. Key questions: Under what circumstances do I act out of fear rather than hope? Do I focus on scarcity, instead of on abundance? Is my attitude more about victimhood instead of mastery? What would the result be if I made different choices?
3. **Realising.** In this phase, the participants make clear choices about personal mindsets and behavioural shifts; they identify "sustaining practices" to help them act on their insights, and reflect on how they will engage their private networks for the challenges and support they will need during the rest of their change journey.

After these workshops, small groups should convene to offer peer accountability and advice. After several weeks, there should be a further facilitated session to take stock of changes in behaviour.

The authors acknowledge that this approach will sound unduly "soft" to some. But it seems to have a transformational impact on everyone – from engineers in Holland to investment bankers in the US to government officials in the Middle East to employees in South Korean conglomerates. While some organisations put all their staff through such a workshop, they can also achieve remarkable impact through a critical mass of people manager/leaders, which should be about 25-30 per cent of the total. The authors note that in those cases, the leaders eventually shed the mentality of "if only they would change" and replaced it with a profound sense of "if it's to be, it's up to me."

Not every successful change programme we have seen uses these techniques. The authors note that in their experience, every change programme that used them (in the context of other recommended interventions) had been successful, and in time frames that were far faster than most leaders had expected. The effect can be remarkably positive when organisations grapple with how to thaw what's often referred to as the frozen middle – a change-resistant layer of middle managers.

PART FIVE

V

Innovation

CHAPTER THIRTEEN

How to Foster Innovation

 INTRODUCTION

Corporate creativity is not about how creatively you can present your data on PowerPoint or Excel. Despite considerable investments in time and money, innovation has been a frustrating pursuit in many companies, according to an article published in the *Harvard Business Review* (*HBR*).

Innovation initiatives frequently fail, and successful innovators have a hard time sustaining their performance – as Polaroid, Nokia, Sun Microsystems, Yahoo, Hewlett-Packard, and countless others – have found. Why is it so hard to build and maintain the capacity to innovate? The reasons go much deeper than the commonly cited cause: a failure to execute. The problem with innovation improvement efforts is rooted in the lack of an innovation strategy, writes author Gary P Pisano in *HBR* published in June 2015.

Without an innovation strategy, innovation improvement efforts can quickly become a grab bag of much-touted best practices. That includes dividing R&D into decentralised autonomous teams; spawning internal entrepreneurial ventures; setting up corporate venture-capital arms; pursuing external alliances; embracing open innovation and crowdsourcing; collaborating with customers; and implementing rapid prototyping.

There is nothing amiss with any of those practices, per se. The problem is that an organisation's capacity for innovation stems from an innovation system: a coherent set of interdependent processes and structures that dictates how the company searches for novel problems and solutions, synthesises ideas into a business concept and product designs, and selects which projects get funded.

Individual best practices involve trade-offs. And adopting a specific approach generally requires a host of complementary changes to the rest of the organisation's innovation system. A company without an innovation strategy won't be able to make trade-off decisions and choose all the elements of the innovation system.[1]

Every CEO would love to have staff who are innovative and creative. In today's competitive environment, any company that delivers an innovative product or service before its competition is likely to reap massive gains. For example, many of us are familiar with innovative products from Sony, including the Walkman, CD players, MD players and digital movie cameras.

In the Walkman example, the creativity was in tweaking Sony's existing products to come up with a portable tape recorder. The innovation was in marketing the Walkman: a jazzy, portable player everyone could carry, listen to music without disturbing others and play favourite tracks of their choosing.

Definitions

A CIO's prime role is as an advisor to the organisation on the strategic use of ICT. Since ICT is a means to boost the productivity of the organisation, it's the CIO's task to foster creativity and innovation. He or she must introduce new systems and solutions to automate laborious processes or reengineer them. The ITD staff will have to support the CIO and come up with new ideas – involving creativity – and innovation. Let's first define the two intertwining terms – creativity and innovation – in a corporate context.

1. **Creativity.** Creativity has always been at the core of the business. But until recently, it hasn't appeared at the top of the management agenda. By definition, the ability to create something novel and appropriate is essential to the entrepreneurship that gets new businesses started and that sustains the best companies after they have reached some level of scale.

---

[1] https://bit.ly/2YW4BZV.

"But perhaps because creativity was considered unmanageable – too elusive and intangible to pin down – or because concentrating on it produced a less immediate payoff than improving execution, it hasn't been the focus of most managers' attention," authors Teresa Amabile and Mukti Khaire wrote in an *HBR* article published in October 2008.[2]

2. **Innovation.** Gartner defines innovation management as a business discipline that aims to drive a repeatable, sustainable innovation process or culture within an organisation. Innovation management initiatives focus on disruptive or incremental changes that transform the business in some significant way.

McKinsey says innovation, at its heart, is a resource-allocation problem; it is not just about creativity and generating ideas. Yet too many leaders talk up the importance of innovation as a catalyst for growth and then fail to act when it comes to shifting people, assets and management attention in support of their best ideas. The portfolios of these companies tend to go heavy on near-term product improvements and other presumably "high certainties" efforts and much lighter on potential breakthroughs or new business models. These forms of innovation are "less certain" but often hold more significant potential to generate sustainable, new sources of growth and outsized returns.

The main difference between creativity and innovation is the focus. Creativity is about unleashing the potential of the mind to conceive new ideas. Those concepts could manifest themselves in any number of ways, but most often, they become something we can see, hear, smell, touch or taste. However, creative ideas can also be thought experiments within one person's mind. Creativity is subjective, making it hard to measure.

Innovation, on the other hand, is entirely measurable. Innovation is about introducing change into relatively stable systems. It's also concerned with the work required to make an idea viable. By identifying an unrecognised and unmet need, an organisation can use innovation to apply its creative resources to design an appropriate solution and reap a return on its investment.

Organisations often chase creativity, but what they need to pursue is innovation. Theodore Levitt puts it best: "What is often lacking is not creativity in the idea-creating sense but innovation in the action-producing sense, i.e. putting ideas to work."[3]

---

[2] https://bit.ly/3grBSBR.
[3] https://bit.ly/3e0eYQp.

Innovation is the ability to implement a creative or new idea, a discovery or a new way of doing things. Take data, for example. Ever since the advent of computing, data needed to be structured, or organised objectively for computers to make sense of them. All RDBMS (relational database management systems) relied on structured data.

That left out the whole array of unstructured data, like images, sounds and analogue files. The creativity was in coming up with a new way to handle unstructured data, with the introduction of Hadoop. The innovation was in taking the idea to implement HDFS (Hadoop Distributed File System), which in turn gave birth to BDA (big data analytics).

I believe having teams with creative thinking does not happen by accident or divine blessing. Companies need to nurture the creativity of their staff by providing an environment that is conducive to innovation. Alex Osborn, known to be the father of brainstorming and a founder of the Centre for Studies in Creativity, once remarked: "Creativity is so delicate a flower that praise tends to make it bloom while discouragement often nips it at the bud."

Case Study A

At the turn of the millennium, all companies had to look for ways to handle the Y2K (Year 2000) rollover. The healthcare industry was at particular risk since it dealt with human lives. In Singapore, many hospitals ran database solutions based on mainframe-based information management systems.

However, there were also other solutions based on ERP (enterprise resource planning) that were Y2K compliant. Many companies began to migrate to the new ERP systems to avoid being hit by the Y2K bug.

Most Singapore hospitals, however, ran their operations on older noncompliant ERP systems.

In a private healthcare group in Singapore, they were using a HIS (hospital information system), which was not Y2K compliant. To resolve the issue meant having to invest heavily on upgrading the older systems. The CIO had to either get the higher budget approved or find a creative solution to this problem.

The CIO found out that hotels were using an ERP system that was not only Y2K compliant but also not as expensive. The CIO presented his plan to the top management. Hotels are like hospitals; both have beds and rooms; both have extensive materials management systems involving laundry, drugs, consumables. Even the budgeting systems are complicated.

However, clinical processes like pharmacy, pathology, radiology and nursing need different systems. The CIO had to source for clinical management systems integrated with the ERP system. The CIO checked with all the vendors; one of them had a system that was in use in major hospitals in Europe; they would work with the CIO's team to tweak their design for the Singapore market. In due course, the integrated system was implemented at the hospital, saving it time and money.

FOSTERING INNOVATION

"Keeping the lights on" is not a source of competitive advantage of the ITD. Outsourced vendors can do this better than the ITD. The department should instead be the beacon of creativity and innovation. By creating and fostering an environment conducive to creativity and innovation, the CIO can reap benefits such as a drop in staff turnover, increased job satisfaction, higher motivation and involvement and an increased sense of achievement amongst employees.

Mind-set Metrics

How can you create a vibrant social environment in the ITD? One of the low hanging fruits that I would often use is the celebration of success. How does this work? The CIO can allow team members to share creative ideas on a collaboration platform like SharePoint. The person who gestates the idea can share it with others – thereby fostering teamwork and camaraderie.

Ensure that you allocate adequate resources, especially money and time, to your team to get the ideas to pilot stage. Highlight these small projects at different milestones to celebrate with your staff. It could be something simple, like a banner for the most creative, most improvised, or most valuable idea of the month or quarter. The celebration could involve giving the winning person or team a trophy or certificate.

- ■ **Reward.** There is no reward without risk. As the CIO, you must encourage your staff to take some level of risk and an allowance to make mistakes. Encourage the team to adopt an "offensive" strategy of taking the lead – instead of a "defensive" approach of waiting for change to be thrust upon them, or wishing to maintain the status quo. That can only happen when management is ready to forgive mistakes and allow staff to have a second chance to rework on an idea or innovation. That does not mean that you should tolerate foolhardiness or constant negligence.

Staff empowerment is a vital factor in influencing creative behaviour. That means allowing teams the freedom to decide what to do or how to accomplish a task. Top management must encourage employees to innovate. Provide incentives for staff to contribute ideas through a staff suggestion scheme (SSS). Encourage staff to participate in work improvement programmes, quality improvement schemes, innovation teams, and hackathons. Good ideas should be publicised throughout the organisation to instil a sense of pride in the employees who have contributed to them.

- ▨ **Celebrate.** A corporate culture marked by free sharing of information, open cooperation and collaboration across levels and departments, between management and workers, enables employees to develop ideas in teams. Encourage joint projects across departments; they usually result in higher-quality innovation.

Reward and celebrate employees who have come up with good ideas. If the concept leads to massive savings and profits, share a percentage of the profits or savings with the individual or team. Some companies go a step forward; they help their employees to patent their innovations and allow them to get a share of the royalties received.

- ▨ **Motivate.** Frederick Herzberg (April 18, 1923–January 19, 2000) was an American psychologist who was a very influential thinker in management. He is most well-known for introducing job enrichment and the Motivator-Hygiene theory. His 1968 article "One More Time, How Do You Motivate Employees?" sold more than 1.2 million reprints by 1987 and was the most requested article from the *HBR*. "It's the job of a manager not to light the fire of motivation, but to create an environment to let each person's spark of motivation blaze," he once wrote.

Creativity is not about ordering employees precisely what they should do to change a process or produce a solution. It is best to set broad goals and leave the rest to the staff's collective imagination. The CIO can help smooth the process by encouraging continuous innovation, offering a platform for staff to share ideas, hold informal discussions to stimulate creativity, eliminate factors that undermine creative thinking, and strive to achieve an optimal balance between current and future goals.

Case Study B

Samsung is one of the most innovative conglomerates on earth. Their innovation management strategy entails deploying an experienced "creative elite" to take the lead with new projects, ensuring they are primed to incorporate the best practices and yield maximum KPI. Samsung's creative elite use open innovation, and corporate tech scouting approaches.

Samsung uses the TRIZ methodology for innovation. TRIZ is the Russian acronym for the "Theory of Inventive Problem Solving". According to TRIZ principles, whatever problem you're facing, somebody, somewhere, has already solved it (or one very like it). Creative problem solving involves finding that solution and adapting it to your problem.

Once the more precise picture gets formed, Samsung uses relevant scientific, technological or corporate teams to deliver the expertise and resources for the new project to proceed. Samsung's creative elite combine TRIZ techniques with scouting approaches to acquire new knowledge, remain on the cutting edge of modern scientific practices, and expand their core abilities to maintain project ROI.

Samsung's strategic partnership with the Russian Academy of Science, for example, uses TRIZ to pinpoint gaps in the market where lucrative innovation efforts can succeed. Samsung's creative elite works with members of the Academy to help develop an array of products, ranging from new LED bulbs to 3D mapping technology.[4]

 DIGITAL DIVIDE

In 2007, I attended an APEC e-commerce conference in Tokyo. The Asia-Pacific Economic Cooperation (APEC) is an inter-governmental forum of 21 member economies in the Asia-Pacific. It was set up in 1989 to promote free trade across the Asia-Pacific region. The APEC HQ is in Singapore. The APEC is one of the highest-level multilateral blocs and oldest forums in the Asia-Pacific region. Member countries include ASEAN, Japan, Australia, New Zealand, South Korea, China, Mexico, Chile, Peru, Russia, Canada, and the United States.

The APEC conference I attended was a gathering of distinguished personalities from the region with one goal: prepare the region for the Internet Age. The state of readiness of APEC countries ranged from low to excellent, given the composition of members, so the discussion swung from one end to another.

What struck me most at this conference is not the e-commerce competency of the nations but the frequent mention of the words, "Digital Divide".

---

[4] https://bit.ly/2W9TFGb.

That signified the widening chasm between the digital haves and the digital have-nots. This chasm occurs at many levels, from a national one to each household in a nation.

The digital divide must also be a key concern for you and other CIOs. CIOs operate in a parallel digital universe. It may seem that in a technological landscape, where we stick to standards and integrate solutions in a shared operating environment, our world is flat. That's not true.

Our technological world is only flat in the data centre. Outside of that, it touches our customers, staff, suppliers, government regulators and others. Our flat world may not connect with some of these stakeholders. However, for our organisation to prosper, it must reach out to both the digital haves and the have-nots. The company must find new markets, reach out to new customers and close the digital gap where feasible.

Closing the Gap

At a basic level, the digital haves are those who benefit from ICT, either at home or at work. Unfortunately, the digital have-nots are usually ones with low incomes and less access to education in general. They would invariably get left out of the digital revolution sweeping the world. Some digital have-nots may be from the vulnerable segments – the elderly, the mentally challenged, the very young and those that actively eschew technology.

Closing the digital gap is primarily the role of government. The ideal is the PPP (public, private partnership) model where the government involves the private sector and SMEs (subject matter experts) to work together to help close the gap. That has always been the Singapore way and has worked wonders.

- **Training.** The best way to close the digital gap is to offer avenues for continuous education and training to the staff (the organisation's responsibility) and the citizens (the government's commitment). At a technical level, training helps your team boost ICT skillsets, which is the organisation's responsibility. At a national level, avenues for training and upskilling makes the population IT literate.

Our discussion is limited to the organisation. How can the company boost IT literacy? One way is to offer focused on-the-job training. A better way is to send specific members of the staff for external courses, which are readily available and conducted by the IHLs (institutes of higher learning). Some of these courses lead to formal qualifications and are expensive. Companies can offer to co-pay for certification as a reward for staff who excel in their work and have a positive attitude.

Within the ITD, the CIO can set up training classes conducted by your IT staff for the BUs. Developing courses and training material will give your IT teams a strong sense of achievement. The bonding and trust in groups and the organisation are immense. The teachers and the taught can get together to resolve issues and problems either during a crisis or otherwise.

- **Coaching.** Coaching is an ideal way to upskill staff, especially on new products, solutions or services. Don't confuse coaching with mentoring. Mentoring is a long-term process based on mutual trust and respect; coaching is for a short period. Mentoring is more about creating an informal association between the mentor and mentee; coaching follows a more structured and formal approach.

A business mentor has the first-hand experience of the mentee's line of work; a business coach need not have hands-on experience of the kind of work the coached does. The prime objective of a business mentor is to help develop skills that are relevant for the mentees in their present job, as well as the future; the priority of a business coach is to improve performance that impacts the current position.

Both mentors and coaches benefit businesses. Companies should be transparent on what their priorities are and what kind of support they seek. With the right help, small businesses can become more productive, profitable and competitive.

- **Volunteering.** There are already many national initiatives to help Singapore's population to be ICT-literate. Primary school children have been exposed to IT since 1997. Singapore's First Master Plan for Education, launched in 1997, focused on setting up the necessary infrastructure for schools and training teachers to use ICT for teaching and learning. It was implemented in three phases, starting with 22 schools in Phase-I and extended to all schools by 2002.

The Second Master Plan for Education ran from 2003 to 2008; it focused on the effective integration of ICT into the curriculum for engaged learning. Both master plans were intended to equip students with ICT skills by integrating ICT into the curriculum. We're now in Phase-IV.

At the international level, the digital divide is quite apparent, where a segment of the population is below the poverty line and has no recourse to any education. In Singapore, most people would have had some contact with computers, but not everyone is at the same level of literacy. Some families cannot afford to own a computer, let alone get access to upskilling on ICT.

It is with this in mind that community groups – in the PPP model – have embarked on a project to refurbish old PCs and then sell them at low cost to the lower-income households. That is laudable, but not enough. Owning a PC does not make one digitally literate. The person has to know how to use the PC to search for relevant information, carry out electronic transactions, communicate with others, and all this securely.

As an IT professional, you have a social and moral responsibility to help the less privileged benefit from the digital revolution. Please volunteer your time and services to industry associations, community groups and government agencies to bring ICT to the masses and help bridge the digital divide.

The ITD Divide

To be sure, there is a digital divide within the ITD in all organisations. That's because the level of technical skills in the ITD team is not the same. Given that ICT covers a whole array of technologies, it's tough for every member of the team to be well-versed in all aspects of ICT. Here's what the ITD divide looks like:

- **Within ITD.** I remember when I had a large team of COBOL developers, we faced a digital divide issue. They had to learn C, then a new programming language. There was considerable resistance. We had a digital divide of those who understood C and those who did not want to. At another time, we had to migrate to a new ERP solution. Once again, there was resistance to change, resistance to learning new ways of doing the same tasks, and a resultant digital divide.
- **Within BUs.** In the early days of computerisation, the accounts department ran on Lotus-123. The accountants developed complex macros in Lotus-123. When we implemented an ERP system, they wanted the ERP data to flow into the Lotus-123 spreadsheets; that was difficult to accomplish. At another time, sales directors wanted paper reports with 255 columns generated by the new ERP system for the daily sales performance. They refused to look at the data on their PC monitors.

■ **Within vendors.** The ICT vendors who sell you fancy gadgets and gizmos are themselves not digitally savvy. Just a few years ago, my team had implemented electronic invoicing and POs (purchase orders). I wanted all our vendors to send their invoices electronically, via email or file transfers. But most vendors insisted that we accept – and issue – paper documents and manually sign each page. It was for legal and audit departments. As long as vendors do not cross over to the next generation of electronic processes, we will continue to have a digital divide.

■ **Within customers.** Customers can range from B2B (business-to-business) to B2C (business-to-consumer) and B2G (business-to-government). Most customers have some level of digital literacy, in the sense that they can write emails, surf the Net and connect to social media on their smartphones. But that's not enough. Customers need to ensure that their PCs or phones have some level of data and cybersecurity. They also need to follow acceptable cyber-hygiene practices to keep themselves – and your organisation – safe from malware.

 TOP TIPS

Teamwork is essential to any company's success. To compete in the market requires teams that can generate ideas faster and handle vast amounts of complex datasets. Teams now have access to unprecedented levels of customer data, powerful creative tools, and ML (machine learning) algorithms to foster innovation. These new insights and tools are also disrupting the process of innovation itself; it's not just that products and services that are getting more complex, but the process of innovation itself is too.

Building high-performing teams require leaders who can meet these complex demands. Leaders must ensure that projects are delivered on time and budget while managing a diverse set of groups with different personalities and skillsets. They need to adjust to a changing workplace, foster collaboration between in-office and remote workers and remain focused amidst a cacophony of distractions. That can seem like a tall order; it can, however, be done if you adopt the right leadership habits. Here are five practices that leaders use to help their teams achieve new heights of creativity.

How to promote innovation in your company? Here are six tips from author Hilary Thompson's blog in *The Boss Magazine*.[5]

---

[5] https://bit.ly/3dYcsKF.

1. Leverage Outside. Leverage external resources to inspire. There is a slew of in-house resources you can use to boost your team (recognition and doughnuts are always welcome). But good leaders also include outside resources into their inspirational bag-of-tricks.

To jumpstart the process, look within your community and leverage local resources. You could invite a local business owner or thought-leader to ignite interest and offer some unique perspectives on your target market. Set up "escape rooms" to practice teamwork and problem-solving skills. Or schedule a "wine and painting" (or similar) sessions to spark collective creativity.

If your local community doesn't seem qualified, you could send emails with a list of inspiring podcasts and blogs to your teams. Or you could set aside lunch-and-learn sessions by streaming a documentary on tech topics then discuss it collectively. Including outside resources of any kind helps to broaden your motivational strategy and to diversify your team's knowledge. It also shows them that there is an abundance of opportunities and resources outside the office to motivate themselves.

2. Build Balance. Build balanced teams. Influential leaders know how to hire for and build balanced teams to maximise innovation. You can do this by hiring individuals with the characteristics of successful innovators. Promising innovators are persistent, proactive, opportunistic, as well as formally educated. However, fostering innovation takes more than throwing a bunch of PhDs in a room and expecting magic.

To start with, you need people who understand the realities of the market vis-à-vis the limitations of your company. You should then balance that group with entrepreneurs who innovate by pushing against those limitations. If you get too many conservative opinions, then and the work will stagnate. If you get too many "out-of-the-box" thinkers, then the ideas could become impractical. The ideal: the push-and-pull with a balanced team could result in innovative approaches with workable ends.

3. Allocate Resources. Allocate resources wisely – value resource scarcity. Managers who motivate their team recognise that necessity is the mother of invention. Ergo, having a limited set of tools might inspire your team to get more from them. Fewer resources also help increase focus. Too many choices push teams into the "weeds" or results in "analysis paralysis".

Resource scarcity could also lower financial investment and resultant oversight. With less to answer for from corporate HQ, your team could gain autonomy. Moreover, big budgets could lead to big expectations and high pressure on teams, both of which could stifle creative thinking and shift the effort from innovating for new designs to solving budget constraints. Resource scarcity also forces your managers to keep small teams. Too many members can complicate decision-making. That can lead to social loafing and lower productivity.

4. Set Clear Goals. Set specific goals for the team. Leaders who inspire creativity are habitual goal setters. They avoid vague generalisations like "Do a great job!" or "Let's work hard." Highly effective leaders start projects with clearly-defined goals or objectives, timelines, and tasks for the team and its members. The leaders then follow up with evaluations and adjustments to fine-tune processes and strategy.

Having guardrails and limitations raises the team's focus and fosters innovation. Managing a team with an attitude that "there are no rules" could leave them rudderless. Giving them too much freedom can become a creativity deterrent. An inspiring leader should lay that groundwork at the very start.

One critical component of setting specific goals is to be able to match individual team members with specific tasks that are both difficult and aligned to their skillset. Both, commitment and motivation may increase when individuals feel task-specific confidence. And with a strong commitment and appropriate feedback, team members are more likely to succeed.

5. Trust More. Trust more than control. Ineffective leaders micromanage their team. They keep a detailed account of who's doing what and when they're doing it. But managers who innovate exhibit firm leadership characteristics such as trust, openness, and courage. Inspiring leaders build a safe workspace which, encourages and embraces failure and rewards new ideas.

These crucial traits are the antidote to the biggest killer of innovation and creativity: fear. When a team starts feeling anxious and worried, their attention often turns inwards, to self-preservation. Risk aversion could set in, with team members weighing the pros-and-cons of innovating something that could be ridiculed. In such an environment, members may feel they won't fail if they don't try.

To be a manager who fosters creativity and innovation, you need to model the creative process yourself. You could use these five habits as a guideline to exhibit innovation. Brainstorm unique solutions to assemble the right mix of people. Find ways to wrangle the resources you need from a tight budget. Set specific goals using team-building exercises. In short, don't just rely on your managerial or leadership style to foster innovation. Use your process to exhibit it.

CHAPTER FOURTEEN

How to Manage Big Data

 INTRODUCTION

Right from the mainframes era to the present, the one output that computers have consistently been producing is reports. They were rudimentary during the days of Big Iron, and they're sophisticated in the current days of Big Data. In the interim, we have gone through templates and formats, and a slew of reports in accounting, financial reporting, materials management, human resources, and others.

And now we have an information deluge; we're all drowning in data and information. We want instant insights, real-time results and accurate predictions. But we have to also contend with the flip side of tech: concerns about data security, confidentiality and privacy. It's akin to walking past your neighbourhood trash can and finding a slip of paper with the bank account details of your neighbour or yourself!

That's where regulatory compliance comes into play. Corporate presentations are no longer limited to just finance and accounting, but must also be compliant to stringent regulations and controls. Such data regulations cover manufacturing, supply chain, CRM, buying behaviours, among others. The emergence of cloud computing has made BI and BA (business intelligence and business analytics) and big data available online and in real time. Businesses make decisions based on these insights every day, and errors, if any, get magnified.

As the CIO, you're the custodian of your organisation's data, and in many cases, compliance is your responsibility. You have to ensure that your team has put data governance and compliance policies in place, despite increasing demands from the business to share PII (personally identifiable information) for BDA (big data analytics). Data thus becomes a two-edged sword. That's because customer information remains in the archive after the customer leaves or a partner terminates their relationship.

Data Governance

As the CIO, data governance and security are two of your primary responsibilities. Your organisation would have accumulated tonnes of information that's in your data stores, and you have to ensure that the data is safe, secure and appropriately stored. Data is the new oil, crude oil, to be precise.

Like crude oil, data is a vital asset because of its ability to provide insights, intelligence and wisdom embedded in it. Your competitors would love to get hold of your data to find out your corporate strategies and business initiatives. Therefore, data and information are the responsibility of the CIO. The governance of data is so crucial that many large corporations now have a CDO (chief data officer).

In the past, electronic or digital data was in the custody of the CIO. You need to involve various end-user teams (internal customers) to give access to, define, and agree on the usage of data, especially when you deploy new software or new applications. You also need their feedback after the implantation is over.

That is important because data is subject to regulatory compliance. For example, the accounting department would need to comply with GAP; the finance department will need to be PCI (payment card industry) compliant. The PCI DSS (data security standard) is a set of protocols to ensure that companies that process, store, or transmit credit card information maintain a secure environment.

Sales and marketing would need data to book orders, generate reports, present trends, forecast sales numbers, and manage advertising and marketing campaigns.

Here are three issues that you need to keep in mind as the custodian of data in your organisation:

1. Confidentiality. Keeping critical information confidential and secure is vital. Only authorised staff should have access to information, and that, too, on a needs basis. But how exactly can you keep data safe?

That involves technical solutions, stringent policies and guidelines, and vigorous enforcement. For those authorised to have access, passwords and 2FA (second-factor authentication) are required. For keeping out external elements, your data security team can use tools such as firewalls and IDS (intrusion detection systems). What is necessary for your organisation depends on the risk profile and tolerance, as well as the vertical segment. Banking and healthcare verticals need stringent security.

It would also be wise to appoint a CISO (chief information security officer), who can either report to the CIO, or in some organisations, even to the CEO. An organisation that does not have a robust information security system and management is likely to suffer a loss of business, and more likely, reputation.

2. Integrity. Data integrity refers to the maintenance, accuracy and consistency of data over its entire life cycle. It is a critical aspect in the design, implementation and usage of any system that stores, processes or retrieves data. Sometimes it is used as a proxy term for data quality. While data validation is a prerequisite for data integrity, data integrity is the opposite of data corruption.

For information to be useful to people in the organisation, extracted data from the databases must be accurate and consistent. Using inaccurate, inconsistent and incomplete information to derive business intelligence will fail the business because you can't formulate business strategies, and you can't make business decisions on incorrect data. Such "dirty" data can cost your organisation dearly, with competitors running after your business, and regulators gunning for your noncompliance.

3. Availability. Data availability is the process of ensuring that data is available to end-users and applications, when and where they need it. It defines the degree or extent to which information is readily usable along with the necessary IT and management procedures that tools and technologies require.

If information is the lifeblood of an organisation, it cannot stop flowing from your data stores to where it is needed. That means that the infrastructure supporting the information systems must be robust enough to prevent any outages. And if there are outages, there must be BC-DR (business continuity and disaster recovery) procedures to ensure that such data outages do not cripple the organisation.

BIG DATA ANALYTICS

What is big data? Gartner defines big data as high-volume, high-velocity and high-variety information assets that demand cost-effective, innovative forms of information processing that enable enhanced insight, decision-making and process automation.

Oracle defines big data as more massive, more complex datasets, especially from new data sources. These datasets can be so voluminous that traditional data processing software can't manage them. These massive volumes of data can address business problems you wouldn't have been able to tackle before. The 5Vs of big data are:

1. **Volume.** The amount of data is a factor. With big data, you'll have to process high volumes of low-density, unstructured data. That can be data of unknown value, such as Twitter data feeds, clickstreams on a webpage or a mobile app, or sensor-enabled equipment. For some organisations, this might be tens of terabytes of data. For others, it may be hundreds of petabytes.
2. **Velocity.** Data velocity is the fast rate at which data arrives. Usually, the highest speed of information streams directly into memory versus being written to disk. Some Internet-enabled smart products operate in near real time and will require real-time evaluation and action.
3. **Variety.** Variety refers to the many types of data that are available. Traditional data types were structured and fit neatly in a relational database. With the rise of BDA, data comes in new unstructured data types. Unstructured and semi-structured data types, such as text, audio and video, require additional preprocessing to derive meaning and support metadata.
4. **Veracity.** Veracity refers to inconsistencies and uncertainty in data, and sometimes the quality and accuracy of data are difficult to ascertain. Data can come via a multitude of data dimensions resulting from multiple disparate data types and sources. For example, data in bulk could create confusion, whereas less amount of data could convey incomplete information.
5. **Value.** Much of the data is of no use to the company, unless you turn it into something useful. Data in itself is of no use or importance unless it gets analysed into something valuable to extract information. Hence, you can state that value is the most important V of all.

The history of BDA started in 2003 with the birth of Hadoop. According to its co-founders, Doug Cutting and Mike Cafarella, the genesis of Hadoop was the Google File System paper published in October 2003. This paper spawned another one from Google: "MapReduce: Simplified Data Processing on Large Clusters". Development started on the Apache Nutch project but moved to the new Hadoop subproject in January 2006. Doug Cutting, who was working at Yahoo at the time, named it after his son's toy elephant. The initial code factored out of Nutch consisted of about 5,000 lines of code for HDFS (Hadoop Distributed File System) and about 6,000 lines of code for MapReduce.

Hadoop 0.1.0 was released in April 2006. The HDFS and its add-ons could, for the first time, analyse both structured and unstructured data. That was an important milestone. In February 2008, Yahoo launched what it claimed was the world's most extensive Hadoop production application. Called the Yahoo Search Webmap, it ran on a Linux cluster with more than 10,000 cores and produced data used in every Yahoo web search query. In June 2009, Yahoo opened its Hadoop source code to the open-source community.

In 2010, Facebook claimed that it had the largest Hadoop cluster in the world with 21 petabytes of storage. In June 2012, Facebook announced that the data had grown to 100 petabytes; later that year it announced that the data was expanding by half a petabyte per day. By 2014, almost all multinational corporations were using Hadoop.

BDA Tools

Hadoop has seen its heyday. Now there is a slew of BDA tools that you could use to great advantage. Here's a list of 15 BDA tools – in random order – that companies could consider for their business and teams.[1]

1. **Apache Hadoop.** Apache Hadoop is a software framework used for clustered file systems and handling big data. It processes datasets utilising the MapReduce programming structure. It is an open-source framework and is written in Java; it thus offers cross-platform support. More than half of the Fortune 50 companies deploy Hadoop, including Amazon Web services, Hortonworks, IBM, Intel, Microsoft, Facebook, and others. Free to use under Apache license.

[1] https://bit.ly/2Z4t4MJ.

2. **CDH.** Cloudera Distribution for Hadoop (CDH) focuses on enterprise-class deployments of Hadoop. It is open source and has a free platform distribution that encompasses Apache Hadoop, Apache Spark, Apache Impala, and others. It allows users to collect, process, administer, discover, model, manage and distribute unlimited data. CDH is a free version. Enterprise versions are available on a per-node cost from Cloudera.

3. **Apache Cassandra.** Apache Cassandra is an open-source distributed NoSQL DBMS (database management system) constructed to manage vast amounts of data spread across numerous commodity servers to deliver high availability. It uses CQL (Cassandra Structure Language) to interact with the database. Some companies using Cassandra include Accenture, American Express, Facebook, General Electric, Honeywell, Yahoo, and others. Free for use.

4. **Knime.** Knime stands for Konstanz Information Miner. This is an open-source tool used for enterprise-level reporting, research, CRM, data and text mining, integration, data analytics, and business intelligence. It supports Windows, Linux, and Apple OS X operating systems. Some companies using Knime include Comcast, Johnson & Johnson, Canadian Tire, among others. Knime platform is free. They also offer other commercial products which extend the capabilities of the Knime analytics platform.

5. **Datawrapper.** Datawrapper is an open-source platform for data visualisation that aids its users to generate simple, precise and embeddable charts very quickly. Its primary customers are newsrooms. Some names include The Times (London), Fortune, Mother Jones, Bloomberg, Twitter, and others. It offers a free version and customisable paid options.

6. **MongoDB.** MongoDB is a NoSQL, document-oriented database and is written in C, C++, and JavaScript. It is an open-source tool that supports Windows, OS X, Linux, and Solaris. Its main features comprise aggregation, ad-hoc queries, BSON format, indexing, replication, server-side execution of JavaScript, schema-less, capped collection, load balancing and file storage. Some companies using it include Facebook, eBay, MetLife, Google, among others. It offers paid enterprise versions.

7. **Lumify.** Lumify is an open-source tool for BDA integration, fusion, and visualisation. Its primary features comprise full-text search, 2D and 3D graph visualisations, link analysis between graph entities, integration with mapping systems, automatic layouts, geospatial and multimedia analysis, and real-time collaboration through a set of projects or workspaces. Lumify is free for use.

8. **HPCC.** HPCC stands for High-Performance Computing Cluster. That is a BDA solution over a highly scalable supercomputing platform. HPCC, also called as DAS (Data Analytics Supercomputer), was developed by Lexis-Nexis Risk Solutions. The tool, written in C++ and a data-centric language known as ECL (Enterprise Control Language), is free to use.

9. **Apache Storm.** This is a cross-platform, distributed stream processing and fault-tolerant computational framework. The developers include Backtype and Twitter. It is written in Clojure and Java. The architecture is based on customised spouts and bolts to describe sources of information and manipulations to permit batch and distributed processing of streams of data. Users include Groupon, Yahoo, Alibaba, the Weather Channel, and others. Free to use.

10. **Apache Samoa.** Somoa stands for Scalable Advanced Massive Online Analysis. Samoa is an open-source platform for big data stream mining and machine learning (ML). It allows you to create distributed streaming ML algorithms and run them on multiple DSPEs (distributed stream processing engines). Free to use.

11. **Talend.** Talend Open Studio for big data offers free and open-source license. Its components and connectors include Hadoop and NoSQL. It provides community support only. Open studio for big data is free. For other enterprise-grade products – BD Platform, and Real-time BD Platform – it offers subscription-based flexible costs.

12. **RapidMiner.** This Is a cross-platform tool which offers an integrated environment for data science, ML and predictive analytics. It comes under various licenses that provide small, medium and large proprietary editions, as well as a free edition that allows for one logical processor and up to 10,000 data rows. Companies like Hitachi, BMW, Samsung, Airbus, and others have been using RapidMiner.

13. **Qubole.** Qubole data service is an independent, big data platform that manages, learns and optimises on its own from your usage. That lets the data team concentrate on business outcomes instead of addressing the platform. Users include Warner Music Group, Adobe, Gannett, among others. Qubole comes under a proprietary license that offers a business and an enterprise edition. The business edition is free and supports up to 5 users. The enterprise edition is subscription-based.

14. **Tableau.** Tableau Is a software solution for BI and BA (business analytics) which present a variety of integrated products that aid in visualising and understanding their data. The software contains three main

products – Tableau Desktop (for the analyst), Tableau Server (for the enterprise), and Tableau Online (to the cloud). Tableau Reader and Tableau Public have been recent additions. Tableau can handle all data sizes and is easy to use for technical and non-technical users. Users include Verizon Communications, ZS Associates, Grant Thornton, and others.

15. **R.** R is one of the most comprehensive languages for statistical analysis. It is open-source, multi-paradigm and dynamic software environment. Written in C, Fortran and R, it is used by statisticians and data miners. Use-cases include data analysis, data manipulation, calculations, and graphical display.

Case Study

In 2012, *The New York Times* published a story under the headline "How Companies Learn Your Secrets." The article discusses, among other things, how and why a marketing team at Target tried to build a model to predict which shoppers were pregnant. This story shows that Target's BDA operation made predictions about intimate details with astonishing precision.[2]

The story is about a girl receiving a coupon book featuring maternity items. Target probably sent out many similar coupon books to many people. If Target just sent out maternity coupon books at random, this exact scenario could have still happened. Some of the randomly assigned coupons books would certainly reach pregnant women by chance, and some of those pregnant women might have had fathers who didn't know that they were pregnant. One of those fathers might have gone to a store to complain. That's the postmortem analysis by blogger Colin Fraser, published in *Medium* in January 2020.[3]

I'm citing this case study not to go into the pros and cons of BDA, but highlighting your role as CIO and how you should deal with it. My approach would be to adapt and adopt best practices from the banking industry, where they treat a customer's bank account details and actions as being strictly confidential. You're the de facto custodian of the organisation's data and have responsibility and accountability for all the organisation's stakeholders, including customers. That way, you will be compliant and protected.

---

[2] https://nyti.ms/2NZ7RNG.
[3] https://bit.ly/31JHrrv.

 **TOP TIPS**

Big data is still relatively new in many organisations, especially in Asia. The importance and significance of BDA in business processes and outcomes have been evolving. Here are some of the essential best practices that implementation teams need to increase the chances of success.[4]

- **Gather.** Gather your business requirements before gathering data. Begin big data implementations by first gathering, analysing and understanding the business requirements. That is the first and most essential step in the BDA process. Align every big data project with a specific business goal.
- **Approach.** Approach BDA from a business perspective. "Implementing big data must be a business decision, not an IT decision." That's a beautiful quote that wraps up one of the most essential best practices for implementing big data. BDA solutions are successful when they are approached from a business perspective, and not from the IT/engineering standpoint. IT needs to get away from the premise of "Build it, and they will come" to "Solutions that fit defined business needs".
- **Use.** Use an agile and iterative approach for implementation. Usually, big data projects start with a specific use-case and dataset. Throughout the performance, the organisation needs to evolve as teams understand the data. That happens once they touch, feel and start to harness its potential value. Use iterative implementation techniques and agile to deliver quick solutions based on current needs; don't focus on big bang apps development. When it comes to the practicalities of BDA, the best practice is to start small by identifying specific, high-value opportunities, while not losing sight of the big picture. Achieve these objectives with this big data framework: Think Big, Act Small.
- **Evaluate.** Evaluate data requirements. Whether a business is ready for BDA or not, carrying out a full evaluation of data coming in and how to utilise it for business advantage is ideal. This process typically requires input from your business stakeholders. Together you analyse what data needs to be retained, managed and made accessible, and what data you can discard.

---

[4] https://bit.ly/2VOEYrU.

- **Ease.** Ease skills shortages with standards and governance. There is a growing shortage of big data analytics professionals who can manage and mine massive datasets. Short of offering hefty signing bonuses, the best way to overcome potential skills issues is to standardise big data efforts within an IT governance programme.

- **Optimise.** Optimise knowledge transfer with a CoE (Centre of Excellence). Establishing a CoE to share solution knowledge, plan artefact and ensure oversight for projects can help minimise errors. Whether big data is a new (or needs more investment), transfer the soft and hard costs across the enterprise. Another benefit of using CoEs is that it will help drive the big data and general information and solutions architecture maturity in a more structured and systematic process.

- **Embrace.** Embrace and plan your sandbox to test prototypes and performance. Permit your data scientists to construct their data experiments and prototypes by using their preferred languages and/or programming environments. After a successful proof of concept, they can reprogramme and reconfigure these implementations with an IT turnover team. Sometimes, it may be not easy even to know what exactly you are looking for. That's because the technology is often breaking new ground and achieving results that were previously labelled as "can't be done".

- **Align.** Align with the cloud operating model. Create BDA sandboxes on-demand and resource management needs to have control of the entire data flow, from pre-processing, integration, in-database summaries, post-processing, and analytical modelling. A well-planned private and public cloud strategy – involving both provisioning and security – should play a crucial role in supporting the changing requirements. Public clouds can be provisioned and scaled up instantly. In cases where quick in-and-out prototyping is required, this can be very effective.

- **Associate.** Get the team to associate big data with enterprise apps. The value of big data should be associated with enterprise-focused application data. Companies should set up new capabilities and leverage their existing investments in infrastructure, platform, business intelligence and data warehouses, and not discard them as being obsolete. Investing in integration capabilities can help knowledge workers correlate different types and sources of data, forge associations and make meaningful discoveries.

- **Embed.** Embed analytics and decision-making by infusing intelligence into operational workflow/routine. For BDA to be a competitive advantage, organisations need to make "analytics" like the way they conduct business; analytics must become part of the corporate culture. Nowadays, the competitive advantage of data-driven organisations is no longer just a good ally, but a "must-have" and a "must-do". The range of analytical capabilities emerging with BDA and the fact that businesses can be modelled and forecasted is becoming a common practice. BDA need not be in silos in teams, but instead made a part of the day-to-day operational function of front-end staff.

CHAPTER FIFTEEN

How to Ensure Enterprise Security

 INTRODUCTION

There are three historical elements to security – data security, information security and cybersecurity. Data security is about securing your data. There is a subtle difference between data and information. Data consists of facts or details from which information is derived. Individual pieces of data are rarely useful alone. For data to become information, data needs to be put into context. The management of data – and therefore, information – has gone through waves of innovation.

Simply put, information is data that has some meaning attached to it. For example, the sequence of numbers "12122012" is just data. Once it is under the "date" field, it is interpreted as December 12, 2012, which signifies that the "data" has turned into "information." Therefore, information security is about protecting the information, which may be either structured, unstructured or semi-structured.

Cybersecurity is about security data and information that is online. Kaspersky defines cybersecurity as the practice of defending computers, servers, mobile devices, electronic systems, networks and data from malicious attacks. Cybersecurity includes the following categories:[1]

- **Network security.** This is the practice of securing a computer network from intruders, whether targeted attackers or opportunistic malware.
- **Application security.** This focuses on keeping software and devices free of threats. A compromised application could provide access to the data it is designed to protect. Successful security begins in the design stage, well before a program or device is deployed.
- **Information security.** This protects the integrity and privacy of data, both in storage and in transit.
- **Operational security.** This includes the processes and decisions for handling and protecting data assets. The permissions users have when accessing a network – and the procedures that determine how and where data may be stored or shared – fall under this umbrella.
- **BC-DR.** Business continuity and disaster recovery define how an organisation responds to a cybersecurity incident or any other event that causes the loss of operations or data. DR policies dictate how the organisation restores its functions and information to return to the same operating capacity as before the event. BC is the plan the organisation falls back on while trying to operate without specific resources.

Right from the early days of computing, securing information was the prime function of the ITD head, and later, the CIO. However, in the mainframe era, security was not a significant issue for three reasons: One, not many people were conversant with the workings of the computer, so apart from computer engineers, no one else could mess with the massive machines. Two, access to the mainframe was controlled; only a few people in the finance and administrative departments had access. Three, the mainframe was well protected by sturdy security software.

When computing cascaded down to the desktop, other peripheral systems – such as LANs (local area network), and later, WANs (wide area networks) – began to appear in corporate buildings. More people now had access to computers, and information security became a vital issue. Many corporate databases that stored important and mission-critical information shifted from the mainframes to client-server systems. The risks rose. Therefore, backing up and protecting information assets became paramount.

---

[1] https://bit.ly/2OTL5Hs.

With the advent of the Internet, computers got interconnected to the outside world. While access to the Internet allowed the organisation to receive information from suppliers, partners and customers, it also meant that the outside world could access the organisation's computer systems. Some of those trying to access them were malicious actors.

Security Pointers

CIOs need to know the common threats to information security to be able to deal effectively with them. Here are some pointers for the CIO:

- **Policy.** The greatest threat is the lack of a security policy to govern the access – both physical and virtual – to networks, systems and data. A formal information security policy should establish the rules, guidelines and definitions for the organisation and prevent inconsistencies in the handling of resources; this can introduce risks. A sound security policy will also act as the management's commitment to ensure security policies are followed across the board. It will list expectations for involvement, accountability and behaviour of staff. The ITD should carry out regular inspections to ensure that all staff comply with the policy.
- **Awareness.** The other side of the security policy is security awareness. Lack of knowledge or understanding of acceptable information security practices – as well as employee indifference to security issues – could be detrimental to the organisation. Information security awareness should be regularly reinforced to all employees to establish the right security procedures and principles. Sound personal security practices should become second nature for all staff.
- **Stakeholders.** It is not enough to just keep your employees in the loop. You should also include your key stakeholders – such as suppliers, channel partners, distributors and retailers – to be security-aware and compliant. That's because your systems are connected to your stakeholders and their users. If your stakeholders are not compliant, they could compromise your organisation's information or cybersecurity. As a CIO, the buck stops with you, so please ensure internal and external compliance.
- **Hyper-connectivity.** The world is now in the fourth industrial revolution, called IR4.0. That means hyper-connectivity is becoming more common. A range of systems and devices – including robots, intelligent machines, IoT controllers and 5G connectivity – have made interconnections ubiquitous. There is a massive amount of data flowing continually across interconnected systems. The risks have therefore risen manifold.

- **Mind-set.** It is best for you as the CIO to keep Murphy's Law – which states that if anything can go wrong, it will – framed on your wall. That's because of the exponential rise in cybercrime. In 2019, Cybersecurity Ventures predicted that cybercrime would cost the world US$6 trillion annually by 2021, up from US$3 trillion in 2015. That represents the most significant transfer of economic wealth in history, risks the incentives for innovation and investment, and will be more profitable than the global trade of all major illegal drugs combined. So it's better to be prepared than caught unawares.[2]

 ## CIA TRIAD

The CIA (Central Intelligence Agency) was created under the US National Security Act of 1947, which President Harry Truman signed on July 26, 1947. The CIA was officially born on September 18, 1947, with Roscoe H Hillenkoetter as its first director. That CIA dealt with national security.

There's another CIA (confidentiality, integrity, availability), which is more relevant to you, the CIO. Also called the CIA triad, it is a model designed to guide policies for information security within an organisation. Some companies call it the AIC (availability, integrity, confidentiality) triad, to avoid confusion with the US CIA. The three elements of the triad are the three crucial components of security.

The CIA/AIC concept came about at different times. Confidentiality was first proposed in 1976 in a study by the US Air Force. Integrity was introduced in a 1987 paper, *A Comparison of Commercial and Military Computer Security Policies*. Availability was first debated in 1988 when computer uptime began to gain currency. By 1998, the three concepts were banded together as the CIA or AIC model or triad.

Here's an overview of CIA as reported by *TechTarget*:[3]

- **Confidentiality.** Confidentiality is roughly equivalent to privacy. Measures to ensure confidentiality must be designed to prevent sensitive information from reaching the wrong people while making sure that authorised people can access it. It is common for data to be categorised based on the amount and type of damage that could be done if it falls into

---

[2] https://bit.ly/3OEka8g.
[3] https://bit.ly/3fWkG7H.

the wrong hands. More or less stringent measures should then be implemented as warranted.

Safeguarding data confidentiality could involve special training for staff privy to sensitive documents; this training would include security risks that could threaten vital information. Training can help familiarise authorised team members with risk factors and how to guard against them. Other aspects of training should include strong passwords and password-related best practices, as well as information about social engineering methods. This will prevent users from bending data-handling rules with good intentions and potentially disastrous results.

An excellent example of methods used to ensure confidentiality is an account number or routing number when banking online. Data encryption is a standard method used to ensure confidentiality. User IDs and passwords constitute a routine procedure; two-factor authentication is the norm. Other options could include biometric verification and security tokens, key fobs or soft tokens.

Besides, users can take precautions to minimise the number of places where the information appears and the number of times it is transmitted to complete a required transaction. Extra measures should be taken in the case of critical documents, such as storing only on air-gapped computers, disconnected storage devices or, for highly sensitive information, only in hard copy.

That's because access to the computer systems is not limited to the ITD; it also extends to users and external partners. Some non-IT users would have permission to run queries on your databases, access confidential information or even make changes to the data. Similarly, the ITD would have "power users" with access to your databases.

You need to limit access to information, segregate access rights according to roles. The CIO's dilemma is about ease of access (user-friendliness) versus confidentiality (data protection). It is necessary to balance the two. That balance should be based on privacy, or who has access and why.

- **Integrity.** Integrity of data involves maintaining its consistency, accuracy, and trustworthiness over the entire data lifecycle. Data must not be altered in transit, and steps must be taken to ensure that data cannot be changed by unauthorised people (this could mean a breach of confidentiality). Some of these measures would require file permissions and user access controls to implement. Version control could be used to prevent erroneous changes or accidental deletion by authorised user, for example.

Besides, some tools must be in place to detect any changes in data that might happen as a result of non-human-caused incidents such as an electromagnetic pulse (EMP) or server crashes. Some measures might include checksums (or even cryptographic checksums), for verification of data integrity. Backups or redundancies must be in place to restore the affected data to its original state.

- **Availability.** Availability can be ensured by rigorously maintaining all hardware. Perform hardware repairs immediately when needed. Maintain a correctly-functioning OS (operating system) environment that is free from software conflicts. It's also important ensure all necessary system upgrades are done company-wide. Provide adequate communication bandwidth. Work to prevent the occurrence of bottlenecks.

When hardware issues occur, having redundancy with RAID with high-availability clusters can mitigate data disasters. RAID (redundant array of inexpensive disks) refers to a data storage virtualisation technology that combines multiple physical hard disks into one logical unit. Fast and adaptive DR (disaster recovery) is essential for the worst-case scenarios; that capacity is reliant on the existence of a comprehensive DRP (disaster recovery plan).

Organisations should factor in unpredictable events such as natural disasters and fire when setting up safeguards against data loss prevention. A backup copy could be stored in a geographically isolated location, perhaps even in a fireproof, waterproof safe, to prevent data loss from natural or other disasters. Robust security equipment – or software such as firewalls and proxy servers – can also help guard against downtime and vital data blocked by malicious DoS (denial-of-service) attacks and network intrusions.

CIA Challenges

The CIA triad is not foolproof; some challenges must be understood and mitigated:

- **Integrity.** Data exists in three states: data-in-use, data-in-motion and data-at-rest. When data is being used, it is usually secure with underlying SSL (secure sockets layer) protocols. When information is at rest, you need to ensure that there is data integrity on how the data was created, who created it and who modified it. Data created, updated or altered must be owned and accountable by individuals performing specific roles. There are legal and contractual implications for all positions and their actions concerning their data. When you can ensure the integrity of the data-at-rest, users are assured to be able to trust the data.

Data-in-motion can be transmitted or received from other systems or external stakeholders. It can come via a secured network or via the Internet. Data-in-motion can be intercepted or diverted. You need to ensure that you can trust the originator and the recipient. The channel of transmission, receipt and the payload must use high security and integrity protocols.

- **Availability.** Applications availability is about maintaining high uptime – and by default, low downtime. That depends not just on your computer systems running smoothly, but also the networks, interfaces and all other connected systems are working and "available". In the old days, Sun Microsystems had a tagline: *The network is the computer*. That's all the truer today. If your network is down, all systems are down. Your network engineer should ensure that all nodes are running without glitches.

Network latency (or lag) is the amount of time it takes for a packet of data to be encapsulated, transmitted, processed through multiple network devices until it gets to its destination and is decoded by the receiving computer. Some reasons for latency are network interface port saturation, interface errors, packet fragments, upstream provider outages and routing issues. The most common cause of latency is due to packet queuing at any gateway along the course of the packet's travel.

- **Big Data.** Big data poses a significant challenge to the CIA triad. That's because big data consists of massive volumes of data, rapidity or velocity, and the variety of sources of data. Duplicate datasets and DR plans can multiply the already high costs. The main concern of big data is collecting and analysing of all this information; responsible data oversight is often lacking. Whistleblower Edward Snowden brought that problem to the public forum when he reported on the NSA's collection of massive volumes of American citizens' personal data.
- **IoT.** With IoT, privacy is a particular concern. It is necessary to protect the information of individuals from exposure in an IoT environment, in which almost any physical or logical entity or object can be given a unique identifier and the ability to communicate autonomously over the Internet or a similar network. The data transmitted by a given endpoint might not cause any privacy issues on its own. However, when even fragmented data from multiple endpoints is gathered, collated and analysed, it can yield sensitive information.

IoT presents a unique challenge because it consists of so many Internet-enabled devices other than computers, which often go unpatched and are usually configured with default or weak passwords. Unless well protected, IoT "things" could be used as separate attack vectors or part of an "IoT-bot".

In a recent proof-of-concept exploit, for example, researchers demonstrated that a network could be compromised through a Wi-Fi-enabled light bulb. In December 2013, a researcher at Proofpoint, an enterprise security firm, discovered that hundreds of thousands of spam emails were being logged through a security gateway. Proofpoint traced the attacks to a botnet made up of 100,000 hacked appliances. As more and more products get developed with the capacity to be networked, it's crucial to ensure security in IoT deployments.

▪ **Authenticity.** Authenticity is about ensuring that connections to resources are authorised and genuine. A core aspect is identity authentication, at the individual and the machine levels. In today's environment, just an ID and a password are not enough. For mission-critical work environments, it's best to have 2FA (second-factor authentication) such as an RSA security token or an automated SMS (short message service) sent to your mobile phone. RSA is a public-key cryptography system that is widely used for secure data transmission. The acronym comes from the surnames of Ron Rivest, Adi Shamir, and Leonard Adleman, who publicly described the algorithm in 1977. Machine identity (via MAC addresses) can authenticate the user and his computer or phone. More elaborate machine authentication can be added to IoT devices if required. MAC is short for "media access control"; a MAC address is a set of digits that uniquely identifies each device on a network.

Case Study A

Confidential information of 14,200 people with HIV, including their names, contact details and medical information, was stolen and leaked online. The culprit was an American fraudster, Singapore's MOH (Ministry of Health) revealed on January 28, 2019.

Mikhy Farrera-Brochez, the man behind the leak, resided in Singapore from 2008 before being jailed in 2017 for fraud and drug-related offences and lying to the MOM (Ministry of Manpower) about his own HIV status. His partner was Mr Ler Teck Siang, a Singaporean physician who was head of MOH's National

Public Health Unit (NPHU) from March 2012 to May 2013 and had access to the HIV Registry for his work. He was charged under the OSA (Official Secrets Act) for failing to take reasonable care of confidential information regarding HIV-positive patients.

It is an offence under the OSA (Official Secrets Act) for any person to possess, communicate or use any confidential information that could have been disclosed, *The Straits Times* quoted a Singapore Police spokesman on January 28, 2019. The police said they would not hesitate to take stern action, including prosecution, against those who have breached the OSA. Anyone found guilty of the wrongful possession, communication or use of confidential data could be fined up to $2,000, and jailed up to two years.[4]

DEEP DEFENCE

Firewalls and other security tools usually protect corporate computer systems, but they are vulnerable to attacks when incorrectly configured. Having a competent team of IT security staff to ensure the correct configuration of these systems and to handle patches will help the organisation to safeguard against intruders entering through loopholes. It just takes a single breach for all of the safeguards to topple down, as has been proven in many corporate cases.

That's where "layered defence" comes in. Ancient rulers built castles and forts with layers of defence to keep their cities safe. Each layer could withstand a certain amount of enemy pressure before cascading for the next layer to take over. The "layers" consisted of not just soldiers, but also a large expanse of open fields, rivers, crocodile-infested moats, high stone walls, and others.

- **SIEM.** These layers may not have worked when the enemy's offence would have been potent. But they bought the defender a very crucial resource: time. It took time to breach each layer – enough time to either fight or flee. In modern cyber-defence, SIEM (Security Information and Event Management) alludes to a layered defence strategy.

---

[4] https://bit.ly/32QoeVG.

SIEM was coined by Mark Nicolett and Amrit Williams of Gartner in 2005. Gartner says SIEM technology supports threat detection, compliance and security incident management through the collection and analysis (both near real-time and archived) security events, as well as a wide variety of other event and context-based data sources. SIEM's capabilities comprise a broad scope of log event collection, management, analytics and other data across various sources, and operational issues, including incident management, dashboards and reporting.[5]

- ▪ **Pen Test.** Penetration testing, also called pen testing or ethical hacking refers to testing a computer system, network or web app to find security vulnerabilities that a hacker or attacker could exploit. Pen testing can be done manually or via specialised automated software apps. The aim is to gather information about the target before the test, identifying possible entry points, attempt to break in, and report back the findings. Once an attacker has exploited a vulnerability, they may gain access to other systems or applications; the process repeats – looking for new vulnerabilities and attempting to exploit them. This process is referred to as pivoting.[6]

All ICT systems have multiple entry points, different applications and a variety of hardware. All of these may be at various stages of patching or upgrades; professionals maintain them with different experiences and skillsets. As the CIO, it is your responsibility to manage an effective and disciplined team to keep your systems current with patches and upgrades, staff training and mentoring, and oversight of all security policies. Pen testing is one method of finding inherent weaknesses or vulnerabilities.

Professionals offer pen tests with teams of experienced security professionals with advanced testing tools. In the ITD, as systems are designed, deployed and maintained by your team, you will have blind spots. When you just use your internal teams to do a pen testing, they will test areas that they know. Vulnerabilities may be in the regions that you don't know, hence you need to engage an external pen test team.

A good practice is to have an SLA (service level agreement) with external pen test firms and run regular pen tests. Such scheduled events should trigger your ICT team to prepare for the test by ensuring patches are up-to-date, and security monitoring systems are in place to detect these penetrations.

---

[5] https://gtnr.it/3hzFFOn.
[6] https://bit.ly/39mIZJE.

It is also useful for a surprise pen test, at least once a year, where the ITD could be caught napping. That is invaluable as there will always be a temp network router or server in your network that's "invisible." During a scheduled pen test, a "smart" ICT team member may shut down the temporary entities during the pen test and get them to be "live" after the test is over. Surprise pen tests will capture such backdoor systems.

The process of penetration testing may be simplified into five phases:

1. **Reconnaissance.** By gathering important information on a target system. This information can be used to attack the target better. For example, open-source search engines can be used to find data that can be used in a social engineering attack.
2. **Scanning.** Deploying technical tools to further the attacker's knowledge of the system. For example, Nmap can be used to scan for open ports.
3. **Gaining access.** Using the data gathered in the reconnaissance and scanning phases, the attacker can deploy a payload to exploit the targeted system. For example, Metasploit can be used to automate attacks on known vulnerabilities.
4. **Maintaining access.** Maintaining access requires taking the steps involved in being able to be persistently within the target environment to gather as much data as possible.
5. **Covering tracks.** The attacker must clear any trace of compromising the victim system, any type of data gathered, log events, to remain anonymous.

- **White Hat.** A "white hat" hacker is an ethical computer hacker or computer security expert who specialises in pen testing and other testing methodologies to help an organisation secure its information systems. A white-hat hacker is different from a "black hat", or a malicious hacker. While a white hat hacker hacks under good intentions with permission, a black hat hacker does so unauthorised with malicious intent. "Grey hat" hackers are ones who hack with good intentions at times, and sometimes without permission. White hats may also work in teams called "sneakers" or "red teams" or "tiger teams".

While pen testing concentrates on attacking software and computer systems from the start – scanning ports, examining known defects in protocols and apps running on the system and patch installations, for example – ethical hacking may include other things. A full-blown ethical hack might include emailing staff to ask for password details, rummaging through executive dustbins and usually breaking in without the knowledge and consent of the targets.

Only the owners, CEOs and board members (stakeholders) who asked for such a security review of this magnitude are aware. To try to replicate some of the destructive techniques a real attack might employ, ethical hackers may arrange for cloned test systems, or organise a hack late at night while systems are less critical.

In most recent cases these hacks perpetuate for the long-term con (days, if not weeks, of long-term human infiltration into an organisation). Some examples include leaving USB drives with hidden .exe in a public area as if someone lost the small USB drive, and an unsuspecting employee found it and took it.[7]

▧ **SingCERT.** Despite the most effective safeguards, inevitably, incidents that involve security breaches will still occur, and the CIO must have contingency plans to deal with them. It would also be worthwhile to keep an eye on regular updates issued by CSA and SingCERT (Singapore Computer Emergency Response Team).

The CSA (Cyber Security Agency of Singapore) was formed in 2015 and tasked with protecting the country's cyberspace. It is part of the PMO (Prime Minister's Office) and is managed by the MCI (Ministry of Communications and Information). The CSA's core mission is to keep Singapore's cyberspace safe and secure and to power a digital economy and digital way of life.

CSA continuously monitors the cyberspace for cyber-threats to protect Singapore's CII (Critical Information Infrastructure) and to ensure the continuous delivery of essential services to Singapore residents. It analyses the risks that the threats pose and takes mitigation measures to prevent them from causing damage.

"Nonetheless, despite our best efforts, cyber-attacks may still succeed," CSA notes on its website. "To deal with them, we have incident response teams who stand ready to investigate, contain and remediate serious cyber-attacks on our CIIs. CSA also regularly conducts cybersecurity exercises to ensure that our critical sectors are ready to respond promptly and effectively if an attack occurs."

The SingCERT responds to cybersecurity incidents on the Internet. "We are mindful that cyber threats do not respect geographic boundaries. Hence,

---

[7] https://bit.ly/3jAersM.

it is critical for us to have a network of international partners that we can work with to address this common threat," CSA notes. "CSA actively pursues bilateral partnerships, participates in multinational discussions to shape the norms of responsible state behaviour in cyberspace, and drives regional cyber-security capacity building programmes."[8]

Case Study B

In Singapore's worst cyberattack, hackers stole the personal particulars of 1.5 million patients. Of these, 160,000 people, including Singapore's Prime Minister Lee Hsien Loong and some ministers had their outpatient prescriptions stolen. The hackers infiltrated the servers of SingHealth, Singapore's largest group of healthcare institutions with four hospitals, five national speciality centres and eight polyclinics.

The 1.5 million patients had visited SingHealth's specialist outpatient centres and polyclinics between May 1, 2015 and July 4, 2018. The personal data that was illegally accessed and downloaded included their names, national IC numbers, gender, race, addresses, and birth dates. No records were tampered with, and no other clinical patient records (diagnosis, test results and doctors' notes) were breached.

Singapore's Health Minister Mr Gan Kim Yong and Minister for Communications and Information Mr S Iswaran both described the leak as the most severe, unprecedented breach of personal data in Singapore. "This was a deliberate, targeted, well-planned cyberattack," *The Straits Times* quoted David Koh, CEO of the CSA, on July 20, 2018. "It was not the work of casual hackers or criminal gangs."[9]

 TOP TIPS

Here are 10 tips for secure computing from the University of Berkeley in California.[10]

1. **Awareness.** Be aware that you are a target for attackers. Don't ever think, "It won't happen to me." Everyone of us is at risk, and the stakes

---

[8] https://bit.ly/3hqZ8QY.
[9] https://bit.ly/39oknQD.
[10] https://bit.ly/3OJwyng.

are high – both for our personal and financial well-being and for our organisation's standing and reputation. Cybersecurity is everyone's responsibility. By remaining vigilant, you are doing your part to protect yourself and others.

2. **Current.** Keep software current. Install software updates for both, your operating system and applications. Install the latest security updates on all your devices: Turn on "Automatic Updates" for your operating system on your devices. Use web browsers that receive frequent, automatic security updates. Ensure that you keep browser plug-ins (Flash, Java, and others) up-to-date.

3. **Phishing.** Beware of suspicious emails and phone calls. Hackers use various social engineering ploys and decoys. Cyber-criminals will try to trick you into divulging confidential information such as your login ID and password, or even your credit card details. Phishing scams can be carried out via the phone, text messages or through social networking sites; the most common is by email. Any official-looking email, text or phone call that asks for confidential information should be treated with suspicion.

4. **Passwords.** Practice good password management. Most of us have quite a few passwords to memorise; it's easy to take shortcuts, like reusing the same password, for example. A password management programme can help you to maintain unique and strong passwords for all your accounts. These programmes can generate strong passwords, enter your credentials automatically, and remind you to update your passwords periodically.

5. **Attachments.** Be careful what and where you click. It's best to avoid visiting unknown websites or download software from untrusted sources. Shady websites often host malware that will install (often silently and automatically) and compromise your personal or work computer. If attachments or URL links in the email are suspicious for any reason, delete it; don't click on it. ISO suggest using Click-to-Play or NoScript browser add-on features to prevent automatic downloading of plug-in content and scripts that can contain malicious code.

6. **Physical.** Do not leave your devices unattended. Securing your devices physically is as important as their securing them technically. If you have to leave your laptop, phone, or tablet for any period of time – lock it up so others cannot access it. If you keep confidential information on a USB drive or external hard drive, ensure the data is encrypted. For desktop computers, lock your screen (in sleep mode) or shut-down the computer when not in use for a longer period.

7. **Safeguard.** Safeguard confidential data. Be aware of "protected or restricted data" that you come into contact with and its associated restrictions. Keep high-level protected data (such as credit card information, student records, health information, and others) outside of your laptop, workstation, or mobile devices. Use encryption when storing or transmitting sensitive information. Securely delete or wipe out sensitive data files from your system when they are no longer needed.

8. **Mobile.** Use mobile devices safely. Lock your mobile device with a PIN or password. That's because most of us rely heavily on our mobile devices, and they are very susceptible to attack. Never leave your mobile devices in public. Install apps from trusted sources only, (Apple AppStore, Google Play, for example). Keep your device's operating system up-to-date. Don't click on URL links or attachments from unsolicited emails or texts. Most handheld devices support data encryption; there are also apps that can do this specially for mobile operating systems.

9. **Software.** Install strong antivirus and anti-malware apps. Install these programmes only from known and trusted sources. Ensure your device automatically updates virus definitions, engines and software to protect all the apps and data on your device.

10. **Backup.** It is best to back up your data regularly. That's because if you become a victim of a security incident, the only guaranteed solution to get your computer or device to start functioning again is to erase and re-install the system, apps and data.

PART SIX

VI

Future

CHAPTER SIXTEEN

The Future of Money

*Keith Carter**

INTRODUCTION

Here's a parable as old as time itself. Called *The Parable of the Talents*, it was shared by none other than Jesus Christ: Before going on a journey, a rich man summoned his servants and entrusted his property to them based on their capability. To the first he gave five talents (let's assume that's $5,000); to the second, $2,000; and the third, $1,000. He then proceeded on his journey.

After a few years, the master returned and asked each what they had done with his "seed capital". The first servant said he had used the money to trade and made $5,000 more; this delighted the master. The second servant said he had invested the sum and doubled it; the master was pleased with him.

*Keith Carter is an Associate Professor at the NUS School of Computing, Director of the NUS Fintech Lab, and Co-Director of the Crystal Centre, a fintech think-tank that prepares candidates with skillsets in innovative thinking and data-driven decision-making. He's the author of the Amazon bestseller, *Actionable Intelligence: A Guide to Delivering Business Results with Big Data, Fast!* (Hoboken, NJ: Wiley, 2014). He has an MBA from Cornell University and a bachelor's in Electrical and Computer Systems Engineering from Rensselaer Polytechnic Institute. Before joining NUS, he worked at Estée Lauder and Accenture. His mission is to help businesses, governments and people succeed with actionable intelligence.

The third servant said he had dug a hole in the ground and buried his master's money. The master was furious. "You ought to have invested my money with the bankers, and at my coming, I should have received what was my own with interest," the master rebuked the man.

That short parable offers some specific lessons: One, even back then banking was a critical institution with products that would help people earn interest. Two, accounting was a core skill that became mainstream once the Egyptians invented papyrus or paper. Three, seed capital as a concept was commonplace.

According to historical records, the oldest known printed text originated in China one year after Christ was born. *The Diamond Sutra*, a Buddhist book from Dunhuang, China from around 868 AD during the Tang Dynasty, is said to be the oldest known printed book. It was created with a method known as block printing, which utilised panels of hand-carved woodblocks in reverse.

Fast-forward a few centuries. Fintech was probably born in the fourteenth century with the introduction of paper money. This money would be protected in the central location instead of having to carry in a bag or hide in your house. In due course, banks and insurance were available for the rich to protect their assets.

Fintech or financial technology in the modern sense is a more recent innovation. "Banking is necessary, banks are not," Bill Gates said this in 1994; this mantra led to the first wave of fintech. Following Silicon Valley's obsession with disrupting incumbent industries, numerous fintech were ready to challenge every aspect of banking and deliver better banking services directly to consumers. "Armed with the recent Millennial disruption index, where 71 per cent of respondents claimed they'd rather visit the dentist than listen to their bank, everyone was convinced that the days of incumbent banks were numbered," according to a blog post on Hernaes.com.[1]

The circle was complete only once the Internet took off. Advances in Internet technologies allowed people to communicate with family and businesses to transact across the world. In the current environment, the pertinent question would be: Is the business running at the speed of banking, or is banking running at the rate of business? The short answer: They should both be trying to keep up the needs of their customers.

Financial technology combines technology and innovation to compete with traditional financial methods in the delivery of financial services. It is

---

[1] https://bit.ly/2ZZVR5v.

an emerging industry that uses tech to improve activities in finance. Gartner defines fintech as technology providers that approach financial business in innovative (sometimes disruptive) ways through emerging technologies. Fintech can fundamentally change how a financial services institution's products and services are created, distributed and generate revenue.

Fintech is a broad topic so I will focus on how to go about "delighting customers" by making timely, relevant offers with data. Also called "actionable intelligence", it is about having the right information in the right person's hands at the right time to improve outcomes. Anticipating the needs of customers and how they want their money to be used is critical. In the story Jesus shared, the servant who got $1,000 hid the money and returned it to his master without recording any gains. The servant misunderstood the rich man's risk tolerance. He did not pay attention to some of the social media data, rhetorically, at that time:

▪ The rich man wanted to reap what he did not sow; invest in businesses or transactions that would provide a return on other people's work. Today we call this "making money work for you".
▪ He would not return for some time. This meant the investment needed to be medium term with some liquidity, because they didn't know when the rich man would return and ask for his money.

Understanding the customer comes from both – the transactions and social media. Merely providing $1,000 was not enough information for the servant to know what to do with it. He had to understand what the rich man did with external data, data that typically only a "relationship manager" can gain from understanding the social circle or today's social media. Banks using fintech are not just looking at the transactions; they are also looking at behaviours, so they can be more like the servant that received $5,000, invested the money and returned it on time to the rich man. He was immediately contracted to do even more money management. Businesses owners and individuals alike appreciate being taken care of.

 ## BANKING ON DATA

Currently, banks come in all shapes and sizes, right from small community banks that offer account opening and closing, payments, loans and interest payments, usually regulated by government policies, to the large multinational ubiquitous ones. It is the large banks that interest everyone.

Banks that have been in business for at least 30 years have grown larger through acquisitions, but are typically encumbered by legacy systems that were installed decades ago, and some continue with it. Over time, they added more features, products and services that have been cobbled and patched together. Apart from money, banks have a surfeit of data – historical and current, fiduciary and transactional. All of that data needs to be used to answer strategic business questions; this is done by accurately capturing, intelligently analysing, taking action and monetising value achieved.

Many of them turn to the humble Microsoft Excel to view and analyse data from all these systems. Excel is the default banking software and the most popular BI (business intelligence) tool used for insurance and private wealth. When new customers approach a bank to set up a personal wealth account, the relationship managers share their ideas, portfolios and calculations on Excel.

Some banks have digitally transformed themselves to offer services that transcend traditional banking, such as being able to order food, buy movie tickets, book a cab, make peer-to-peer payments or use various concierge services. DBS PayLah is a mobile wallet, which can be downloaded as a mobile app for peer-to-peer payments. PayNow is a funds transfer service that lets users of nine banks transfer funds in Singapore dollars to anyone else with an account with one of these nine banks: DBS/POSB, UOB, OCBC, Citibank, HSBC, Maybank, Standard Chartered, BOC, and ICBC.

Pepper

In Israel, Pepper is a mobile bank created by the 117-year-old Bank Leumi. Pepper enables customers to manage their finances entirely via their smartphone. Bank Leumi felt that DX (digital transformation) wasn't going to be enough, so it created a new bank using technology at its core, with no legacy systems. "Now more than ever, customers – especially millennials – aren't willing to accept age-old banking experience," says Pepper CEO Lilach Bar David. "They expect a radically different kind of experience."

Pepper provides the services this generation of consumers expects, including:

▪ Online account opening and signup of products without visiting the branch.
▪ Nearly instant payments.
▪ Suggestions on how to save.

Most people carry out all their transactions online. Whether they are buying airline tickets, booking a cab or checking out an Airbnb rental, some visit retail stores to check out electronic gear or clothing. Once they have made up their minds, they leave the store and order it online; this is called "showrooming".

But what about B2B (business-to-business) transactions? B2B customers are under tremendous pressure to fulfil their customers' B2C requests, who want to know where their products are and when they will arrive. Apart from an efficient supply chain, it's the movement of money – which is the movement of data – that needs to happen rapidly. That's where banks come into the picture.

Banks and insurance companies are assured about high profits and regulatory protection. Governments have set up walls to ensure that the incumbents don't fail. They want to make sure that some start-up doesn't collect all the money and run away, as Wirecard did.

Wirecard

Wirecard was founded in 1999 in Munich, Germany, backed by venture capital funds. It was a payments processor, and its business model was to help websites collect credit card payments from customers. In 2005, Wirecard took over the listing of a defunct call centre group – which avoided the scrutiny of an IPO – and was listed on the Frankfurt Stock Exchange.

"It then had 323 employees and the core of its business was managing payments for online gambling and pornography," the *Financial Times* reported on July 25, 2020. "In March 2018, in Wirecard's Singapore HQ, the group's legal staff began an investigation into three members of the finance team. The probe was launched after an internal whistle-blower raised allegations about a plan to fraudulently send money to India via third parties in a scheme known as round-tripping."[2]

Regulatory barriers set up by most governments helped traditional banks allow time to catch up on new tech. Some smart banks started running incubators and fintech labs, and invited start-ups to try their products and ideas in exchange for sharing funding, space and, sometimes, data. The PoC (proof of concept) could result in one of these outcomes:

- The start-up does amazingly well; the bank then offers equity to leverage the technology.

---

[2]https://on.ft.com/2D7IhnX.

- The start-up fails, but has a great potential; the bank then buys the start-up.
- The start-up fails, but the founders show promise; the bank then hires the founders.

At the core of it all is data. Until recently, banks have not leveraged data, apart from checking an applicant's credit rating – or considering at a company's assets – for approving loans. And, of course, for regulatory compliance in confirming KYC (know your customer) forms.

Many financial services companies subscribe to OSINT (open-source intelligence), which is data collected from publicly available sources to be used in an intelligence context. OSINT is not related to open-source software or collective intelligence. For example, OSINT can provide a great deal of actionable and predictive intelligence from public, unclassified sources.

Grab

Let's look at Grab's business model and its effect on customers. Grab Holdings Inc is a Singapore-based company that offers a range of services, including ride-hailing, food delivery, consumer and financial services on a single mobile platform. It operates in Singapore, Cambodia, Indonesia, Malaysia, Myanmar, Philippines, Thailand and Vietnam. It was the region's first "decacorn" (start-up with a valuation of over US$10 billion), with a valuation of US$14 billion as of 2019. Banks are now being challenged by the nonbanks like Grab, which has more than 86 million users.

When you buy food from Grab or goods from Lazada, your credit card is instantly charged, but the goods don't come for several minutes, hours or maybe days, depending on the product. You, however, get a commitment that the goods will be delivered. Grab, Lazada and other platforms don't own inventory; they only act as an intermediary between the seller and the buyer; this is called a "two-sided economy."

Such two-sided economy platforms have revolutionised the way B2C (business-to-consumer) is done. The bank, as an intermediary, is transparent and seamless. Compare this with going to the bank. There's no instant gratification because interest is paid after 6 to 12 months. Moreover, interacting with the bank is:

- Painful having to haggle with the bank for a loan.
- Begging the bank for fees to be waived.
- Failing to get the online system to work as expected.
- Trying to register for a mortgage with the fear of rejection.

Contrast this with being able to store money on your Grab wallet while you continue to use Grab to:

- Book a taxi to go to your destination.
- Order your favourite dishes from a restaurant without having to wait in line.
- Avoid going out in the rain by having the goods you ordered delivered to you.
- Even apply for a loan with Grab PayLater, which allows you to pay 30 days after purchase.

The concept of the "everyday bank" is already one that Grab has brought to life with its nifty app. The app provides services we need every day, the ability to store money, transact and be a facilitator of business. Indeed, it contains our data and as a result, acts as a bank although it is not regulated like one. It is on the front page of most people's phones. It's these types of companies that are making Bill Gates' statement come true: "banking is necessary, but banks are not."

These days, both consumers and businesses expect immediate gratification:

- Consumers: Want a product, use an app (Amazon Prime, Grab, Alibaba); it's delivered.
- Businesses: Want a website, use an app (Freelance.com, Godaddy.com, MS Azure); it's delivered.

Banks erred in thinking that their B2B (business-to-business) customers would be satisfied with slow, multiday money transfers using traditional methods. Every business needs to know one key tenet – your customers will stay with you until they find something faster, cheaper or better; cryptocurrencies offer all three.

Cash to Crypto

Make transactions even faster by moving from cash to crypto. A cryptocurrency is a digital or virtual currency that is secured by cryptography on a secure, verified ledger, which makes it quite impossible to counterfeit or double-spend. Many cryptocurrencies are decentralised networks based on blockchain tech. Cryptocurrencies follow these rules of economics:

- Currency needs "flow" to be valuable.
- Usage and flow allow the currency to be equated to goods and services.
- The more frequently it's used, the more anchored is its value.
- Governments want their currency to be used inside their country and if possible, internationally.
- Financial systems need to enable people to store value and earn interest in that currency.
- Monetary controls should be under regulatory purview; that's why cryptocurrencies struggle.
- Currencies need to be exchangeable for transactions to occur.
- High volatility in the currency will make buyers and sellers want to hedge the risks.
- The greater the volatility, the higher the risk and more expensive to do business in that currency.

Money as most people know it involves cash or "fiat currency", which is legal tender whose value is backed by the government that issued it, such as the USD, the GBP, the SGD and the Euro. This approach differs "commodity currency" or money whose value is underpinned by some physical good such as gold.

Cryptocurrency is "virtual currency". It was born when the American cryptographer David Chaum created an anonymous cryptographic electronic money called eCash in 1983. In 1995, he implemented it through Digicash, an early form of cryptographic e-payments, which required special software to withdraw "fiat currency" from a bank and embed the transaction with encrypted keys before it could be sent to a recipient. That made cryptocurrency to be untraceable by the issuing bank or any third party.

A store of value built on top of cryptography is nothing new; banks have been using mainframe computers since the 1950s to digitally store a customer's data and records of how much money one has with the bank. So the concept of digital money is not new. However, for once, there are competitors in the financial industry imbued with the ability to issue alternative currencies, in an attempt to challenge the dominance of banks and the global financial system.

Cryptocurrencies – such as bitcoin – are used outside existing banking and governmental institutions and are exchanged over the Internet. Cryptocurrencies try to maintain their value by:

- Offering interest, like a bank; the US SEC said that this was illegal.
- Pegging to physical assets; the US regulators said that this would be taxable.
- Selling it as equity in a company; the US SEC said this was illegal.

As a result of the above, many cryptocurrencies failed to take off. The few that were left – such as Bitcoin, Ethereum and Ripple – are under attack in different ways, usually in terms of reputation. The Chinese Central Bank–backed digital currency, as well as another backed JPMorgan, were also issued.

Blockchain

That's where blockchain could add value. Blockchain is a system in which a record of transactions made in bitcoin or another cryptocurrency is maintained across several computers that are linked in a peer-to-peer network. Blockchain technology offers high security and guaranteed delivery at the cost of speed. The most prominent use of blockchain currently is with cryptocurrency.

Blockchain is very secure; you can add permissions to it so that only specific parties can access that information. You can programme a workflow so it can act as an intermediary collecting one condition from one party and another condition from another party, then executing a mutual finalised contractual obligation so that everyone is satisfied.

Blockchain can be used for secure messaging. Blockchain has redundancy built in with multiple nodes on the network. If one node fails, another can pick it up and ensure it gets to its final destination. Privacy protection is also encrypted, so it's hard for intermediaries to read that information if access is denied. Here's a list of projects that could be appropriate for blockchain:

Potential projects	Highly secure, encrypted with authentication	Guaranteed delivery with fault tolerance	Chain of custody of data	Slow, costly accurate transactions	Workflow and payments enabled
Real estate	Needed	Needed	Bonus	Needed	Needed
Daily local payments	Not needed	Not needed	Not needed privacy issue	Problem	Needed
Public company filings	Needed	Needed	Needed	Needed	Needed
Stock market transactions	Needed	Needed	Not needed	Problem	Needed

You could consider using the table to confirm your use-case for blockchain. If any column causes a problem, you could either make a custom blockchain that fixes the problem or wait until the technology matures. Blockchain holds great promise as a communications tool. However, there are still issues that need to be fixed, so financial services and IT departments should approach this tech conservatively.

Another potential use-case: high-value logistics. Blockchain can manage shipments from the factory to the retail store. ANZ Bank ran a test to ship from Sydney to Melbourne and track it using blockchain. However, they ran into a problem: the factory was not equipped with blockchain tech. The factory was two hours away from Sydney and fixing the issue was impossible as the receiving distributor could not handle the new tech.

Blockchain can be deployed for secure data transfer data between companies. Currently, EDI (electronic data interchange) happens between two computers to exchange standard business documents such as purchase orders, invoices, inventory levels and shipping notices. EDI software solutions facilitate the exchange of business documents and data across a variety of platforms and programmes.

The problem? In the 1990s, each EDI implementation cost about $50,000; the technology was developed, and large enterprises spent up to $100,000 or more to implement EDI that ran over phone lines. Currently, EDI also runs on the Internet.

These investments in EDI, made over the span of 20 years, are the key reason why blockchain wasn't implemented between corporations. Merely sending data about purchase orders, invoices and quotations did not add enough value for the companies to transition.

- What's the future of money? Here are some points to consider, based on an EY whitepaper:[3]
- Across the European Union, account-to-account payment services are proliferating.
- Canada, Australia and Singapore are among the nations that are licensing non-banks to initiate digital and mobile payments.
- In Asia, China's WeChat Pay and Alipay, which mix low-cost, transactional functionality with shopping and lifestyle features, are leading the way.
- In the United States, cheques are still widely used and only 53.5 per cent of card transactions use modern EMV chip and pin authentication in 2018.

---

[3]https://go.ey.com/2IiuRIk.

▪ The mobile money operator (MMO) model – where consumers transfer mobile phone credit – is strong in sub-Saharan Africa, led by Kenya's M-Pesa, which has since expanded to Afghanistan, South Africa, India, Romania and Albania.
▪ In Latin America, many people remain unbanked, despite a government push towards electronic payments to curb corruption.

Ultimately, banks need to keep up with the speed businesses expect, or they risk being replaced by organisations that facilitate business faster, cheaper and better, enabled by digital transformation. With globalisation, businesses have access to banks worldwide; therefore, the local banks need to understand their customer more. Local banks are competing globally because transactions can arrive virtually from anywhere. Will customers entrust their money to a wallet or a store that will provide convenience, security and financial growth? Bankers need to ask themselves, which servant they will be? The one that paid attention to the rich man's needs, or the one that just stored the money and lost it all.

CHAPTER SEVENTEEN

The Future of Work

*Teo Chin Seng**

 INTRODUCTION

To understand the future, you need to understand the lessons learned from the past. Here's one from humanity's pre-industrial past:

In the late 1800s, many cities in the then "developed world" were literally drowning in horseshit. For these cities to function, they were dependent on thousands of horses to transport people and products. For example, in London in 1900, there were more than 11,000 horse-drawn "Hansom" cabs and a thousand horse-drawn buses, each needing 12 horses per day. That's 50,000 horses in London, alone, notes a post on Historic UK.[1]

---

*Mr Teo Chin Seng has been in the ICT industry for about 35 years. He has held senior management positions in leading companies in Singapore, China, Middle East Asia and the United States. Most recently, he was SVP of Global ICT in DP World where he led its digitalisation across 78 terminals in 40 countries. His previous positions include group CIO at NHG, and senior management roles in NIPSEA, ST Engineering, Dubai World, Parkway Group Healthcare, and as Executive Director of iCity Lab (Smart Cities) in SMU. Mr Teo has mentored tech start-ups and helped companies in digital transformation.

[1] https://bit.ly/2JHQTor

The problem was that each horse could produce up to 15 kg of manure a day, usually deposited on the open road. Other than the stink of horseshit, it also attracted an enormous number of flies and other insects, which then spread typhoid fever and other diseases.[2]

What changed the game? The Ford Model T, which was introduced on October 1, 1908, with the steering wheel on the left. The engine and transmission were enclosed; the four cylinders were cast in a solid metal block; the suspension used two semi-elliptic springs. The car was simple to drive, easy to clean, and cheap to repair. It was affordable at US$825 in 1908, equivalent to US$23,480 today.

Henry Ford's revolutionary assembly-line manufacturing process ensured that the price was reduced every year. Sales crossed 250,000 by 1914. By 1916, as the price dropped to US$360 – equivalent to US$7,828 in 2015 dollars – for the basic touring car and sales reached 472,000. The future of how people lived, worked and played had changed forever. Technology brought affordable machines to ordinary people. It increased human productivity and "drove" the global economy for the next 100 years.

As the electrification of cities began to take shape, there was more disruption, with older coal, steam and gas-based industries started to use electricity to power their engines. That had a cascading effect on manufacturing, health care, chemical engineering, transportation, and others. What are the learnings from the past that we can extrapolate for the future?

- **Silos.** In the past, knowledge was in silos, usually learned through apprenticeships. The blacksmith, for example, knew how to shape a sheet of iron into a sharp, gleaming sword. The goldsmith knew how to turn a lump of misshapen yellow metal into a shining piece of jewellery. The only way that this intricate knowledge could be passed on was by one-on-one coaching, mentoring, apprenticing. In today's world, there are also silos of experience in companies – called tacit knowledge – that needs to be captured so that future generations of digital artisans can turn it into meaningful insights.
- **Platforms.** In the old days, basic models or platforms existed, though they were not called that. For example, the sheet of iron is a platform; it can be moulded into a sword, a saucepan, a horseshoe, a cart screw, or whatever was possible in eighteenth-century technology. Today's platforms

---

[2] https://bit.ly/2DbfiiE.

are digital, such as Windows 10, Red Hat Enterprise Linux, or cloud-based PaaS (Platform as a Service). The concept is the same, but the medium has changed – from wood to metal to silicon to virtual. Digital platforms are a means to scale and propagate the use of technology.

▪ **Upgrades.** At the beginning of the last century, electricity-powered indus-trialisation moved labour from rural villages to urban cities. Every upgrade brought disruption as well as the promise of higher productivity and ease. That effect is seen most profoundly in the semiconductor industry. Driven by Moore's Law, the shrinking of the physical dimensions of the chip while boosting its capacity revolutionised the world. Semiconductor miniaturi-sation helped raise a swathe of industries, ranging from data processing to optical computing, telecommunications to e-commerce, industrial auto-mation to robotics, and big data to AI. Technology upgrades disrupt and change the behaviour of people, businesses and governments, with regu-lations and legislation following in due course.

▪ **Intelligence.** Every technology upgrade has given the machine a boost in smartness or intelligence. Electricity allowed people to work at night, run fans, cooking appliances and have air-conditioning at home and in the office. Digitalisation likewise is making our environments safer, our man-ufacturing more efficient, the devices that help us smarter. As is evident during the Covid-19 lockdown, you can get all the amenities by sitting at home; all you need is a mobile phone and an Internet connection. You can order food and drinks, teleconsult with your doctor or broker, and down-load books or movies.

The Digital Dimension

Digital technology is now crossing physical human borders, especially with robotics and AI. This borderless digital world requires that technology leaders who are the traditional innovators like Samsung or new players like Tesla need to create products, solutions and services with the world as the marketplace; solutions can be adapted and localised easily for each unique market. They must be acceptable to the culture, legal, regulatory and language requirements of each country.

Digital technology helps drive changes in five dimensions:

1. **The base.** The base technology could be at the silicon, the chipset and the material level. In the digital world, it can be the operating system or OS. The base is the platform. It provides a medium on which different

applications can be written, moulded and run, and new products can be created. For example, Windows or Red Hat Enterprise Linux or Lithium battery or electric motor would be the base platforms.

2. **The systems.** Systems-level refers to the higher platform with standards and integration. That enables multiple technologies to be run and integrated with the systems or machinery. On the cloud, PaaS could be considered as the system that includes the base (OS) and other core applications.

3. **The software.** Software applications are the layer that runs on the systems that, in turn, run on the base OS. The software applications may have integration with higher-level applications such as robotics, blockchain, ML (machine learning) and AI.

4. **The data.** The data is not part of the core application stack. Data comes from outside the stack, which may be internal (data within the organisation) and external (data from outside the organisation). Without data, none of the above three layers can work. Access to data – seamlessly and securely – is crucial.

5. **The community.** The community can be the users, either within or outside the organisation. It can be other businesses (B2B), consumers (B2C), or regulators and government agencies (B2G). The community contributes the 4Vs of data: volume (the amount of data generated), variety (data coming from different sources such as social media), velocity (the speed at which data is generated), and veracity (the authenticity of data, or the filtering of fake news, for example).

THE EVOLUTION OF WORK

Over the last hundred years, work has evolved as machines have replaced workers in many tasks. On balance, however, technology has created more jobs than it has displaced. Technological progress has transformed living standards. Life expectancy has gone up; primary healthcare and education are widespread, and most people have seen their incomes rise. And yet, fears of robot-induced unemployment often dominate discussions over the future of work.

The World Bank's World Development Report for 2019, *The Changing Nature of Work*, addresses these issues, analysing what exactly is changing and what needs to be done. The report argues that, on balance, concerns about robot-induced unemployment appear to be unfounded. Instead, the future of work gets driven by the competing forces of automation and innovation.[3]

To be a leader who can adapt by leveraging the five dimensions of work, you need to figure out which changes in your organisation can be transformational or gradual, which must be disruptive, abrupt or revolutionary, and which requires creativity and innovation. The ability to distil through the fast pace of technology developments, a keen eye to identify new business models, and the foresight to bring people, technology and new ways of doing things will become the hallmark of a technology leader.

The New Normal

The "old normal" was based on a linear way of working around a physical workplace. The "new normal" is a digitally enabled way of living that cuts down on physical interactions, propagates information and increases mobility. Unlike the current physical workplace that aggregates people together around "work", in the new normal, people will aggregate around "value".

"Factors such as the growth of freelancing, 24-hour everything, mobility, crowdsourcing, and gamification have unleashed the workforce, freeing it from many traditional bounds and constraints," according to a Deloitte blog. "Indeed, one of the fastest-growing workforce segments is the alternative worker – one who works off-campus and outside of an organisation's official talent balance sheet.

"Also, the rise of platform technologies has made it easier for organisations to use crowdsourcing to tackle tough challenges. And technologies such as AI augmented reality, and robotic process automation allows work to be out-sourced to robots."[4]

The linear and physical delivery of work will change with the increasing use of digital technology. The supply chain will become more integrated and smarter, manufacturing will be more autonomous, and agriculture will become more mechanised with the help of robots.

The pandemic requires isolation of human communities to prevent the spread of Covid-19. This isolation has created a use-case for work to continue despite the bulk of employees being at home, using video conferencing for meetings. The remote workforce has already made working from home the

---

[3] https://bit.ly/31Y4L4Z.
[4] https://bit.ly/3e7IBQ6.

new normal. Even after a vaccine is developed, many companies plan to continue with remote working.

Here's a snapshot of what has changed in our recent past:

- We are not constrained to buy only from our neighbourhood stores.
- We can buy online from oversea stores and get products delivered to our doorstep.
- We do not need to go to the library; we can download and read – or listen to – electronic books.
- We don't need the Yellow Pages; all of that information is an online search away.
- We can communicate through texting or via video or audio calls.
- We don't need satellite dishes; our cable set-top-box can stream the channel we wish to watch.
- Broadband Internet and smart devices allow us to work, play, buy or sell what we want 24/7.

We have been following a linear method of working that evolved from the industrialisation era. That meant working with a defined job scope, at a physical location, for a specific company, and being paid a fixed amount at a fixed duration, such as once per month or fortnight. Covid-19 has changed all this, almost overnight. During the lockdown, we accelerated the use of technology around work, redefined our supply chains and changed how we interacted and communicated.

A TALE OF TWO COUNTRIES

In 1859, about 160 years ago, the noted English author Charles Dickens' historical novel, *A Tale of Two Cities*, was published. The story is set in London and Paris before and during the French Revolution. It tells the story of a French Doctor, Manette and his 18-year-long imprisonment in the Bastille in Paris. He is released and travels to London to live with his daughter, Lucie, whom he had never met. The story is set against the conditions that led up to the French Revolution.

We're currently living during the technology revolution with a surging pandemic that's upset most lives worldwide. So it is apt to call this section *A Tale of Two Countries*, both of which are at the forefront of technological and societal change, helped by strong governments that believe in innovation.

The need for new skills has accompanied the introduction of new technologies in the workplace since the Industrial Revolution. However, the adoption of automation and AI will mark an acceleration over the shifts of even the recent past.

"The need for some skills, such as technological as well as social and emotional skills, will rise, even as the demand for others, including physical and manual skills, will fall. These changes will require workers everywhere to deepen their existing skill sets or acquire new ones. Companies, too, will need to rethink how work is done within their organisations," according to a McKinsey article published on May 23, 2018.

"Over the next 10–15 years, the adoption of automation and AI technologies will transform the workplace as people increasingly interact with ever-smarter machines. These technologies, and that human-machine interaction, will bring numerous benefits in the form of higher productivity, GDP growth, improved corporate performance, and new prosperity. Still, they will also change the skills required of human workers."[5]

The Rise of China

In my view, the last two decades that saw the rise of China is an excellent example of how disruption benefitted a country. China is unique in the adoption of technology. China has leapfrogged a generation, going from fixed-line telephony to fibre-optics and mobile 3G. China's lack of IT legacy cut down a massive overhead of trying to migrate different generations of technology. Its late start in the technology journey was transformed into an advantage that accelerated the velocity of digitalisation.

China did not follow the Western world's trajectory of technology adoption. China's colossal landmass, population density and economic, cultural and social diversity helped it adapt and leverage technology in different ways, evolved other solutions, and multiple layers of social classes. It was like having an entire world in one country. China could implement, deploy, customise and innovate technology solutions for its cities, markets and consumers, based on geography, ethnicity and stage of economic development.

China's massive investments in infrastructure, especially roads, ports and broadband gave an enormous boost with its low-cost manufacturing capabilities, making it the manufacturing hub of the world. It is no longer the

---

[5] https://mck.co/3gzuuVo.

low-cost factory; it has moved up the value chain by innovating and making complex products.

China's vast domestic market of 1.4 billion people, coupled with a digitally savvy generation with rising disposable incomes created an ecosystem to help it leapfrog in innovation. Massive upgrades in bandwidth, mobile networks and civil service computerisation enabled China's state-owned enterprises to roll-out end-to-end solutions that was not possible in most other countries.

Parallel technology giants evolved successfully in China from these unique factors. Here's a listing of China's top tech companies, published by Pandaily on January 17, 2020.[6]

- OnePlus: Smartphone leader with OnePlus7, 7Pro and 7T models.
- ByteDance: News aggregation app called Toutiao with AI-driven content.
- Huawei: 5G leader. Plans to build undersea fibre optics cable from China to Chile.
- Xiaomi: Smartphones and IoT maker, has a presence in all ASEAN countries. They are selling smart TV now.
- Tencent: WeChat is the most used social media app. They announced US$2 billion investment in a short video platform, Kuaishou.
- Oppo: Smartphone leader. They released the ColorOS smartphone operating system. They invested US$7 billion on R&D.
- Alibaba: Cloud major. Its 11.11 Shopping Festival grossed US$38.4 billion last year in gross revenue.
- Meituan Dianping: Bought Mobike. It was rated the world's most innovative company by FastCompany in 2019. Valuation of US$76 billion is third-largest, after Alibaba and Tencent, ahead of Baidu.
- TaoBao: This is similar to Amazon.com.
- Baidu: This is similar to Google search.

Here's a case study on how the Chinese government plans for the future, excerpted from a *New York Times* article that was published in *The Straits Times* on July 7, 2020.[7]

Mr Ma Zhaoxu, China's Vice-Minister of Foreign Affairs, said that from March through May 2020, China exported about 70.6 billion masks. The

---

[6] https://bit.ly/2BBoVXJ.
[7] https://bit.ly/3Iw4ZWC.

entire world production was about 20 billion in 2019, with China accounting for half. China also foresaw the vital importance of nucleic acid test kits, which can detect coronavirus infections. China's Ministry of Science and Technology had identified the kits as a "targeted development" industry in 2017 itself.

The Ministry's decision was part of China's US$300 billion "Made in China 2025" industrial policy to replace imports in many vital industries, including medical devices. The Ministry has called for raising China's share of the local market by 30-40 percentage points in each category of medical supplies.

However, a few economic policy experts in China think that the country may be going too far. Tianyancha, a Chinese data service, noted that more than 67,000 firms had registered in China in 2020 to make or trade masks.

"Many mask-manufacturing enterprises, especially SMEs that came into the picture much later and did not possess strong foundations. They would have to face closure when they have a surplus of masks and profits begin to plunge," Mr Cai Enze, a retired deputy mayor and economic planner in central China, wrote in an essay in April 2020. "That marks the start of a crisis." Still, the broader industry in China appears to be better prepared for the future.

The Singapore Sling

In November 2018, Singapore's EDB (Economic Development Board) launched an international ad and promotion campaign using the tagline, *Singapore, the Impossible Story*. The EDB released a series of "Impossible" films showing Singapore's rise as a business-friendly tech hub for the world. The first ad featured Singapore's separation from Malaysia – when the world doubted Singapore would ever amount to anything. Other clips laud the success of Grab founder Anthony Tan, One Championship founder Chatri Sidyodtong and editor-in-chief of *The Asian Scientist Magazine*, Dr Juliana Chan.

Can Singapore continue to be a global technology leader? The challenges are many: small domestic market, small population size, no natural resources, high cost of living, and scarcity of land. On the positive side, we have a robust digital infrastructure, an effective PPP (public, private partnership), a technocratic government, robust physical infrastructure, good governance and a digital-native-ready population. Here are some salient points worth considering for the future:

- **Work with less.** Singapore has to adapt to working with less. If we look at all our successful pillars of the economy, tourism, infrastructure, housing, transportation, and others, we need to start using SoSE (System of Systems Engineering) style of thinking. While systems engineering is a well-established field, SoSE represents a challenge for the present systems engineers on a global level. In general, SoSE requires considerations beyond those usually associated with engineering to include socio-technical and sometimes socioeconomic phenomena. In the simplest form, SoSE aggregates many systems together to achieve a common purpose, like multiple systems running on a cruise ship. Even though its roots are in engineering, the methods and approaches have evolved into other areas of modelling, analysis and design.[8]

- **New normal ready.** During the circuit breaker, Singapore residents were asked to stay home to reduce community infections. Initially, there were constraints on efficient food deliveries. That gave rise to last-mile food delivery solutions from Grab, Deliveroo, Food Panda and others. But the answer was not just about food deliveries. Traditional restaurants and hawker centres also had to be ready for the "new normal" with electronic storefronts, e-payments, and tie-ups with delivery firms. When you implement SoSE principles, you design operation scenarios to test how the removal of components or subsystems will affect the core.

- **Ready to learn.** Singapore's small size and population density allow us to adapt and digitally transform our companies, especially SMEs, quickly. We have learnt from China to approach disruptions with technology-based solutions. Singapore has always been proud that it is a global player, not just a regional player, especially when it comes to technology adoption. Going forward, we need to get the masses to be ready to learn, by providing them with the means, the opportunities, and the incentives.

- **Diversified delivery.** Trade and logistics are Singapore's lifelines. In the last few decades, being a physical hub was crucial. Our strategic location as the gateway between the East (China, India and ASEAN) and the West (North America and Europe) served us well. In the future, physical location won't matter; digital business will. Can we create strategic value as a strategic digital hub as well? Yes. We're also the region's data centre hub, and our Internet connectivity with the rest of the world is as good as can be. Smart aggregation of information to create new knowledge will help us continue to be a digital logistics hub.

---

[8] https://bit.ly/3fq4pqx.

▪ **Fulfilment models.** When the pandemic struck, initially there were shortages of medical supplies and all international supply chains were disrupted. We diversified our sourcing, we asked our Residents' Committees to be the last mile to distribute masks to all households, and we ramped up the availability of hospital beds, including using cruise ships as treatment centres. We even began importing eggs from Poland, something we had never done before. All of this proves that Singapore is resilient, Singapore is agile, and together, we will define new roles and definitions of work in the postpandemic world.

The bottom-line: The future of work will undergo constant change and should be more about creating value. It is apt to quote McKinsey in closing: The world of work is changing. AI, automation and robotics will make this shift as significant as the mechanisation in prior generations of agriculture and manufacturing. While some jobs will be lost, and many others created, almost all will change.

CHAPTER EIGHTEEN

Why Ethical AI Matters

James Lau Oon Beng*

 INTRODUCTION

The term *artificial intelligence* (AI) was first coined by the late Emeritus Professor of Computer Science at Stanford University, John McCarthy (September 4, 1927–October 24, 2011) at the Dartmouth Summer Research Project in 1956. He had invited researchers from various disciplines, including language simulation, neuron nets and complexity theory. Prof McCarthy picked the name AI for its neutrality, to avoid highlighting one of the tracks being pursued at the time for the field of "thinking machines" that included cybernetics, automata theory and complex information processing.

John McCarthy was born in Boston, Massachusetts to an Irish immigrant father and a Lithuanian Jewish immigrant mother. John was brilliant. He

---

* Mr James Lau Oon Beng is a lawyer with 27 years' experience in both contentious and noncontentious international cross-border transactional and dispute-resolution, acquired through a combination of private practice at leading law firms and in-house roles at Fortune 500 companies. He is currently Chief Legal Officer and Company Secretary of NatSteel Holdings Pte Ltd, a wholly owned subsidiary of Tata Steel Ltd. Tata Steel is a Fortune 500 company and was named as one of the 2020 World's Most Ethical Companies by Ethisphere for the ninth time, in February 2020.

graduated from Belmont High School two years early and was accepted into Caltech at age 17 in 1944. He developed the LISP programming language family in 1958, which is the second oldest programming language after FOR-TRAN, significantly influenced the design of the ALGOL programming language, popularised time-sharing, and invented "garbage collection," which is a systems methodology in AI.

Prof McCarthy spent 40 years teaching at Stanford University and received the 1971 Turing Award for his contributions in the field of AI, the US National Medal of Science and the Kyoto Prize. He died at his home in Stanford on October 24, 2011, at age 84.

AI is a buzzword today. Simply put, AI is about getting computers to perform tasks or processes that would be considered intelligent if done by humans. A more formal definition comes from the English Oxford Living Dictionary: "AI is the theory and development of computer systems able to perform tasks typically requiring human intelligence, such as visual perception, speech recognition, decision-making, and translation between languages."

While AI might be about programming, ethics is about values. In Singapore, AI has the potential to become a US$960 million market in 2022 and US$16 billion market by 2030, with a compound annual growth rate of 42.2 per cent, according to data collated by IMDA. That includes a wide range of technologies used to analyse, organise, access and provide advisory services.[1]

On January 23, 2019, Minister for Communications and Information Mr S Iswaran released an AI Model Governance Framework at the World Economic Forum in Davos. The AI Model Governance Framework was the first in Asia to provide detailed and implementable guidance to private and public sector organisations on the responsible use of AI.

The AI Model Governance Framework is not a set of prescriptive rules. "I think that AI technology is too new and too nascent to have very firm rules," Mr Iswaran said. "But this is a good collaborative approach to try and shape the principles that will govern it."

In ICT (info-communications technology), when you write software, you are judged based on your intentions for which the programs are written. Software is written with specific outcomes in mind, such as accounts reconciliation and enabling e-commerce. Such "linear software" will precisely do what it's intended to, and nothing more. But software for AI and ML (machine learning) is not linear; it is circular, dynamic and is supposed to learn from examples that

---

[1] https://bit.ly/3fGMfS6.

are either set by humans, or by machines. That adds a new dimension, and that's where the question of ethics comes up.

AI systems are not based on a fixed linear logic (where we can attribute a crime to the programmer); it is based on reasoning, interpretation, analytics and outcomes. So if there are unintended consequences from the use of AI, who is responsible? The programmer? The company that developed the software, or the one that used it?

AI ETHICAL ISSUES

With increasing digitalisation, you may have access to massive datasets of a given population, such as their employment, race, income, criminal records and financial history. You may also get access to images from social media, like photographs, video footage and biometric information. Juxtaposing all this, you can compile a reasonably accurate profile of specific individuals, which could be used for legitimate purposes by authorised organisations (like law enforcement) or commercial use (targeted marketing). The ethical issues arise when there are false positives, such as identifying the wrong person for a crime.

Statistical Discrimination

AI is not appropriate or suitable where its use will entrench and reinforce discrimination and racism. For example, AI is used to predict the risk of re-offending, also known as predictive recidivism, as well as the use of facial recognition by law enforcement to identify criminals.

Predictive Recidivism
▪ United States

An often-cited article, "Machine Bias," showed that software used for predictive recidivism is biased. Here's a real-life example: In 2014, Brisha Borden was running late to pick up her god-sister from school when she spotted an unlocked kid's blue Huffy bicycle and a silver Razor scooter. Borden and a friend grabbed the bike and scooter and tried to ride them down the street in the Fort Lauderdale suburb of Coral Springs.

Just as the 18-year-old girls realised they were too big for the tiny conveyances – which belonged to a 6-year-old boy – a woman came running after them saying, "That's my kid's stuff." Borden and her friend immediately dropped the bike and scooter and walked away. But it was too late; a neighbour who witnessed the heist had already called the police. Borden and her friend were arrested and charged with burglary for the items, valued at a total of US$80.

Compare their crime with a similar one: The previous summer, 41-year-old Vernon Prater was picked up for shoplifting US$86.35 worth of tools from a nearby Home Depot store. Prater was the more seasoned criminal. He had already been convicted of armed robbery and attempted armed robbery, for which he served five years in prison, in addition to another armed robbery charge. Borden had a record, too, but for misdemeanours committed when she was a juvenile.

Yet something odd happened when Borden and Prater were booked into jail: A computer program spat out a score predicting the likelihood of each committing a future crime. Borden, who is black, was rated a high risk. Prater, who is white, was rated a low risk.

Two years later, we know the computer algorithm got it precisely backwards. Borden has not been charged with any new crimes. Prater is serving an eight-year prison term for subsequently breaking into a warehouse and stealing thousands of dollars' worth of electronics.[2]

■ **United Kingdom**

In March 2020, a review by the West Midlands' Police Ethics Committee concluded that there was a coding error that rendered inaccurate and unreliable the AI system under development – called most serious violence (MSV). The MSV was supposed to predict which of the 2.4 million people in the West Midlands Police database – and which of the 1.1 million people in the West Yorkshire Police database – would commit their first violent offence with a gun or knife in the next two years.

"As a result of the failure of MSV, the police have stopped developing the prediction system in its current form," *Wired* magazine reported in an article titled "A British AI Tool to Predict Violent Crime Is Too Flawed to Use," on August 9, 2020. "It has never been used for policing operations and has failed to get to a stage where it could be used. However, questions have also been raised around the violence tool's potential to be

---

[2] https://bit.ly/3f2rxLy.

biased toward minority groups and whether it would ever be useful for policing."[3]

Facial Recognition

■ On June 8, 2020, in a letter to the US Congress, IBM CEO Arvind Krishna indicated that IBM would stop selling general-purpose IBM facial recognition or analysis software. "AI is a powerful tool that can help law enforcement keep citizens safe," Mr Krishna's letter stated. "But vendors and users of AI systems have a shared responsibility to ensure that AI is tested for bias, particularity when used in law enforcement and that such bias testing is audited and reported. National policy also should encourage and advance uses of technology that bring greater transparency and accountability to policing, such as body cameras and modern data analytics techniques."[4]

■ On June 10, 2020, Amazon announced a one-year moratorium on the use of its facial recognition technology by police departments. AWS said it is implementing a one-year suspension on the use of Amazon Rekognition's face comparison feature by police departments in connection with criminal investigations. AWS will allow the technology to be used to help identify or locate missing persons.[5]

■ In June 2020, Microsoft Corp announced it would limit the use of its facial-recognition systems and that it will not sell the controversial technology to police departments until there is a federal law regulating it. The move follows similar decisions by Amazon and IBM as protesters across the US pressed for an end to police brutality and racial profiling.[6]

■ **Legal Developments on the Use of Facial Recognition**

■ **United Kingdom**

Professor Pete Fussey and Dr Daragh Murray of the University of Essex, in their July 2019 report titled *Independent Report on the London Metropolitan Police Service's Trial of Love Facial Recognition Technology*, found that there was an error rate of 81 per cent in facial recognition used by the London Metropolitan Police. The authors concluded that it

[3] https://bit.ly/31TLcJe.
[4] https://ibm.co/39tyuo5.
[5] https://bit.ly/32Tk13v.
[6] https://wapo.st/2CFrwAs.

is "highly possible" the Metropolitan Police's use of facial recognition would be held unlawful if challenged in court. The Metropolitan Police chose not to exercise its right of reply after reviewing the report.[7]

On August 11, 2020, the English Court of Appeal decided that South Wales Police's use of live AVR (automated facial recognition) technology was not in accordance with the European Convention on Human Rights and the UK Human Rights Act 1998 as "it involves two impermissibly wide areas of discretion – the selection of those on watch-lists, especially the 'persons whose intelligence is required' category, and the locations where AFR may be employed."[8]

▓ **United States**

On March 31, 2020, Washington State Governor Jay Inslee signed into law the Act to Regulate use of Facial Recognition, which restricts law enforcement's use of facial recognition, which will come into effect on July 1, 2021. "Unconstrained use of facial recognition services by state and local government agencies poses broad social ramifications that should be considered and addressed," the Bill states. "Accordingly, legislation is required to establish safeguards that will allow state and local government agencies to use facial recognition services in a manner that benefits society while prohibiting uses that threaten our democratic freedoms and put our civil liberties at risk."[9]

Appropriate Uses of Surveillance AI

As discussed, surveillance AI is not appropriate or suitable where its use will entrench and reinforce discrimination and racism.

However, the use of electronic tagging (including, but not limited, to ankle tags) will enable those with lower risk of re-offending, especially with strong family support, to serve part of their sentence at home under the (Singapore) Home Detention Scheme for their rehabilitation and reintegration back into society, thereby helping to reduce re-offending.

"More people who are sent to prison will receive stronger community support, during and after their internment, in a bid to break the cycle of re-offending," *The Straits Times* reported on February 18, 2016. "This is because

---

[7] https://bit.ly/3f4lHcT.
[8] https://bit.ly/3amWcCR.
[9] https://bit.ly/3hF48Sh.

community-based programmes, in which inmates can serve the tail-end of their jail terms outside prison walls, have helped to keep overall recidivism rates 'low and stable,' said the Singapore Prison Service."[10]

Commercial applications and uses of surveillance AI include monitoring hazardous situations, such as centrifugal pressure in nuclear reactors or fire hazards, since humans cannot remain on constant alert. AI systems might be ideal for such jobs, not just for monitoring, but for learning from events and taking action when required, such as alerting engineers to check out a specific incident such as a leaking pump or valve.

Another example comes from Shell's use of AI solutions for preventive maintenance of its oil drilling and mining assets. Shell runs AI on the Microsoft® Azure cloud to predict when maintenance is needed on compressors, valves and other equipment; it helps steer drill bits through shale deposits, and improves the safety of employees and customers.[11]

AUTONOMOUS AND INTELLIGENT SYSTEMS

AI could also be used to detect abnormalities through multiple sensing points and even predict situations before it happens. AI is increasingly being used to carry out more autonomous operations. The self-driving car is one example. But ethical issues arise when they malfunction or where their logical reasoning compromises moral responsibilities. Autonomous vehicles and the Moral Machine experiment are two examples.

Moral Machine Experiment

In June 2016, researchers at MIT (Massachusetts Institute of Technology) created a Moral Machine experiment to gather public preferences using crowdsourcing of personal preferences. In one experiment, a driverless car must choose between two evils – killing two passengers or five pedestrians. This is based on a what is called the "Trolley Problem", which the late philosopher Philippa Ruth Foot (October 3, 1920–October 3, 2010) designed in 1967; it was popularised by the Laurence S Rockefeller Professor of Philosophy at MIT,

---

[10] http://str.sg/ZCgz.
[11] https://on.wsj.com/3jBRTrz.

Judith Jarvis Thomson. As an outside observer, people express their preference on which outcome they think is more acceptable. They can then see how their responses compare with other people. If they are feeling creative, people can also design their scenarios, for others to view, share and discuss.[12]

You can participate in the Moral Machine experiment at https://www.moralmachine.net/. Many have already done so. The experiment has been criticised for fostering bias.

Dr Abby Everett Jaques, Ethics of AI Project lead for the MIT Quest for Intelligence, says that such methodologies make the structural features of one's answer invisible. "The right question isn't what would I do if I were forced to choose between swerving and going straight," she says. "The right question is what kind of world would I be creating if this is the *rule*."[13]

Programming utilitarian ethical principles into autonomous vehicles can produce discriminatory outcomes as collective rather than individual harms are minimised, says Dr Araz Taeihagh, Assistant Professor of Public Policy, and researcher Ms Hazel Si Min Lim from the Lee Kuan Yew School of Public Policy at the NUS (National University of Singapore). "It can introduce new safety risks due to design constraints due to increased opacity of decision-making."[14]

The Moral Machine experiment also presents a false choice and a false ethical dilemma. Based on a survey by the same MIT researchers, survey participants preferred autonomous vehicles with a self-protective model, which protects passengers at all costs. In its media release in Stuttgart on October 18, 2016, Daimler clarified that it is "clear that neither programmers nor automated systems are entitled to weigh the value of human lives."

I believe the decision on what to do in the event of an imminent and unavoidable accident should be made by humans, however flawed or imperfect such decision may be. That is due to the smaller, more limited impact of human-based choices compared to the wide-ranging and far-reaching effects of algorithm-based decisions.

---

[12] https://bit.ly/2Ehmhah.

[13] Abby Everett Jaques, Why The Moral Machine is a Monster, March 2019, at pages 5-6, https://bit.ly/384dWSF

[14] 14Hazel Si Min Lim and Araz Taeihagh, Algorithmic Decision-Making in AVs—Understanding Ethical and Technical Concerns for Smart Cities, (2019) 11(20) Sustainability 5791 at 19 http://bit.ly/3miL2Dh

SOME FRAMEWORKS FOR ETHICAL AI

Principles for ethical AI have been formulated to address ethical challenges and by Singapore, Australia, the European Union, the United Kingdom and the United States, among others.

Singapore

The PDPC (Personal Data Protection Commission) was set up on January 2, 2013, to administer and enforce the Personal Data Protection Act (PDPA) 2012. The aim is to promote and implement personal data protection to foster an environment of trust among businesses and consumers. The PDPC is Singapore's leading authority in matters relating to personal data protection and will represent the Singapore government internationally on data protection related issues.

"In administering and enforcing the PDPA, the PDPC aims to balance the need to protect individuals' personal data and the needs of organisations to use the data for legitimate purposes," the PDPC website notes. "To achieve this aim, the PDPC formulates and implements policies relating to the protection of personal data, including the relevant regulations and Advisory Guidelines, to help organisations understand and comply with the PDPA."[15]

On January 21, 2019, PDPC released its first edition of the Model AI Governance Framework for broader consultation, adoption and feedback. The framework provides detailed and implementable guidance to private sector organisations to address critical ethical and governance issues when deploying AI solutions. By explaining how AI systems work, building acceptable data accountability practices, and creating open and transparent communication, the framework aims to promote public understanding and trust in technologies.

On January 23, 2020, the PDPC released the second edition of the Model AI Governance Framework. The second edition includes additional considerations (such as robustness and reproducibility) and refines the original Model AI Governance Framework for greater relevance and usability.

For instance, the section on customer relationship management has been expanded to include considerations on interactions and communications

---

[15] https://bit.ly/3hBCcyH.

with a broader network of stakeholders. The second edition of the Model
AI Governance Framework continues to take a sector- and technology-
agnostic approach that can complement sector-specific requirements and
guidelines.[16]

International

1. European Group on Ethics. On March 9, 2018, the European Group on
Ethics in Science and New Technologies issued a statement on AI, robotics and
autonomous systems. "Advances in AI, robotics and so-called 'autonomous'
technologies have ushered in a range of increasingly urgent and complex
moral questions. Current efforts to find answers to the ethical, societal and legal
challenges that they pose and to orient them for the common good represent a
patchwork of disparate initiatives," the statement noted.

"This underlines the need for a collective, wide-ranging and inclusive process of reflection and dialogue, a dialogue that focuses on the values around
which we want to organise society and on the role that technologies should
play in it. This statement calls for the launch of a process that would pave the
way towards a common, internationally recognised ethical and legal framework for the design, production, use and governance of artificial intelligence,
robotics, and 'autonomous' systems."[17]

In June 2018, the EC set up an independent High-Level Expert Group on
AI. On April 8, 2019, the High-Level Expert Group on AI released its *Guidelines
for Trustworthy AI*. It stated that trustworthy AI should be lawful, respecting
all applicable laws and regulations; ethical, respecting ethical principles and
values; and robust, both from a technical perspective and taking into account
its social environment.[18]

2. AI4People. In February 2018, AI4People was launched at the
European Parliament, as the first multistakeholder forum bringing together
all actors interested in shaping the social impact of new applications of AI,
including the European Parliament, civil society organisations, industry and
the media. In November 2018, AI4People released its *Ethical Framework for a
Good AI Society: Opportunities, Risks, Principles, and Recommendations*.

"Several multi-stakeholder groups have created statements of ethical
principles which should guide the development and adoption of AI," the

---

[16] https://bit.ly/3jSebp8.
[17] https://bit.ly/32VuLOO.
[18] https://bit.ly/308tfH7.

statement notes. "Rather than repeat the same process here, we instead present a comparative analysis of several of these sets of principles. Each principle expressed in each of the documents we analyse is encapsulated by one of five overarching principles. Four of these – beneficence, non-maleficence, autonomy, and justice – are established principles of medical ethics. A fifth – explicability – is also required to capture the novel ethical challenges posed by AI."[19]

3. IEEE. On March 25, 2019, the IEEE (Institute of Electrical and Electronics Engineers) Global Initiative on Ethics of Autonomous and Intelligent Systems released the current version of its *Ethically Aligned Design, A Vision for Prioritising Human Well-being with Autonomous and Intelligent Systems.*

"As the use and impact of autonomous and intelligent systems become pervasive, we need to establish societal and policy guidelines in order for such systems to remain human-centric, serving humanity's values and ethical principles. These systems must be developed and should operate in a way that is beneficial to people and the environment, beyond simply reaching functional goals and addressing technical problems. This approach will foster the heightened level of trust between people and technology that is needed for its fruitful use in our daily lives," the statement notes.

"To be able to contribute in a positive, non-dogmatic way, we, the techno-scientific communities, need to enhance our self-reflection. We need to have an open and honest debate around our explicit or implicit values, including our imaginary around so-called AI and the institutions, symbols, and representations it generates."[20]

4. OECD. The OECD (Organisation of Economic Co-operation and Development) Principles on AI were adopted in May 2019 by member countries when they approved the recommendation of the OECD Council on AI. On June 9, 2019, the G20 adopted a human-centred approach to AI, guided by the G20 AI Principles drawn from the OECD recommendations. The responsible development and use of AI can be a driving force for a sustainable and inclusive society.

"The benefits brought by the responsible use of AI can improve the work environment and quality of life. It can create a potential for realising a human-centred future society with opportunities for everyone, including women and girls as well as vulnerable groups," the G20 Ministerial Statement on Trade

---

[19] https://bit.ly/3hDTlrB.
[20] https://bit.ly/39zWN3F.

and Digital Economy noted. "To foster public trust and confidence in AI technologies and fully realise their potential, we are committed to a human-centred approach to AI."[21]

5. United States. In May 2019, the United States adopted the OECD Principles on AI. In June 2019, the United States announced support for the G20 AI Principles. On January 7, 2020, the White House Office of Management and Budget and the Office of Science and Technology Policy issued a draft of *Guidance for Regulation of AI Application* containing 10 principles for AI regulation.

"AI is expected to have a positive impact across sectors of social and economic life, including employment, transportation, education, finance, healthcare, personal security, and manufacturing. At the same time, AI applications could pose risks to privacy, individual rights, autonomy, and civil liberties that must be carefully assessed and appropriately addressed. Its continued adoption and acceptance will depend significantly on public trust and validation," the draft noted.

"It is therefore important that the government's regulatory and non-regulatory approaches to AI promote reliable, robust, and trustworthy AI applications, which will contribute to public trust in AI. The appropriate regulatory or non-regulatory response to privacy and other risks must necessarily depend on the nature of the risk presented and the appropriate mitigations."[22]

 ## CONCLUSION

The principles of ethical AI has to be complemented by what is commonly referred to as "virtue ethics", which enables character formation and emphasises living ethically. *Phronēsis* (or practical wisdom) is one of the virtue ethics that the renowned Greek philosopher Aristotle (384–322 BC) explained in his book titled Nicomachean Ethics, as "what is good. for themselves and what is good for human beings in general".

Robert J Sternberg, Professor of Human Development at Cornell University, says that wisdom is in large part a decision to use one's intelligence, creativity and experience for the common good. "Wise individuals do not look out just for their interests, nor do they ignore these interests," he notes. "Rather,

---

[21] https://bit.ly/3f9dhkz.
[22] https://bit.ly/2P6Azgh.

they skilfully balance interests of varying kinds, including their own, those of others, and those of the communities of which they are a part."[23]

Mary Sim, Professor of Philosophy at College of the Holy Cross, wrote in her 2007 book titled *Remastering Morals with Aristotle and Confucius*, that *junzi* (君子) is similar to Aristotle's *phronēsis*. *Junzi* is a person "who conducts himself/herself in a way that wins the trust and cooperation of others, by truly promoting the good of others, rather than promoting his/her own gain at the expense of others."

[23]Robert J. Sternberg, Personal Wisdom in the Balance, in Michel Ferrari and Nic M. Weststrate (editors), The Scientific Study of Personal Wisdom : From Contemplative Traditions to Neuroscience, Dordrecht, Heidelberg, New York and London, Springer, 2013, at page 70.

Epilogue: Innovating in the Trenches

*Jim Lim Shien Min**

S INGAPORE'S LOCKDOWN OR CB (circuit breaker) was initiated on April 7, 2020, after the country reported 120 new cases of Covid-19 two days earlier, the highest daily increase since the pandemic began in end-January. The surge in cases came from multiple clusters involving foreign worker dormitories; this was the second black swan event for Singapore, after the SARS (severe acute respiratory syndrome) epidemic in 2003.

Action plans had to be put in place to ensure that the virus was contained, and the healthcare needs of foreign workers were addressed. However, there were not enough healthcare facilities to house all infected foreign workers, many of whom had mild symptoms. The Singapore Expo Convention Hall and Exhibition Centre was turned into a CIF (community isolation facility) in just a week to care for patients classified as "mild" cases and those on the road to recovery.

* Jim Lim is Executive Education Fellow and Adjunct Lecturer at NUS, and Healthcare Sector Lead at NCS. He was the Founder-CEO of Good Doctor Technology, a joint venture between China's PingAn Good Doctor and Grab. He has held senior management roles, including Huawei APAC (where he was the Digital Transformation CTO), Amdocs, Tech Mahindra and Accenture. Jim has an MBA (Distinction) from Manchester Business School and Bachelor in Engineering (Honours) in Electrical and Electronics Engineering from Nanyang Technological University. He is PMP-certified and has expertise in P&L and customer management, strategic consulting and start-ups.

These facilities were critical as they provided an alternate facility to house infected foreign workers as the 300,000 workers living in the dormitories were methodically tested. That isolation reduced community infection within each dormitory and enabled the better deployment of healthcare professionals.

Covid-19 is highly contagious. When a large group of patients are in one location, we had to consider:

- Minimal contact of healthcare and support staff with each patient to reduce the risk of infection.
- Have a system in place to monitor, diagnose and treat each patient.
- Ensure a high level of safety while delivering telehealth, food and essential supplies.
- Allow patients access to news so that they could communicate with their loved ones.
- Ensure adequate protection for support staff like cleaners, facility- and delivery people.
- Set up a contact-tracing mechanism in the event of an outbreak.

"We are paying close attention to the welfare of the foreign workers," Prime Minister Lee Hsien Loong said in a national telecast on April 10. "They came to Singapore to work hard for a living, and provide for their families back home. They have played an important part in building our HDB flats, Changi Airport, MRT lines. We have worked with their employers to make sure they will be paid their salaries and can remit money home. We will provide them with the medical care and treatment that they need."

On Good Friday, April 10, 2020, Singapore reported 198 new cases, bringing the total across the 2,000-mark threshold to 2,108, most of the new cases were from the dormitories. The increased cases triggered the need to get all the CIFs ready to receive patients. This is where my courageous journey started.

I worked as the healthcare sector lead in NCS (previously known as National Computer Systems). Some of us planned to volunteer to help the national effort to fight Covid-19. The NCS CEO decided that this could not be on an official job assignment, but on a volunteer basis due to the risk of infection, and thus named the team as "Courage Squad" to honour their courageous act. I volunteered as the squad leader for the first batch of six volunteers from NCS who had stepped forward to provide IT support at the Expo CIF, together with IHIS (Integrated Health Information Systems), the technology agency for public healthcare in Singapore.

Singapore has been through earlier outbreaks like SARS in 2003 and had set up quarantine facilities such as the NCID (National Centre for Infectious Diseases) to handle epidemics. However, unlike SARS, Covid-19 is highly contagious, more widespread and tough to diagnose due to some patients being asymptomatic despite being infected. The situation was worsened by the global shortage of medical PPE (personal protective equipment).

All of this presented a challenge when the infected patients were located at the Expo CIF:

- How to perform ADT (admission, discharge, transfer) procedures in a temporary isolation facility that lacked hospital information and management systems?
- How to quickly alert the medical professionals should the patients' vital signs deteriorate?
- How to ensure safety procedures, such as social distancing among the people working at CIF?
- What other precautions needed to be taken to reduce the risk of infection among the working professionals in CIF?
- How to perform contact tracing should someone get infected?

It was not an easy feat to assemble and deploy the Courage Squad within just six hours on a long holiday weekend. We had to quickly find accommodation for them (as a safety measure instead of going home), to work out allowances, get fresh laptops and other supporting materials, and to backfill their replacements. Situational leadership and agile project management skills were demonstrated. Isn't this what a CIO might be asked to do when your CEO asks you to deploy a "tiger team" to serve users at an urgent temporary site?

It was challenging to start a project that did not have a fixed scope in a facility that was not sure of the number of patients to be treated. We also had to procure ICT hardware and software when Singapore had just started its CB, and all economic activity was effectively closed. We carried out the following steps:

- We surveyed the site to know what technology (drones, robots, etc.) we could bring to help.
- We created an equipment and software inventory to track the ever-changing scope due to frequent changes in the number of patients to accommodate.

- For instance, we had to be ready when single-bed cubicles were converted to twin-sharing, and the initially planned three halls expanded to six to accommodate the surge in patient volume.
- We had to contact hardware and software vendors to determine the availability of equipment.
- We had to work around the clock to install, configure and test all the equipment and software.

THE IRON TRIANGLE

This was a crisis project with a specific objective: to offer backend ICT support. We were unsure whether anyone would volunteer since the number of confirmed cases was rising and the CB had just started. To our surprise, we had an overwhelming response; this was our first trophy, to have brave individuals who cared for others and wanted to help. That's why we called our team the Courage Squad to reflect the selflessness and courage of our volunteers. Since the CIF was an infectious facility, we had to control the number of people that could work at the site at any given time, despite our services being available 24/7.

Our handling of resources could be a good case study for CIOs on how to balance risk and resources under extreme time pressure; this is similar to the typical "iron triangle" concept in project management. The iron triangle postulates that:

- The quality of work could be constrained by the project's budget, timelines and scope.
- The project manager can trade between constraints.
- Changes in one constraint necessitate changes in others to compensate, or quality will suffer.

For example, a project can be completed faster by increasing the budget or cutting the scope. Similarly, expanding the scope may require equivalent increases in funding and schedule. Cutting the budget without adjusting the schedule or scope will lead to lower quality. "Good, fast, cheap. Choose any two," encapsulates the iron triangle constraints concisely.[1]

---

[1] https://bit.ly/31sdGJY.

In our case, our iron triangle was constrained by:

- The scope: We did not know how many infected patients would be admitted to the CIF.
- The time: We did not know how long each patient will take to recover.
- The resources: We had to guesstimate the volunteers needed, the number of diagnostics equipment required, and so on.

The quality of healthcare to be provided was at the core of this mission. During the initial two weeks, we thought we were crawling through a minefield every day. Our speed of deployment needed to be balanced with our being infection-free.

On April 25, *The Straits Times* reported that Singapore had three community isolation facilities: D'Resort NTUC Chalet in Pasir Ris, which could hold 500 people; two halls at Singapore Expo that could hold 950 people, with another four halls on the way; and Changi Exhibition Centre, which could keep 2,800 people.

From the lessons we learnt, and as the team became more experienced, we improved the situation by adopting innovative ways of deploying technology and reducing the reliance on human resources. The Courage Squad, together with other volunteers, partners and healthcare workers, helped implement the IT infrastructure and software successfully within a week. We could deliver:

- Level-1 remote helpdesk support services: How to use the devices for data entry for the Telehealth app, and fix or replace any batteries, cables that malfunctioned.
- Level-2 operations and maintenance: Teams had to be trained on how to wear and remove the PPE so that they could enter the "red zone". This was to replace devices or to attend to patient queries if L1 support could not solve the problem.
- Level-3 application support: Engineers used remote login and access on the Telehealth app. These engineers could troubleshoot, debug and provide software patches to resolve issues remotely.

Here are some lessons that we learnt from doing this exercise:

- Every pandemic is different. Covid-19 was very unlike what we had ever experienced.

- It is crucial to be able to adapt to the new situation, as it arises, sometimes suddenly.
- Leveraging technology makes excellent sense, especially telemedicine, robotics, AI and IoT.
- Be humble and cautious when dealing with new unknown viruses, pandemic or otherwise.
- Be agile and flexible, but ensure you and your team have done good baseline planning.
- Don't deploy technologies just because they look "cool"; they must be able to solve problems.
- Good BCP (business continuity planning) is vital; ensure it has been tried and tested recently.
- New SOPs (standard operating procedures) must be in place for this black swan moment.
- Don't be overconfident and stubborn; both are negative attributes that can cost human lives.

 ## IDEAS AND INNOVATIONS

Necessity is the mother of invention. Out of necessity, we innovated and tried new ideas to enable us to do our work safely, provide a high level of healthcare and deliver our services more efficiently. These are some of the innovations that grew from our involvement at the CIF:

- **Telehealth.** The aim was to reduce human-to-human contact while providing excellent healthcare. In CIF, our initial services focused around self-help vital signs monitoring by the infected patients. That was done through the Telehealth applications installed in the iPad. Every patient was given a mercury thermometer, an oximeter, and a blood pressure monitor. We trained every patient to do a self-check using those devices. The readings from those devices were registered into the iPad Telehealth app by the patient. Every patient had to take these readings five times a day and record it. Healthcare workers need not be present to reduce the risk of infection to the healthcare worker.
- **Asset tracking.** The aim was to ensure sufficient inventory while reducing cross-infections. Since there were so many devices, how could asset tracking be done? In the initial stage, the concern was to ensure against contamination by the infected patients. The simple solution was

to use RFID (radio-frequency identification) tags. However, there were not enough RFID tags; due to the circuit breaker, nonessential services were not available. There was also a need for unique RFID tags for iPads due to interference with the regular RFID tags. Fortunately, we managed to get some RFID tags from the National Library and made many calls to source more RFID tags. That made us wonder whether the definition of essential versus nonessential services needs to change? What may not seem crucial would become vital in a situation like this.

■ **Automation.** The aim was to deliver services with less human-to-human contact. Manual data entry was required to input patient records into the Telehealth app. Since the CB had started, it was impossible to arrange all the resources needed. To reduce reliance on human resources, and thereby limit exposure to the virus, automation was high on our agenda. We developed and deployed RPA (Robotic Process Automation) programs to replace manual data entry and remote provisioning and management of mobile devices for secure asset allocation and tracking. Every equipment and device had to be managed all the time remotely. We protected our support team by reducing patient contact, and we protected our patients, given that an external person could carry in an infection.

■ **Contact tracing.** The aim was to keep our support staff, services providers and patients safe. Initially, the temperature taking and workers check-in processes were done in the same way as many others, with security officers and registration booths. It was improved with the use of thermal cameras and later, NRIC (National Registration Identity Card) or access-card scanning. In mid-July, Surbana Jurong began trials on a new contact tracing device and digital check-in system. The technology complemented national contact tracing device "TraceTogether Token" and mandatory digital check-in system "SafeEntry" at workplaces. We tracked our equipment, as well as our healthcare workers, external service providers and patients as they moved within and when they moved in or out the CIF. Contact tracing ensured that we could control infections when we detected a breach.

■ **Robotics.** Robots can be used for some tasks without getting infected. To reduce the need for our support staff to visit the patient cubicles, we sourced commercial robots that we could quickly adapt to replace human tasks. These included service robots (similar to the Pepper robot), which could provide the information when asked, and the Boston Dynamics Robot Dog to act as a safe distancing ambassador. These robots provided safety, efficiency and quality of services. We could envisage their potential in the healthcare world, as well as see them playing a part in our everyday lives.

- **Disinfection.** The aim was to keep the facilities sanitised and ensure that we reduced air and surface transmission. Surgical face masks, hand sanitisers and medical PPE were given to all of us despite the low supplies in the initial stages. Disinfection chambers were installed a month or so later. But a more significant challenge was to sanitise the CIF regularly throughout the day. We wanted to reduce the risk of surface infection as the supporting workers could be infected when they come in contact with a contaminated surface. Disinfection is labour-intensive, and since we used chemicals, it could cause damage to the cleaner's health. In Singapore, companies in robotics, such as Otsaw and Sesto robotics, redesigned their robots to handle disinfection services in office buildings and shopping malls.

- **TOW.** TOW stands for Telehealth on Wheels. There were many devices used at the CIF. Some developed faults and needed to be replaced or repaired. We had a limited number of ICT personnel on-site to serve so many patients. Every time one of us had to enter the "red zone", we had to suit-up with a PPE. If we had to visit multiple patients in multiple halls, we had to disinfect ourselves after each patient was seen. Each encounter with a patient increased the risk of infecting our staff. That's where the TOW came to our help. It was a trolley fitted with wheels. We placed instructions on how to use the new devices or exchange their current devices on the trolley.

Singapore was in the CB period. We had to find a creative way to fabricate the TOWs. First, we got MOH approval for the IKEA warehouse to be opened for us to select the tables that we could use. Next, we sourced for wheels that could be fixed to the tables. Then, we assembled them. In three days, from idea to completion, 200 TOWs were created at the Expo CIF. Innovation need not be high-tech all the time. Our safety concerns enabled us to find quick and effective ways to deliver a solution. It worked very well, thanks to teamwork and collaboration with other vendors.

- **Agile.** We were using all the principles of "Agile" project management, not by choice, but by necessity, as there was no time to do a "Waterfall" project planning. The dedication and commitment of everyone involved, including NCS senior management, made the Agile methodology work.

Crisis management demands decisive actions; the risk is mitigated by a team of experienced professionals who are committed to the success of the project. Some SOPs were inherited from the SARS experience, such as the medical PPE procedures. But Covid-19 was more widespread and sometimes asymptomatic (unlike SARS). We found that the rules of managing Covid-19 kept changing as we discovered more. Our quick adaption to change were Agile processes that were effective in this crisis. Note that we started this project with only a general objective; the details were developed in cycles of iterations.

LESSONS LEARNED

We worked within the boundaries of time and constraints to deliver a technology infrastructure and support for the CIF. There were many lessons that we learned; these will help us if another pandemic occurs. While we experience acceleration and faster adoption of digital technologies across industries, it might be too early to conclude the explicit norms of the "new normal", especially when Covid-19 is still changing how people interact with each other. Besides, any new initiative (whether or not triggered by a pandemic) must be able to address the problem statement, pass the cost-benefit analysis and have clear and differentiating value propositions for it to become a new normal. Here are some suggestions for the present and future innovation:

- ▦ **Gesturing.** Gesturing for device input. On the second day of my volunteering, we faced a unique challenge: how to work on iPads using gloves. Those wearing gloves could not slide the iPad screen, limiting their ability to perform their tasks. While a few mobile phones and tablets offer navigation using hand gestures, these features were not available in the devices that we selected. There is a need for a noncontact input for devices that are used in an infectious environment.
- ▦ **Drones.** Drones to ensure enforcements. At the CIF, we could not have human patrols moving around the facilities to enforce compliance or to detect breaches. Medical personnel needed to ensure that their patients were taking medication and recording their vital signs. We wanted to perform video surveillance and analytics of patient activities, such as recording their vital signs five times a day. The idea of using drones was discussed – and aborted – because pipes all across the ceilings of exhibition halls would cause a technical hindrance. Using technology for

surveillance is a right and nonintrusive way of ensuring compliance during a pandemic.

▪ **Communications and social health.** Patients are in isolation due to infection containment. Workers within the CIF were on restricted access to the outside world and were subject to stringent facility access protocols. There were occasional periods of stress, like a sudden influx of patients or a significant technology breakdown, such as the network failing. Such isolation could impact the mental health of everyone in the CIF.

  ▪ Communication was required with different actors in the CIF; fake news must be monitored.
  ▪ Patients needed to interact with their families and with nurses and doctors.
  ▪ The information had to be effectively disseminated to all relevant parties.
  ▪ Conflict resolution and escalation was a crucial element in a closed environment.
  ▪ Conflicts that were not appropriately managed could result in unhealthy friction in teams.
  ▪ Long hours, isolation and frustrations due to limited resources could result in extreme stress.

   One key area where technology could help would be in formal and informal communications. It could be in the form of collaboration or an email platform with a social media function like Facebook. It should include workflow management and identify interest groups.

▪ **Zero-touch.** During the CB, e-commerce and online deliveries have seen a surge in transactions. Many delivery companies implemented "contactless" deliveries to protect the delivery people and customers by reducing contact, such as signing a receipt. This trend is likely to continue in the new normal. New retail experiences using AR/VR (augmented reality/ virtual reality) technologies could further address the need for high-touch trials such as clothes fitting. Zero-touch is for infection management during this pandemic, but it has become a design parameter for the future of retailing. There is no need to visit a physical store; a remote view via a VR device can be useful during a pandemic.

▪ **Teleconsult.** During the CB, although primary care services were available, many patients opted to teleconsult with doctors. Most teleconsult platforms provide delivery services for prescription medicines. These platforms offer low-touch (physical) as well as high-touch (emotional) interaction between patients and doctors. There is a gap in the patient journey for tele-diagnostics services for an end-to-end seamless experience. For more complex healthcare services where physical visits cannot be avoided, online-offline seamless handover and data integration will be at the core in the future of healthcare.

■ **Culture.** Asian cultures usually comprise face-time for interaction; the pandemic forced everyone to go high-tech and low- or no-touch. Is it possible for Asian audiences to learn to trust each other using low-touch virtual meetings? Can employees be highly productive while working from home? As a home-based worker for the last 15 years, I can say that it can be managed with discipline. NCS recently published a whitepaper, "The Three New Lenses to View Digitalisation in the Post-Covid-19 World." "There should exist a spectrum of touch – from zero-touch to high-touch in the new normal," the paper states. "The ability for organisations to be sensitive and adapt to the different needs of users across the service is a critical success factor for the organisation of tomorrow."[2]

■ **Security.** There is already a steep rise in malware and hacking attacks. Beside enterprise-grade VPNs (virtual private network) for remote login, there is a need for an IIP (Internet Isolation Platform) to allow search and communication while safeguarding enterprise data and systems. For healthcare organisations with highly sensitive data, it would be ideal for network layer segregation using secure and effective networks such as GPON (Gigabit Passive Optical Network). Moreover, ASOCs (Advanced Security Operation Centres) can be set up for companies to get visibility, control and recommendations on their security postures. No technology is fool-proof; proper governance and processes must also be implemented to mitigate security threats.

The ancient Chinese saying, 危机 (*Weiji*) is formed by two words – "threat" and "opportunity" – which implies that in each threat, there is an opportunity. That is akin to Nicholas Taleb's "Black Swan Theory" to have robustness against adverse events while exploiting positive events.[3]

It is essential to leverage technology to tackle problems and use innovation to resolve issues that are sure to crop up in the "new normal" that's impacting all of us.

---

[2] https://bit.ly/2DFBMsn.
[3] https://bit.ly/2UbcRSp.

Index

A

ABAP, programming training, 113
access, gaining/maintenance (pen test phases), 201
account-to-account payment services, increase, 218
Acton, Brian, 69
Act to Regulate Use of Facial Recognition, 238
Adleman, Leonard, 198
admission, discharge, transfer (ADT), procedure, 249
Advanced Security Operation Centres (ASOCs), setup, 257
Agile project management principles, usage, 254–255
AI4People, launch, 242–243
Aikido way, 124–125
Alibaba (outsourcing case study), 69–70
AliPay, 218
Allen, David, 58
always-on operation, 135
Amabile, Teresa, 167
Apache Cassandra, 184
Apache Hadoop, 183
Apache Samoa, 185
Apache Storm, 185
application security, 192
apprenticeships, 104–105
  scheme, 105
artificial intelligence (AI), 104 *see also* ethical AI
  ethical issues, 235–239
  surveillance AI, uses, 238–239
  term, coinage, 233
Artificial Intelligence Model Governance Framework, 234
Asian Computer Service (ACS), payroll project delivery failure, 9

Asia-Pacific Economic Cooperation (APEC), 171
asset tracking, 252–253
attachments, loading (caution), 204
audio/video, unstructured data, 38–39
augmented reality/virtual reality (AR/VR), usage, 256
authenticity, 198
automated facial recognition (AVR), usage, 238
automation, 253
autonomous systems, 239–241
availability, 196, 197 *see also* confidentiality, integrity, availability
  custodian responsibility, 181

B

Babbage, Charles, 15–16
banks, data usage, 211–219
Barrick, Marilyn, 124
"Benefits of Infrastructure Outsourcing, The" (Sayer), 66
Beyond Performance 2.0 (Keller/ Schaninger), 160
big data
  5Vs, 182
  challenge, 197
  management, 179
  Oracle definition, 182
big data analytics (BDA), 158, 182–186
  advice, 187–189
  case study, 186
  history, 183
  tools, 183–185
black hat hacker, 201
blockchains, 104, 217–219
  redundancy, 217
bodies, certification, 107–108

brainstorming, 177
Brandenburg Gate, Reagan speech, 1
breaks, taking (information overload
    avoidance), 60
Bukit Merah Central, wall removal, 1–2
bulletin boards (BBs), usage, 144
business
    CIO alignment, 159–160
    mentor, experience, 173
    processes, ITD automation, 18
    rules, 38
business analytics (BA), 179
business continuity, disaster recovery
    (BC-DR), 192
    case studies, 83–86
    importance, 32
    planning, process, 77
    plans, protocols (inclusion), 34
    procedures, emphasis, 31
    requirement, 28
    trial runs, implementation, 10
business continuity plan (BCP), 80
    requirement, 30
business disruption plan, 79–81
    reason, 79
business intelligence (BI), 179
    impact, 37
business resumption plan (BRP), 79–81
    development, steps, 80–81
business-to-business (B2B)
    community, 224
    transactions, 213
business-to-consumer (B2C)
    community, 224
    requests, 213
business-to-government (B2B)
    community, 224
business units (BUs), 154
    customer information database
        sharing, 120
    data mart ownership, 41
    deliverables, agreement, 83
    digital divide, 174
    insights, 52
    ITD, BRP interface, 81
    ITD communications, maintenance, 143
    ITD support, absence (complaint), 141
    organisational usage, 74–75
    PC support unit setup, 7
business users (BUs), involvement, 17

C
Cafarella, Mik, 183
Cantey Technology, BC-DR case study, 84
capability (conflict minimisation step), 122
Capability Maturity Model Integration
    (CMMI), 132, 139
Capability Maturity Model Level 3 (CMM L3)
    Certification, creation, 132
Capability Maturity Model (CMM), maturity
    levels, 136
Capex project, 27
Carnegie-Mellon University (CMU), 132
cash, crypto conversion, 215–217
Cassandra Structure Language (CSL),
    usage, 184
Central Provident Fund, DCs (impact), 25–26
centre of excellence (CoE), usage/
    establishment, 188
certification, 106–111, 135–139 *see also* staff
Certification for IT Project Managers (CITPM),
    SCS implementation, 108
change
    advice, 160–161
    agent, 155–159
    case study, 154–155
    communication, 157
    handling, 153
    initiator, role, 157
    leaders, support, 157
    metrics, 156–157
    mind-sets, 154
    reactions, 156
    requests, usage, 143
    resistance, reasons, 154
Changing Nature of Work, The (World Bank
    World Development Report), 224–225
Chan, Juliana, 229
chatbots, KMS evolution, 57
Chew, Sok Chuang, 11, 12
chief data officer (CDO), 180
Chief Information Officer (CIO)
    case study, 51–53
    database access, 37
    DW project advice, 42–44
    emotions, management, 117
    expectations, 92
    information role, 51–53
    issues, management, 116–117
    ITD change, 156
    ITD operational cost responsibility, 135

ITD staff support, 166
journey, 159–160
management actions, 92–93
raw data control, 39–40
responsibility, 180
success, factors, 131
chief information security officer (CISO),
appointment, 181
chief knowledge office (CKO),
responsibilities, 57
China
impact, 227–229
innovation, increase, 228
tech companies, list, 228
technology adoption, 227
Christensen, Rod, 148
Chuang, Kwong, 3
circuit breaker (CB), initiation
(Singapore), 247, 250
City of Atlanta, ransomware (BC-DR case
study), 83–84
Clark, Richard E., 96
Click-to-Play browser, usage, 204
client-facing data, retrieval, 40–41
client-server computing, impact, 36
client-server systems, openness, 23
cloud computing, emergence, 27, 47–48
Cloudera Distribution for Hadoop (CDH), 184
cloud service provider (CSP), 135
marketplace, 27
usage, 29
coaching, 173
Cobb, Stephen, 33
COBOL, usage, 28, 93, 174
code of practice/code of ethics, 104–105
cold site, 78
Cold War, cessation (Malta Summit
declaration), 1–2
Colombo Plan, 6
Committee of Sponsoring Organisations
of the Treadway Commission
(COSO), 139
commodity elements, outsourcing (focus), 66
communications
chains, establishment, 83
conflict minimisation step, 121
flow, maintenance, 143–144
requirements, 256
community isolation facility (CIF)
infected patient placement, challenge, 249

lessons, 255–257
usage, 247–250
company
departments, business value
grouping, 21–22
failures, 79
focus, improvement, 64
training roadmap, 112
transformation, 230
complacency, impact, 160
computer-aided design and drafting (CADD)
system, HDB introduction, 2
Computer Services Department (CSD)
issues/problems, 3
management, 7
name, change, 52
Siow appointment/role, 51–52
Siow relocation/staff meeting, 2–4
superscale status, 3
transformation, 7, 10
computer virus, BC-DR case study, 85
computing
on-demand approach, 68
security, advice, 203–205
confidentiality, 194–195
custodian responsibility, 181
confidentiality, integrity, availability (CIA)
triad, 194–199
big data, impact, 197
case study, 198–199
challenges, 196–198
conflict
analysis, 118–122
internal conflicts, 119
occurrence, minimisation (steps), 121–122
conflict, causes, 116–117
conflict resolution
action, plan, 118
Aikido way, usage, 124–125
case studies, 117–118, 120–122
process, 115
consistency (conflict minimisation step), 121
contact tracing, usage, 253
content management system (CMS), 56
continual service improvement, 138
Continuous Quality Improvement, 134
contracting, outsourcing (contrast),
64–65
Control Objectives for Information and Related
Technology (COBIT), 137

core, focus (outsourcing), 66
corporate culture,
    information (sharing), 170
Courage Squad, 248–250
Covid-19
    DC case study, 33
    impact, 247–250
    lockdown, 223
    spread, prevention, 225–226
creative elite, deployment, 170–171
Creative Futuring process, 159
creativity
    fostering, 166–167
    innovation, contrast, 167
Critical Information
    Infrastructure (CII), 202
critical systems approach, 32
cross-training, 56
crowdsourcing, 165, 225
cryptocurrencies
    economics rules, 215–216
    failure, 217
    virtual currency, 216
cultural issues (KMS example), 55
culture, face-time requirement, 257
customer
    collaboration, 165
    delight, 211
    digital divide, 175
    expectations, IT regulations (ITD
        balance), 141
    satisfaction levels, decrease, 79
customer relationship management (CRM), 37
    company migration, 19
    development, 36
    importance, 135
    running, 31
    structured data, 38
Cutting, Doug, 183
cyberattack, Committee of Inquiry (COI)
    report, 96
cybercrime, increase, 194
cybersecurity, 191–192, 204
    categories, 192
Cyber Security Agency of Singapore (CSA),
    formation, 202

D
Daskal, Dolly, 155
data, 35

4Vs, 224
assumptions/constraints, 38
backup plan, 80
client-facing data, retrieval, 40–41
custodian, responsibility, 180–181
data-in-motion, transmission, 1907
EMP, impact, 196
governance, 54, 180–181
lake, usage, 40–42
loss, safeguards, 196
machine-generated data, 39
mart, concept, 40–41
models, formal structure, 50–51
owner groups, agreements, 43
project sponsor/management meetings, 43
raw data, 47
security, 191
semi-structured data, 50–51
storage, expense/accessibility, 47–48
structured data, 38, 50
transformation rules, 38
types, 42, 50–51
unstructured data, 38–39, 50
user expectations, management, 43
data analytics supercomputer (DAS), 185
database management system (DBMS), 184
databases, ITD power user access, 195
data centers (DCs), 25
    BC-DR, importance, 32
    case studies, 32–34
    complexity, 27
    critical systems approach, 32
    DRP/BCP requirement, 30
    The Engineering Project (TEP), electricity
        cost analysis, 26
    environmental monitoring system (EMS),
        importance, 31
    evolution, 28–32
    flooring, construction, 29
    infrastructures, expense, 27
    in-house/outsource question, 27–28
    location, selection, 29
    management, 29–32
    operations, attention/emphasis, 31
    operators, need, 26
    ownership/lease, question, 26–27
    physical security, pretection, 30
    power outages, protection, 29
    secondary DC, maintenance, 30
    staffing, importance, 31

upgrading, 29
virtual security, protection, 30
data management, 39–42
  case study, 42
  changes, 37
  mainframes, usage, 36
  waves, 36–37
Data Processing Management Association
  (DPMA), 105
dataset owners, communication, 43
data warehouse (DW)
  building, problems, 41
  designer, role, 42–43
  design, internal marketing plan
    development, 43
  problems, avoidance, 43
  project, advice, 42–44
  project, political climate
    (discussion), 43
  usage, 40–42
Datawrapper, 184
David, Lilach Bar, 212
daydreaming (information overload
  avoidance), 60
DBS Bank/IBM, outsourcing lesson, 73–74
DBS PayLah (mobile wallet), 212
Decision Support System (DSs), setup, 41
deep defence, 199–203
  case study, 203
deep learning (DL), 104
delegation (information overload
  avoidance), 60–61
deliverables, defining, 83
denial-of-service (DoS) attacks, 196
dial-in modems, usage, 29
Difference Engine, 15
digital divide, 171–175 *see also* Information
  Technology Department
  gap, closure, 172–174
Digital Equipment Corp., 90
digital technology, impact, 223–224
digital transformation (DX), 212
DiplomIngenieur Bauingenieurwesen (Bachelor
  in Civil Engineering award), 6
disaster recovery (DR), 77, 196 *see also*
  business continuity, disaster recovery
disaster recovery plan (DRP), 80, 196
  requirement, 30
document management system (DMS), 56
  setup, 54

documents, preservation, 39
drones, usage, 255–256

E
eat the frog (information overload
  avoidance), 59–60
Eberts, Jake, 59
Economic Development Board (EDB), 229
electromagnetic pulse (EMP), impact, 196
electronic data interchange (EDI),
  implementation cost, 218
Electronic Data Systems (EDS)/US Navy,
  outsourcing lesson, 72
electronic medical record (EMR), 94
Electronic Numerical Integrator and Computer
  (ENIAC), construction, 25
email
  derail (information overload avoidance), 59
  habits, Microsoft tracking, 49
  structured data status, 38
emotions, management, 117
employee suggestion schemes (ESS), KMS
  example, 56
end users
  assistance, 141
  behaviour, collection, 37
  query operational databases, avoidance, 41
energy, conservation (information overload
  avoidance), 60
Enterprise Control Language (ECL), 185
enterprise resource planning (ERP), 37
  company migration, 19
  DC, impact, 31
  development, 36
  ITD management, 130
  management, 130
  running, 28
  software, updates/upgrades, 16
enterprise resource planning (ERP)
  systems, 174
  configuration problem, 123
  merger, 70
  usage, 168–169
enterprise-scale DCs, 25
enterprise security, ensuring, 191
environmental monitoring system (EMS),
  importance, 31
error reporting tool (ERT), usage, 143
ethical AI, 233
  frameworks, 241–244

Ethical Framework for a Good AI Society
(AI4People), 242
ethics, values (relationship), 234
European Community (EC), High-Level Group
on AI report, 242
European Group of Ethics in Science and
New Technologies, statement, 242
everyday bank, concept, 215
executive information system (EIS),
evolution, 41–42
extended BRP (EBRP), creation, 81
external entity, identification, 64
external parties, IT activities
(outsourcing), 64
external resources, leveraging, 176
external training, 112–113

F
facial recognition, 237
usage, legal developments, 237–238
facilities services, redundancies (service
provider responsibility), 27–28
Factor Analysis of Information Risk
(FAIR), 139
failure (fail fast), 10–12
Farrera-Brochez, Mikhy (fraud/drug
charges), 198–199
FatPipe wireless open-access research
platform (FatPipe WARP),
implementation, 85
favouritism (conflict minimisation step), 121
feedback
database (KMS example), 55
encouragement, 143–144
financial technology (fintech), 210–211
fires, BC-DR case study, 86
firewalls, usage, 31
first-level resolution (FLR), 148–149
Fishbone Root Cause Analysis, 134
Foot, Philippa Ruth, 239–240
Ford, Henry, 222
FORTRAN, usage, 28
fourth industrial revolution (IR4.0), 193
Frederick the Great II, 3, 4
freelancing, impact, 225
frequently asked questions (FAQs), 144, 149
Friga, Paul N., 122
fulfilment models, 231
Fussey, Pete, 237
future, invention, 158–159

G
G20, AI Principles, 243–244
Gaille Media, BC-DR case study, 86
gamification, 225
Gandhi, Mahatma, 155–156
General Data Protection Regulation (GDPR), 109
Germany, Slow residence, 5–6
gesturing, usage, 255
Getting Things Done (Allen), 58
Gigabit Passive Optical Network (GPON), 257
GitHub (outsourcing case study), 70
Gleichstellungsbeirat, 5
Globe2 variant, 85
goals, setting, 177
Google (outsourcing case study), 70–71
Goole NHS Foundation Trust, BC-DR
case study, 85
Gorbachev, Mikhail, 1
governance *see* data
case study, 131–132
certifications, 135–139
ensuring, 129
government-linked companies (GLCs), talent
valuation, 91
Grab Holdings Inc., 214–215, 229
Gramm-Leach-Bliley Act, 138
graphical user interface (GUI),
patch (usage), 23
Greenleaf, Robert K, 4
grey hat hacker, 201
groups, training roadmap, 111–112
"Guardians of Peace" hackers, impact, 33
Guidance for Regulation of AI Application (White
House), 244
Guidelines for Trustworthy AI (EC High-Level
Group on AI report), 242

H
Hadoop, 183
Hadoop Distributed File System
(HDFS), 168, 183
"Handling Conflict in Relationships the Aikido
Way" (Barrick), 124
hard disk, upgrade process, 16
hard skills, 122
head of department (HOD), threat, 119
Heinla, Ahti, 71
help desk, 144, 149–150
ITD responsibility, 147–148
setup, advice, 151–152

helpless desk, 148–149
Herzberg, Frederick, 170
high-performance computing cluster
(HPCC), 185
Hochschule für Technik (HFT) Stuttgart,
Siow attendance, 5, 12
Hong Kong Housing Authority, deal
(Siow advice), 10
Housing and Development Board (HDB)
CADD system, introduction, 2
CIO appointment, 2
data, inventory request (case study), 42
DCs, impact, 25–26
HQ, wall (breaking), 1–2
IBM mainframe, batch processes, 17
journey, learning organisation, 55
PCs/email accounts, issuance, 48
Singapore Quality Award, 55
Vision2000 (strategic IT plan), 52–53
Y2K case study, 20
Y2K transition, ease, 8
Hsien Loong, Lee, 203, 248
human resources department (HRD),
interactions, 119
human resources management (HRM)
changes, 17
training, inadequacy, 115
human resources (HR) system, problems, 8–9
hurricanes, BC-DR case study, 86
hyper-connectivity, importance, 193

I
IBM, 90
mainframe, batch processes, 17
outsourcing lessons, 71–74
IEEE *See* Institute of Electrical and
Electronics Engineers
images (unstructured data), 39
implementation (QMS project failure
reason), 133–134
individuals
conflict, 118
training roadmap, 112
induction programme, 99
Industrial Revolution workplace, technologies
(impact), 227
infocommunications technology (ICT)
(info-communication technology),
10, 104, 141
employee tools, 22

professionals, presence (Singapore), 20
staff, exit, 21
information dump, 58
flow, 35–37
security, 192
information overload, 47
avoidance, advice, 58–61
defining, 48
occurrence, 48–49
Information Services Department (ISD), 7, 131
name, change, 52
Information Systems Audit and Control
Association (ISACA), 137–139
information systems (IS) organization,
software/services delivery, 129
information technology (IT)
governance, 138–139
knowledge, shelf life, 106
managers, skillsets, 92
outsourcing policy, setup advice, 74–75
porous industry description, 103
Project Management Certification
Programme, 81
skills, 105
support services, ITD provision, 150
training, roadmap, 111–113
Information Technology as a Service
(ITaaS), 135
Information Technology Department (ITD), 16
business/operating models, retooling, 22
business process automation, 18
business units, BRP interface, 81
business units, communication flow
(maintenance), 143
capabilities/considerations, customer
expectations (gaps), 133
change, CIO (impact), 156
change, resistance (reasons), 154
competitive advantage, 169
conflicts, 119
control, loss, 63
core team (construction), certifications
(impact), 113
cost reduction overemphasis, impact, 67
DC construction, 31
demands, 111
digital divide, 174–175
end-users, ITD contact, 148
IBM mainframe, batch processes, 17
ICT change, 157

Information Technology Department (ITD)
(continued)
    IT quality policy, 130
    legacy, 20–24
    mainframe maintenance, 22–23
    management, complexity, 134–135
    operation, cost (CIO responsibility), 135
    peacetime housekeeping procedures, 28
    power use access, 195
    project delivery organisation, organisation/
        management, 131
    QMS, impact/consideration, 132, 134
    rejuvenation/replacement retooling, 23
    resignations, impact, 94
    retooling, 21–24
    running, external service provider
        responsibility, 63
    self-restructuring/reinvention, 154
    service delivery problems, external risk
        exposure, 27
    skillsets/vacancies, 21
    skunkworks, setup, 91
    software apps/system components, usage/
        identification, 32
    software process, development, 136
    sourcing plan, presence, 74
    staff inspections, 193
    standby site operation, 78
    strategic IT plan, formation, 159
    structures/capabilities, retooling, 21–22
    structures, centralisation/
        decentralisation, 141
    systems implementation, 64
    systems/services improvement, 143
    talent, 98
    technology/delivery, retooling, 22
    total costs, understanding, 74
    training strategy, 159
    Y2K, impact/outcome, 78
Information Technology Department
        (ITD) teams
    certification, 145
    DW, impact, 41
    quality, increase, 135
Information Technology Infrastructure
        Library (ITIL), 137–139, 145–146
    concepts, 138
Information Technology Management
        Association (ITMA), 105
Information Technology Service Management
        (ITSM), 137–138

information technology (IT) staff
    open costs, 94–95
    quitting, hidden costs, 94
    retention, problem, 63–64
    turnover, 89
information technology (IT) talent
    hiring, 90
    need, 20
InfoWeb, online launch, 8
Infrastructure as a Service (IaaS), 27, 135
infrastructure outsourcing, 66–69
innovation, 252–255
    advice, 175–177
    case study, 168–169, 170–171
    definitions, 166–168
    fostering, 165, 166, 169–171
    management, defining, 167
    ML algorithms, impact, 175
    open innovation, 165
    suggestions, 255–257
Inslee, Jay, 238
Institute of Electrical and Electronics
        Engineers (IEEE), Global Initiative on
        Ethics of Autonomous and Intelligent
        Systems, 243
institute of higher learnings (IHLs), 103
integrated circuit (IC), components
        (doubling), 16, 106
integrated development environment
        (IDE), usage, 29
Integrated Health Information Systems
        (IHIS), 248
    career change, 10
integration
    problem-solving theme, 123
    QMS project failure reason, 134
integrity, 195–196 see also confidentiality,
        integrity, availability
    custodian responsibility, 181
intellectual property (IT), 53
intelligence, increase, 223
intelligent systems, 239–241
internal conflicts, 119
internal marketing plan, development, 43
International Federation of
        Information Processing (IFIP),
        IT qualifications, 107
Internet Isolation Platform (IIP), 257
Internet of Things (IoT), 104
    devices, 37
    privacy, concern, 197–198

Internet servers, usage, 31
internship programme, 105
interpersonal/inter-BU communications,
    absence, 155
Iron triangle, 250–252
ISO9001 standard, 132, 135
ITD *see* Information Technology
    Department

J
Jaques, Everett, 240
JavaScript, server-side execution, 184
JAVA, usage, 29
job groups, training roadmap, 111–112
Journey to the East (Greenleaf), 4
JP Morgan/IBM, outsourcing lesson, 72

K
Kasesalu, Priit, 71
Keller, Scott, 160
key performance indicators (KPIs), 52
Khaire, Mukti, 167
King Frederick the Great II *see* Frederick
    the Great II
knowledge management (KM), 53–58
    case studies, 54–55, 57–58
    examples, 55–57
knowledge management system (KMS)
    creation, 54, 57
    examples, 55–56
    processes, 55
knowledge transfer (optimisation), CoE
    (usage), 188
know your customer (KYC) forms, 214
Koh, David, 203
Kosal, Chuck, 123
Kostanz Information Miner (Knime), 184
Koum, Jan, 69
Krishna, Arvind, 237
Kwong Yong, Chuang, 6

L
Lai, Tung, 8
large businesses (LBs), talent valuation, 91
layered defence, usage, 199
learning, encouragement, 157
legacy
    factors, 17
    ITD legacy, 20–24
    third dimension, CIO consideration, 17–18
    Y2K scare, 18–20

legacy systems
    functioning, problem, 16–17
    handling, 15
    maintenance costs, increase, 22
    relevance, 21
    Y2K Bug, impact, 19
Levitin, Daniel J., 58–60
Levitt, Theodore, 167
lightning, BC-DR case study, 84–85
Lim, Christina, 4–5
Lim, Edward, 9
Lim, Hazel Si Min, 240
Lim, Hng Kiang, 7, 8
local area networks (LANs), 192
    inclusion, 26
Loong, Lee Hsien, 96
Lumify, 184

M
"Machine Bias," 235
machine-generated data, 39
machine identity, usage, 198
machine learning (ML), 104
    algorithms, impact, 175
mainframe systems, cost
    (comparison), 22–23
Malta Summit, Cold War declaration, 1–2
management
    skills, 92
    theory, 6
managers
    CIO expectations, 92
    skillsets, 92
    valuation, 91–92
manufacturing resource planning (MRP),
    development, 36
MapReduce, 183
Master Data Management (MDM)
    requirement, 38
    solution, 37–39
    tool, usage, 38
Ma Yun, Jack, 69
McCarthy, John, 233–234
McChrystal, Stanley, 61
McKinsey Mind, The (Rasiel/Friga),
    122–123
measurement metrics,
    outsourcing, 66–67
media access control (MAC), machine
    authentication, 198
mediation, usage, 120

mentoring
  activities, checklist, 97–98
  advice, 101
  case study, 100
  metrics, 96–101
  programme, 99
  rationale, 100
  schemes, 98–100
  schemes, implementation, 101
mentors, quality (importance), 99–100
Microsoft Sharepoint, usage, 54
migration strategies, types, 19
mind-set
  metrics, 169–170
  security awareness, 194
miniaturisation, impact, 26
Ministry of Finance (MOF) oversight, impact, 9
mobile devices, usage (safety), 205
mobile money operator (MMO) model, 219
Model AI Governance Framework
  (PDPC), 241–242
Møller-Maersk, DC case study, 32–33
Monetary Authority of Singapore (MAS), 74
money, future, 209, 218
MongoDB, 184
Moore, Gordon Earle, 16, 106
Moore's Law, 16, 24, 26, 106
Moral Machine experiment (MIT), 239–240
most serious violence (MSV), 236
multifactor authentication, usage, 33
multimedia, data source, 38–39
multitasking, avoidance (information overload
  technique), 59
Murray, Daragh, 237

N
National Centre for Infectious Diseases (NCID),
  setup, 249
National Computer Board (NCB)
  civil service computerisation, 104
  support, 108
National Computer Systems (NCS), 248
  career change, 10
  senior management, involvement,
    254–255
National Public Health Unit (NPHU), 198–199
National Registration Identity Card
  (NRIC), 253
National Service military training, Slow
  enlistment, 6

Navitaire/Virgin Atlantic, outsourcing
  lesson, 72–73
network
  BC-DR case study, 85
  extension, 26
  latency (lag), 197
  security, 192
network-attached storage (NAS), usage, 31
new normal, 230, 255
Nicolett, Mark, 200
Nmap, usage, 201
Northern Lincolnshire, BC-DR case study,
  85
NoScript browser, usage, 204
*Note on the Application of Machinery to the
  Computation of Astronomical and
  Mathematical Tables* (Babbage), 15
NotPetya attack, 32–33
Nutch, 183

O
objectivity (QMS project failure reason), 133
office automation, DC (impact), 32
Office Automation Masterplan (OAM), 48
office politics, resolution, 119
Official Secrets Act (OSA), 199
"One More Time, How Do You Motivate
  Employees?" (Herzberg), 170
open innovation, 165
open-source intelligence (OSINT), 214
operational data, 42
operational security, 192
Optical Character Recognition
  (OCR), usage, 39
organisational conflict, 116
organisational data, classification, 42
organisational knowledge, 17
Organisation of Economic Co-operation and
  Development (OECD), Principles on AI
  (adoption), 243–244
organisations, confrontations, 116
Organised Mind, The (Levitin), 58, 59
outsourcing
  advice (Forrester Research), 67–68
  case studies, 69–71
  consolidation, 68
  contracting, contrast, 64–65
  control/initiative, balance
    (maintenance), 68
  cost, flexibility (contrast), 67

evolution, 22
failures, lessons, 71–74
infrastructure outsourcing, 66–69
IT outsourcing policy, setup advice,
74–75
knowledge/expertise, retention, 68
long-term approach, 67
optimisation, 63
relationship, management, 68
service desk outsourcing, 148
virtualisation, 68
overload *see* information overload
Ozzie, Ray, 48

P

Pareto principle, usage, 77
password management, practice, 204
patching (migration strategy), 19
payment card industry data security standard
(PCI DSS), 180
PC officer, technical staff reporting, 7
peacetime housekeeping procedures, 28
penetration testing (pen test), 200–202
phases, 201
people management skills, 92
Pepper (mobile bank), 212–213
Pepper (robot), 253
PERL, usage, 29
Personal Data Protection Act (PDPA), 109
Personal Data Protection Commission (PDPC),
setup, 241
personalisation (problem-solving theme),
123
phishing, suspicion, 204
physical security, protection, 30
Pisano, Gary P., 165
Platform as a Service (PaaS), 27, 31, 135
platforms, 222–223
Platt, Lewis, 58
points of presence (POPs), 85
Politics of Information Management, The
(Strassman), 51
Post Implementation Review (PIR), setup, 143
power users, database access, 195
predictive recidivism, 235–236
presencing, participant involvement, 161
problem solving
creative problem solving, 171
process, 121, 122–123
themes, 123

process management, emphasis, 36
project failure, 81–82
scoping, impact, 82
project management, 81–83, 108–111
advice, 82–83
changes, documentation, 83
complexity, 130–131
problems, 82
skills, 6, 110
Project Management Body of Knowledge
(PMBOK), 131
Project Management Institute (PMI),
108, 131
project management meetings (PMMs),
conducting, 144
project managers
attributes, 109, 111
project managers, certification, 108–109
project plan, usage, 82–83
proof of concept (PoC), impact, 213–214
prototyping, implementation, 165
public, private partnership (PPP), 172, 229
Public Service Commission (PSC), Siow
application/acceptance, 5
Python, programming training, 113

Q

QMS
ITD considerations, 134
Quality Assurance Unit (QAU), creation,
132
Quality Circles, 134
Quality Management System (QMS)
ITD consideration, 134134
methodology, 132–135
principles, 133–134
projects, failure (reasons), 133–134
standards, 134–135
quality policy, quality goal (inclusion), 130
quantum computing, 104
Qubole, 185
Queensland/IBM, outsourcing lesson, 71
questionnaire, usage, 143

R

R (statistical analysis package), 186
radio-frequency identification (RFID) tags,
usage, 253
random access memory (RAM), impact, 36
ransomware, BC-DR case study, 83–84

RapidMiner, 185
rapport (conflict minimisation step), 121
Rasiel, Ethan M., 122
raw data, 47
    CIO control, 39–40
Reagan, Ronald, 1
realising, actions, 161
real-time data, management/
        coordination, 37
reconnaissance (pen test phase), 201
recovery time objective (RTO), 78
red teams, 201
redundant array of inexpensive disks
        (RAID), 196
red zone, team entry, 251
reengineering benefits, acceleration, 64
rejuvenation, expense, 23
Relational Database Management System
        (RDBMS), usage, 50
remote workforce, impact, 225–226
research files (KMS example), 55
resources, allocation, 176–177
return on investment (ROI), expectation
        (achievement), 67
reward, risk (combination), 169
risk
    aversion, 177
    tolerance, 211
Rivest, Ron, 198
Rivest, Shamir, Adleman (RSA), 198
Robot Dog (Boston Dynamics), 253
Robotic Process Automation (RPA) programs,
        usage, 253
Robotics, 253–254
Royal Bank of Scotland (RBS), outsourcing
        lesson, 73

S
SamSam attackers, 84
Sarbanes-Oxley Act, 138
SARS
    impact, 249
    SOPs, inheritance/usage, 255
Saxberg, Bror, 96
Sayer, Phil, 66
scanning (pen test phase), 201–202
Schaninger, Bill, 160
Scharmer, Otto, 161
scoping, impact, 82
Sebregts, Yuri, 239

secondary DC, maintenance, 30
secure sockets layer (SSL) protocols,
        usage, 196
security see data
    advice, 193–194
    awareness, 193
    policy, absence (threat), 193
    requirement, 257
Security Information and Event Management
        (SIEM), 199–200
segregation (migration strategy), 19
semi-structured data, 50–51
Senge, Peter, 160
sensing, leader involvement, 161
Servant as Leader, The (Greenleaf), 4
servant leadership, 3–5
service desk outsourcing, 148
service level agreement (SLA)
    compliance, 22
    pen tests, usage, 200
    repair, 65
    requirement, 28
    usage, 31, 78
service strategy/design/transition/
        operation, 138
Shamir, Adi, 198
Shamoon wiper malware, impact, 33
shared database, development
        (questions), 120
shared files (KMS example), 55
Shin, Laura, 58
Siang, Ler Teck, 198–199
Sidyotong, Chatri, 229
silos, 222
Simba, BC-DR case study, 86
Sin, Chong Yoke, 10
Singapore
    circuit breaker (CB), initiation, 247, 250
    community isolation facilities, 251
    company transformation, 230
    disinfection, procedure, 254
    ethical AI framework, 241–242
    First Master Plan for Education, 173
    fulfilment models, 231
    new normal, 230
    recidivism rates, 239
    SARS, impact, 249
    Second Master Plan for Education, 173
    technology, leadership, 229–231
    trade/logistics, importance, 230

Singapore Computer Emergency
    Response Team (SingCERT),
    202–203
Singapore Computer Society (SCS), 105
    certification scheme, 107–108
Singapore Health Services (SingHealth),
    cyberattack, 95–96
Singapore Information Management
    (SIM), 105
Singapore Quality Award, 55
Singtel, 10
Siow, Alex
    CSD relocation/staff meeting, 2–4
    DiplomIngenieur Bauingenieurwesen
        (Bachelor in Civil
        Engineering award), 6
    HDB CIO appointment, 2
    project management skills, 6
    PSC acceptance, 5
    Public Administration Medal
        (Silver) award, 8
    staff members, relationship, 8
    win-win formula, 9
Siow, Iris, 11–12
Siow, Ivan, 11–12
situational analysis, exercise, 119
skillsets, 104–106, 149 *see* information
    technology; managers
Skills Framework for the Information Age
    (SFIA), certification, 107
skunkworks, setup, 91
Skype (outsourcing case study), 71
Slack Technologies (outsourcing case
    study), 70
small and medium businesses (SMBs),
    talent valuation, 91
small business, tech support
    (reasons), 146–147
Smith, Brad, 237
Snabe, Jim Hagemann, 32
sneakers, 201
social health, impact, 256
social media (SM)
    leverage, 39
    platforms, usage, 144
social networking tools, 57
soft skills, 122
    enhancement, 98
Software as a Service (SaaS), 27, 31, 68

vendor, usage (risk factors), 73
Software Engineering Institute (SEI)
    setup, 136
Software Engineering Institute (SEI), CMMI
    development, 139
Sony Pictures, DC case study, 33–34
source code, changes, 18
South East Asian Regional Computer
    Confederation (SEARCC), IT
    standards, 107
spam filters, impact, 49
Squandered Computer, The (Strassman),
    69–70
staff *see* information technology staff
    certification, 135–139
    empowerment, 170
    mentor, ability, 99–100
    motivation/mentoring, 89
    training, advice, 114
    training/certification process, 103
staff suggestion scheme (SSS), usage,
    144, 170
stakeholder
    management skills, 92
    security awareness, 193
standardisation (QMS project failure
    reason), 134
StarHub, career change, 10, 150
statistical discrimination, 235–238
storage area networks (SANs), usage, 31
Storage as a Service (StaaS), 27
Strassman, Paul, 51, 69–70
strategic data, 42
streamlining (problem-solving theme), 123
structured data, 38, 50
Suan, Tan Poh, 8
subjectivity (QMS project failure reason),
    133
subject matter experts (SMEs), 172
    availability, 22
    nomination/vote, 54–55
supplier, monitoring/managing, 68
supply chain management (SCM)
    company migration, 19
    development, 36
    integration, 37
surveillance AI, uses, 238–239
sustaining practices, 161
System of Systems Engineering (SoSE), 230

T

Tableau (software), 185–186
tactical data, 42
Taeihagh, Araz, 240
tag tasks (information overload avoidance), 59
Talend Open Studio, 185
talent *see* information technology talent
   case study, 95–96
   costing, 93–96
   valuation, 90–91
Tallinn, Jaan, 71
Tan, Anthony, 229
Tan, Serene, 9–10
teams, 175
   balanced teams, building, 176
teamwork, advice, 175–177
technical integration, 17
technical knowledge, changes, 17
technical staff, inertia, 155
technology
   impact, 227
   integration/innovation skills, 92
   management, strategic approach, 142f
   support, reasons, 146–147
telcos, leased lines (usage), 29
teleconsult, option, 256–257
telehealth, 252
Telehealth on Wheels (TOW), 254
The Engineering Project (TEP), electricity cost analysis, 26
Theory of Inventive Problem Solving (TRIZ) methodology, usage, 171
Thompson, Hilary, 175
Thompson, Judith Jarvis, 240
tiger teams, 201, 249
TraceTogether Token device, 253
tracks, covering (pen test phase), 201
training, 158–159, 172 *see also* staff
   case study, 113
   conflict minimisation step, 122
   external roadmap, 112–113
   provision, 157
   roadmap, 111–113
transparency (problem-solving theme), 123
"Trolley Problem," 239–240
trusted business processes, 18
trust, increase, 177
Turban, Efraim, 8

two minutes (information overload avoidance), 58
two-sided economy, 214

U

Unilever (outsourcing case study), 70
United Kingdom
   facial recognition, usage (legal developments), 237–238
   predictive recidivism, 236–237
United States
   facial recognition, usage (legal developments), 238
   predictive recidivism, 235–236
unstructured data, 38–39, 50
upgrades, usage, 223
U-process, phases, 160–161
user *see* business users; end users
   expectations, management, 43
   IDs, usage, 195
   interfaces, usage, 41
   power users, database access, 195
   support, 144–147
US Navy/Electronic Data Systems (EDS), outsourcing lesson, 72

V

vendors, digital divide, 175
Veritas Software Singapore, StarHub customer, 9
Virgin Atlantic/Navitaire, outsourcing lesson, 72–73
virtual currency, 216
virtualisation, 68
virtual machines (VMs)
   security, 30
   usage, 29
virtual private networks (VPNs), usage, 29, 257
virtual security, protection, 30
virus *see* computer virus
vision (conflict minimisation step), 121
Vision2000 (HDB strategic IT plan), 52–53
Vision for Prioritising Human Well-being with Autonomous and Intelligent Systems (IEEE), 243
voice-response systems, usage, 31
volume, variety, velocity, veracy (4Vs), 224
volunteering, 173

W

warm site, 78
WeChat Pay, 218
WhatsApp (outsourcing case study), 69
white hat hacker, 201
wide area networks (WANs), 192
  inclusion, 26
Williams, Amrit, 200
Wilson, Glenn, 59
win-win formula (Siow vision), 9
Wirecard (payment processor),
    213–214
work
  changes, 226
  evolution, 224–226
  future, 221
workflows, usage, 144
workplace conflict, 116

Y

Y2K crossover, preparation, 19
Y2K problem, appearance, 90
Y2K rollover, 78
  handling, 168
Y2K scare, 18–20
  case study, 20
  ITD replacement/rejuvenation process, 23
Yahoo Search Webmap, 183
Yon, Gan Kim, 203
Yuan, Eric, 153

Z

Zeldes, Nathan, 49
Zendesk, advice, 151–152
Zennström, Niklas, 71
zero-touch, importance, 256
Zhaoxu, Ma, 228